Inside *Pierrot lunaire*

Performing the Sprechstimme in Schoenberg's Masterpiece

Phyllis Bryn-Julson
Paul Mathews

THE SCARECROW PRESS, INC.
Lanham, Maryland • Toronto • Plymouth, UK
2009

SCARECROW PRESS, INC.

Published in the United States of America
by Scarecrow Press, Inc.
A wholly owned subsidary of
The Rowman & Littlefield Publishing Group, Inc.
4501 Forbes Boulevard, Suite 200, Lanham, Maryland 20706
www.scarecrowpress.com

Estover Road
Plymouth PL6 7PY
United Kingdom

British Library Cataloguing in Publication Information Available

Library of Congress Cataloging-in-Publication Data

Bryn-Julson, Phyllis.
    Inside Pierrot lunaire : performing the Sprechstimme in Schoenberg's masterpiece /
Phyllis Bryn-Julson, Paul Mathews.   p. cm.
    Includes bibliographical references and index.
    ISBN-13: 978-0-8108-6205-0 (pbk. : alk. paper)
    ISBN-10: 0-8108-6205-0 (pbk. : alk. paper)
    ISBN-13: 978-0-8108-6225-8 (ebook)
    ISBN-10: 0-8108-6225-5 (ebook)
    1. Schoenberg, Arnold, 1874–1951. Pierrot lunaire. 2. Sprechstimme. I. Mathews, Paul,
1968–. II. Title.
ML410.S283B78 2009
782.4'3—dc22   2008026835

∞™ The paper used in this publication meets the minimum requirements of
American National Standard for Information Sciences—Permanence of
Paper for Printed Library Materials, ANSI/NISO Z39.48-1992.
Manufactured in the United States of America.

Contents

Acknowledgments

$\mathscr{W}$e gratefully acknowledge Belmont Music Publishers and the Arnold Schoenberg Center for permission to print the many score examples, manuscript excerpts, and photographs. Similarly, we thank the *Leipziger Blätter* for permission to print photographs of Albertine Zehme, her house, and her family. We also thank the following for their assistance and guidance:

- Theresa Muxeneder and the staff at the Arnold Schoenberg Center
- Susan Clermont and the staff of the Music Division at the Library of Congress
- Maggie Portis and the staff of the Reading Room at the Morgan Library
- Thomas Liebscher of Passage-Verlag and the staff of the *Leipziger Blätter*
- Doris Mundus, of the Stadtgeschichtliches Museum Leipzig
- Gregory C. Richter of Truman State University
- Richard Hoffmann and Kevin Clark
- The Peabody Institute of the Johns Hopkins University and its thenacting director, Peter Landgren, for a faculty development fund that financed a trip to the Arnold Schoenberg Center in Vienna
- Renée Camus and Kellie Hagan at Scarecrow Press
- Deborah Mathews, Donald Sutherland, and our families
- Sharon Gail Levy of the music theory faculty of the Peabody Conservatory, whose moonbeam-oar righted the ship in many rough waters

Note on Abbreviations

*F*ollowing their initial citation, sketches and manuscripts are referenced with the abbreviations designated by Reinhold Brinkmann in the critical report to his edition of *Pierrot lunaire* for the *Gesamtausgabe*. The sketches and annotated copies are preserved at the Arnold Schoenberg Center in Vienna (ASC). The autograph manuscript is at the Library of Congress in Washington, D.C., and the printer's copy is at the Morgan Library in New York. Most of these materials may be viewed on the website of the Arnold Schoenberg Center at http://www.schoenberg.at. Many letters to and from Schoenberg are archived at the Library of Congress but may be viewed in transcript or facsimile at the Arnold Schoenberg Center; these letters are designated (LC/ASC). The following table lists the abbreviation, the source, and the location with archive number where applicable, for each abbreviated citation.

Aa	Early sketch, perhaps of "Die Kreuze"	ASC, number 709
Ab	Copy of the text (*Textvorlage*) with sketches	ASC, number 710–727
Ac	Early sketch for piano	ASC, no number
Ad	A sketch in Schoenberg's concert calendar	ASC, no number
B	Autograph Manuscript	Library of Congress
C	Printer's Copy (*Stitchvorlage*)	Morgan Library
D	First edition of the score	Universal Edition
D1	Schoenberg's first annotated copy of the score (*Handexemplar*)	ASC, no number
D2	Schoenberg's second annotated copy of the score	ASC, no number

Introduction

...für eine Sprechstimme (MELODRAMEN)

$\mathcal{T}$he official title of Arnold Schoenberg's masterpiece as engraved in 1914 is emblematic.[1] The title, which Reinhold Brinkmann called "a thoughtfully designed composition" and Schoenberg's "first statement about his *Pierrot lunaire*," communicates much of what Schoenberg values about *Pierrot*.[2] At the same time, it presents the ambiguity contained in the work. *Pierrot* is in fact "three times seven poems from Albert Giraud's *Pierrot lunaire*," [translated from the original French into] "German by Otto Erich Hartleben." The piece is composed "for a Sprechstimme [speaking part] piano, flute (also piccolo), clarinet (also bass-clarinet), violin (also viola) and cello." However, the designation *melodrama* is curious. If Schoenberg had written *Sprecher* (speaker) instead of *Sprechstimme*—as he had already done in his earlier composition *Gurrelieder*—then it would have been unnecessary to specify *melodrama*. On the other hand, if using the word *Sprechstimme* necessitated the qualification *melodrama*, then why is it simultaneously deemphasized with parentheses and emphasized with capital letters?

Schoenberg spent a considerable amount of time deciding the wording and presentation of the title page shown in ex. I-1.[3] Of particular concern to him was the designation of the genre and how his treatment of the Pierrot poems was not quite a set of songs and yet something more than the melodramas that were then fashionable. In a letter to his publisher soon after completing the work, Schoenberg named the work simply, "*Pierrot lunair* [*sic*] . . . Melodrama-Cycle with an accompaniment" of the same instrumentation.[4] Four months later, the program for the premiere of *Pierrot lunaire*, which served as a rough draft of the title page, included the evocative equation that describes the three cycles of seven pieces: "Three Times Seven Poems from Albert Giraud's '*Songs of Pierrot lunaire*' [our emphasis]."[5] Also, in the program, the word *melodramas* appears in smaller, lowercase letters.

DER ERSTEN INTERPRETIN
FRAU ALBERTINE ZEHME
IN HERZLICHER FREUNDSCHAFT

DREIMAL SIEBEN GEDICHTE

AUS ALBERT GIRAUDS

PIERROT LUNAIRE

(DEUTSCH VON OTTO ERICH HARTLEBEN)

Für eine Sprechstimme
Klavier, Flöte (auch Piccolo), Klarinette (auch Baß-
Klarinette), Geige (auch Bratsche) und Violoncell

(MELODRAMEN)

von

ARNOLD SCHÖNBERG

Op. 21

Example I-1.   Detail of the title page.

These fine details reflect a certain ambiguity about the way the text is presented to the audience. A melodrama, as the term was then understood, was a genre that consisted of a musical accompaniment for a text that was declaimed in a dramatic style. Unlike a song, in which each syllable of the text is fixed in musical notation with a definite duration and pitch, the declamation of a melodrama was fairly free: the text was simply written above the music, as shown in ex. I-2.[6]

Melodrama as a genre dates back to the eighteenth century. However, in the late nineteenth century, despite the disdain of contemporary music critics, the melodrama genre had become quite popular with audiences. Well-known examples included Richard Strauss' *Enoch Arden* (1897) and *Das Schloss am Meere* (1899) and Max von Schilling's *Das Hexenlied* (1904). Audiences came to these works with definite expectations: in a song, the text is sung; in a melodrama, the text is spoken.

Example I-2.   Max von Schilling, _Das Hexenlied_, mm. 224–27.

In _Pierrot lunaire_, the text is not quite spoken and definitely not sung: it is _set_ as a _Sprechstimme_. That is to say, the performer is presented with notation that resembles the notation used for singing, with each syllable of the text fixed for a definite duration and at a definite pitch, as seen in ex. I-3. However, instead of singing the text (except where otherwise noted, as for example in m. 24 of ex. I-3), the performer is instructed to transform it into a Sprechmelodie (spoken melody): the rhythm and pitch are to be observed, but the character of the vocalization should reflect the nuanced sound of speech.

The duality of the Sprechstimme, lying somewhere between singing and speaking, informs Schoenberg's title page. The same duality has informed and challenged performers, scholars, and critics up to the present day. The development of the Sprechstimme, both as a concept and as a description thereof, is an interesting case of the intersection of a composer's creativity and a performer's unique ability.

★ ★ ★

Albertine Zehme, a singer and actress who specialized in reciting melodramas, commissioned Schoenberg to compose _Pierrot lunaire_ to her specifications. Having already performed musical recitations of the Pierrot poems, she wanted Schoenberg to provide music that would complement what she considered a unique style of declamation. She expected a work that would transcend the normal constraints of the melodrama genre.

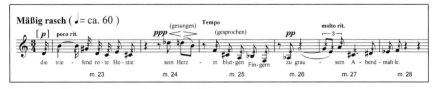

Example I-3.   "Rote Messe," mm. 23–28.

Schoenberg initially understood that the work was to be a set of melodramas. He describes them as such in his diary entry of 25 January 1912, noting he had "received a proposal to compose a cycle, 'Pierrot lunaire' for an intended recital by Frau Dr. Zehme," and that he would "handle the melodramas" if he could renegotiate the terms.[7] Not long thereafter, he discussed *Pierrot* with Anton Webern, who described the project to Alban Berg: "[Schoenberg] is composing for, as he says, an extremely talented woman—who is, naturally, Viennese (that which is good comes hence)—melodramatic music to poetry that she recites [*vorträgt*]."[8] In the months and years that followed, Schoenberg never hesitated to describe *Pierrot* as the *Pierrot melodramas*.

On the other hand, Albertine Zehme did not initially describe *Pierrot* as melodrama; the word does not appear in association with *Pierrot* in her letters to Schoenberg. A sense of her expectations can be determined from a letter to Schoenberg from his business manager, Emil Gutmann, dated 24 February 1912. Gutmann describes a letter he received from Zehme in which she clarifies that she did not want the resulting work designated a melodrama, but rather "music to spoken words or spoken songs." Gutmann continues, "She gave her rationale in a long explanation, the upshot of which is that she is not a speaking machine [*Sprechenmaschine*] but rather a trained musical interpreter."[9]

After a few weeks of discussions, Schoenberg and Zehme finally agreed to terms for the composition, premiere and tour. In the contract, signed 10 May 1912, the work is described as "at least twenty poems as melodramas with piano accompaniment and possibly two other accompanying instruments."[10] Despite this final arrival at a description of the piece as melodramas, it is nevertheless clear that in the exchange of letters predating the start of composition, we see an almost fluid intermingling of the concepts of *singing* and *speaking*. Thus, the ambiguity of singing and speaking, and of melodrama and song cycle, is foreshadowed before Schoenberg composed his first sketch.

Two days after signing the contract, Schoenberg composed the first melodrama, "Gebet an Pierrot," which ultimately became the ninth of twenty-one melodramas. The first three measures from the draft of "Gebet," quite similar to the final published version, are shown in ex. I-4.[11] From the first complete measure of this sole draft of "Gebet," we see Schoenberg implementing a style of recitation that seems to ask the reciter to be sufficiently accurate as to make a distinction between F-sharp and F-natural.[12]

What did Schoenberg expect to *hear* when he wrote the recitation part for "Gebet"? What did he hear when the piece was rehearsed and performed? These questions can never be answered. However, it seems likely that the answers to these questions do not align, and Schoenberg did not hear what he expected to hear. Schoenberg's description of the sound he wanted changed almost immediately and continued to change for the next thirty years.

Example I-4. "Gebet an Pierrot," mm. 1–3: autograph manuscript and transcription.

Schoenberg ultimately called the recitation part a *Sprechstimme*, or literally *speech part*, in much the same way *flötestimme* is a flute part and *geigestimme* is a violin part. In a preface to the score, he explained that the melody given in the Sprechstimme was not meant to be sung but rather transformed into a *sprechmelodie*. Later writers have used the word *Sprechstimme* to refer to the sound and technique required to perform *Pierrot*, but it is worth noting that Schoenberg initially coined the term *Sprechstimme* to indicate that a part of the texture was for musical speech.[13] The preface continues to explain that the rhythm should be executed exactly as written, and that the performer must consider the nuance of the speaking voice, which gives a pitch but then leaves it immediately by rising or falling.

Schoenberg's preface, considered in detail in chapter 3, provides valuable clues as to how the Sprechstimme should sound. However, there is still ambiguity. Consider the three measures of the recitation in ex. I-2. Are the first three notes of recitation truly meant to be G, E, and A-sharp? Is it permissible to use the same intervals transposed? Is it permissible to just have three notes where the second is the lowest and the third is the highest?

The preface also talks of leaving the note immediately by rising and falling. Such a technique of *portamento* is dependent on the durations assigned to each note: the longer the duration, the slower the *portamento*. Comparing the first measure to the second measure of "Gebet an Pierrot," we note that the durations increase as the intervals increase, as shown in ex. I-5. The augmented-fourth between the E-natural and A-sharp must be covered in less than a single sixteenth note; the augmented-octave must be covered in less than two sixteenth notes. In these two examples, the size of the pitch interval roughly corresponds to the length of the duration. However in the third measure, we encounter the longest duration in ex. I-5—two-thirds of a half note. The significantly longer duration is paired with one of the smallest intervals, two half-steps between B and A. This seems counterintuitive: if one is to give the note and leave it immediately, and it can be done sufficiently fast as to travel over an octave in less than the duration of an eighth note, then how does one travel the pitch interval of a major second for a duration larger than a quarter note?

★ ★ ★

This small book is about the performance of the Sprechstimme in *Pierrot lunaire*. We maintain that solutions to performance problems such as the inconsistencies revealed in ex. I-5 are best found by relating the Sprechstimme, or recitation, to the entire motivic structure of each melodrama. Only through such a contextual understanding can the Sprechstimme truly function as a kind of speaking that can, in Schoenberg's words, "contribute to a musical form." Our task is complicated by Schoenberg's later statements, the statements of his associates and students, Schoenberg's use of Sprechmelodie in other pieces, and the recording he conducted in 1940. However, we will show that Schoenberg's

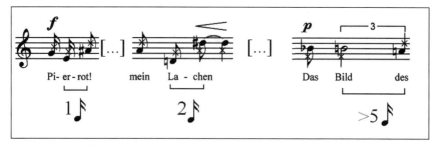

Example 1-5.   Pitch intervals and durations in "Gebet an Pierrot," mm 1–4.

often-cited later statements about Sprechmelodie are not always directly applicable to *Pierrot*, and that these sometimes contradictory statements suggest that Schoenberg changed his mind about how the Sprechstimme should be performed. As our questions about "Gebet an Pierrot" suggest, there are three categorically different realities about the sound of Sprechmelodie—the sound Schoenberg wanted to hear when he composed, the sound Schoenberg heard at the premiere, and the sound Schoenberg prescribed for later performers.

In chapter 1 we detail the development of the Sprechmelodie concept. Chapter 2 summarizes Schoenberg's development in the years immediately preceding the composition of *Pierrot*. As such, it treats the metamorphosis of Schoenberg's musical language and the foundation of Albertine Zehme's interest in the amalgam of singing and speaking. Therein, we hope to reexamine the role of Albertine Zehme, who has been largely overlooked in previous literature on *Pierrot*. In chapter 3, we review the primary sources.

The principal substance of our argument is the score itself. We conclude the first part of the book with chapter 4, which explains the principles of our analysis. Drawing on Schoenberg's writings and a wealth of more recent scholarship, we emphasize the conflicts in aesthetics and musical praxis that Schoenberg sought to resolve as he composed *Pierrot*. The second part of the book provides an analysis of each melodrama with a particular view toward relating the Sprechstimme as an equal part in the texture and demonstrating that the pitches found in the recitation are as fully integrated into the fabric of the piece as the pitches in any of the instrumental parts.

NOTES

1. We will use Schönberg's later, Anglicized spelling throughout the text, although he did not adopt that spelling until he fled Nazi Germany in 1933.

2. Reinhold Brinkmann, "The Fool as Paradigm: Schönberg's *Pierrot lunaire* and the Modern Artist," in *Schönberg and Kandinsky: An Historic Encounter*, ed. Konrad Boehmer, vol. 14, *Contemporary Music Studies*, ed. Peter Nelson and Nigel Osborne (Amsterdam: Harwood Academic Publishers, 1997), 139. Strictly speaking, Brinkmann was discussing the title as it appears on the program at the premiere, with some small changes detailed above.

3. Reinhold Brinkmann, *Melodramen und Lieder mit Instrumenten. "Pierrot lunaire," op. 21: kritischer Bericht, Studien zur Genesis, Skizzen, Dokumente*, Reihe B Band 24, Sämtliche Werke. Mainz: B. Schott's Sohne, 1995.

4. Letter to Emil Herzka, 20 June 1912, excerpted in Brinkmann 1995, 230–31. While it was typical for both Schoenberg and Zehme to waver on the final *e* in *Lunaire*—indeed, Zehme's 1911 concert with Vrieslander's music was called *Pierrot lunair*—the word is spelled with a final *e* in both Giraud's original and Hartleben's

translation. In both French and German, *Pierrot lunaire* is correctly spelled with a lower case *l* on the second word.

5. Brinkmann 1995, 177. This program is found in *Arnold Schoenberg Self-Portrait: A Collection of Articles, Program Notes, and Letters by the Composer about his Own Works.* ed. Nuria Schoenberg-Nono (Pacific Palisades: Belmont Music Publishers, 1988), 110.

6. Max von Schillings and Ernst von Wildenbruch, *Das Hexenlied* ([Bad Godesberg]: R. Forberg, 1904).

7. *Berliner Tagebuch* quoted in Brinkmann 1995, 225. Albertine Zehme was married to a noted attorney, Dr. Felix Zehme, and as was customary, Schoenberg addressed her with her husband's title: *Frau Dr. Zehme.*

8. Anton Webern to Alban Berg, 11 February 1912, quoted in Brinkmann 1995, 225.

9. Emil Gutmann to Schoenberg, 24 February 1912, quoted in Brinkmann 1995, 226.

10. Schoenberg-Nono, 109; reprinted in Brinkmann 1995, 227.

11. Arnold Schoenberg, *Pierrot lunaire*, Manuscript Score [1912]. The Library of Congress, Washington, DC (henceforth Source B), 1. The changes in the engraved edition are very minor. The published score is in score order, the recitation dynamics are above the staff, and extraneous staves are removed. The low notes in the clarinet are made staccato. He eliminates the slur from the piano part. Schoenberg later added the metronome marking *half note = ca 60*. Finally, and most significantly, the notation of the *Sprechstimme* changed from x-ed noteheads to standard noteheads with an x on the stem.

12. The labeling of staves in this draft is confusing. Schoenberg used large sheets of paper with 64 staves. For convenience, he divided these sheets and composed on the smaller pieces. Because the staves were close, he skipped staves between instruments. Clearly, he was making these decisions as he began to draft the work and changed his mind about where to write the clarinet part.

13. Among English writers, *Sprechstimme* is commonly used to mean a technique of vocal production. German and French authors tend to preserve the original meaning of *Sprechstimme*—a part in the texture—and use *Sprechgesang* or *Sprechmelodie* for the sound and technique. These differences are thrown into high relief when Europeans write or speak in English. Thus, Gunther Schuller asks Eduard Steuermann—who was teaching Frau Zehme the *Pierrot* Sprechstimme before Schoenberg coined the term—about the "origin of Schoenberg's idea for *Sprechstimme*," and further notes that "Humperdinck had used Sprechtimme." Gunther Schuller and Eduard Steuermann, "A Conversation with Steuermann," *Perspectives of New Music* 3/1 (1964): 25. Schuller, born and raised in New York, obviously uses *Sprechstimme* to mean the technique since it does not have an article ("*the* Sprechstimme"). On the other hand, in a German-language article from 1947, Peter Stadlen writes about Schoenberg's *Sprechgesang*; in a revised English translation, *Sprechgesang* becomes *Speechsong*. Ten years later, Stadlen revised the article again in German, settling on the by-then conventional *der Sprechstimme*. Peter Stadlen, "Schönberg und der Sprechgesang," in *Bericht über den 1. Kongress der Internationalen Schönberg-Gesellschaft: Wien, 4. bis 9. Juni, 1974*, ed. Rudolf Stephan (Wien: Lafite, [1978]), 202–12. Stadlen's "Schoenberg's Speech-Song," *Music & Letters* 62/1 (1981): 1–11, is a revised translation of his previous essay, while "Die von Schönberg intendi-

erte Ausführungsart der Sprechstimme im 'Pierrot lunaire'," in *Stimme und Wort in der Musik des 20. Jahrhunderts*, ed. Hartmut Krones (Wien: Boehlau, 2001), 109–26, is his third version of the article. We have elected to sidestep this quandary by using *Sprechstimme* to mean only the part of the texture: *the* Sprechstimme. We believe it is best not to generalize the technique of vocal production, because the technique for *Pierrot* is quite distinct from the technique for later works by Schoenberg.

1

Schoenberg and the Development of the Sprechstimme Concept

*A*rnold Schoenberg's legacy as a composer rests primarily on his highly regarded instrumental works, which are the most recorded and most anthologized works in his catalog. However, Schoenberg's early oeuvre is dominated by works composed for the voice. In the twenty-year period before the start of World War I, fourteen of Schoenberg's twenty-two works with opus numbers are compositions for voice.[1] To that number should be added the Second String Quartet, op. 10, the last two movements of which set the poems "Litanei" and "Entrückung" by Stefan George for soprano and string quartet. Moreover, there is a wealth of early vocal works without opus numbers, including the Brettl-Lieder (1901) and thirty-five assorted songs completed before 1903.[2] Finally, Schoenberg completed thousands of pages of orchestration for other composers' operettas, which, at the very least, provided a limited forum for testing novel combinations of voices and instruments.

Significant among these early vocal works, and predating many of them, is the colossal *Gurrelieder* (1900–1903, 1911), an oratorio for chorus, soloists, and a large orchestra. *Pierrot lunaire* and *Gurrelieder* are Schoenberg's most celebrated vocal works, and both employ notated Sprechmelodie. Schoenberg did not complete the orchestration of *Gurrelieder* until 1911, but the short score he completed in 1900 demonstrates a fully realized use of a Sprechmelodie notation similar to the Sprechstimme in the manuscript of *Pierrot lunaire*. See example 1-1.[3] (The text in the excerpt reads: "Sprecher: Herr Gänsefuß, Frau Gänsekraut/Speaker: Sir Goosefoot, Lady Goosespice.")

This chapter summarizes the influences and immediate precursors of Schoenberg's Sprechstimme concept and notation. Particular emphasis is placed

1

Example 1-1.   Heightened detail from the *Gurrelieder* sketches.

on a similar type of speech-melody and notation in Englebert Humperdinck's 1897 dramatic melodrama *Die Königskinder*. Finally, Schoenberg's cabaret experience is considered a possible source of influence. The Sprechstimme concept in these early tonal works is examined to separate the idea of the Sprechstimme from the post-tonal sound world of *Pierrot lunaire*.[4]

★ ★ ★

The first significant use of a speech-melody notated on a staff is found in Englebert Humperdinck's 1897 incidental music to the play *Die Königskinder* (which should not be confused with the 1910 opera of the same name, discussed below). Humperdinck, a conservatory-educated composer, achieved consider-able success in 1893 for his fairy-tale opera *Hansel und Gretel*. *Die Königskinder* is a nursery rhyme in a dramatic adaptation by Ernst Rosmer, the pseudonym of Elsa Bernstein-Porges (1866–1949). Humperdinck tried to convince Bernstein-Porges to convert her play into a libretto for another fairy-tale opera, but she wanted a distinct articulation of the words. As a result, *Königskinder* premiered in 1897 as a mix of genres: a play with songs and melodramas.

For a special *parlando* effect in the melodramas, Humperdinck asked for a rhythmic speech-melody, which he notated with x-ed noteheads.[5] He called the notation "Sprechnoten," and the result "*gebundene Melodrama*" (melodrama *bound*, presumably, with a more nuanced approach to pitch). In the introduc-tion to the score, Humperdinck explains, "the Sprechnoten (♩) that are applied in the melodramatic passages are used for the purpose of indicating the rhythm and inflection of the intensified speech (the melody of the spoken verse) and for placing [the passages] in agreement with the accompanying music. The usual type of notation (♩) is applied to lied passages."[6]

As can be seen from ex. 1-2,[7] the Sprechnoten are clearly in harmonic agreement with the accompanying flute. Indeed, in the first three measures where the flute plays, its low D is repeated three times, forming a perfect octave, fifth, and

Example 1-2. *Die Königskinder* (1897).

unison with a Sprechnote. With no other accompanying instruments, the intonation of these three intervals is exposed and the Sprechnoten must be precise.

Unfortunately, the intonation was probably not precise when the work was performed. Max Brockhaus, who published the score, wrote of disagreements between Humperdinck and the performers late in the rehearsal process.

> Just before the dress rehearsal Humperdinck and Possart fell to wrangling because of the disregard of Humperdinck's instructions about the Sprechnoten. The actors spoke the words of the melodrama with correct rhythms, but ignored the specified pitch, so that the problem of the melodrama, to Humperdinck's understandably great exasperation, remained unresolved.[8]

Much later, Humperdinck reminisced that *Köningskinder* "was a compromise, in which no party actually won much. The musicians complained that their tuning was disturbed by the constant cessation of the music. The actors complained that they could project not over the full *Humperdinckian* orchestra. The words were incomprehensible or ruined by shouting."[9]

Die Köningskinder was met with mixed reviews. Felix Salten offered a justification for the novel approach, noting that Rosmer's "realism" required "freely rolling musical rhythms for the melodies which dwell in the language in which they create."[10] Despite the justification, the technique itself was roundly criticized. The influential scholar and critic Robert Hirschfeld wrote, "It is thus not singing at all, but a continual striving toward fixed pitches, an intensified speech, but not intensified naturally toward song; in the ponderous movement of the melodrama, it serves more to retard us than to support us."[11] In light of continuing enthusiasm for Wagner's operas, critics were particularly careful to distinguish Wagner's prosody from Humperdinck's experiment. In another essay, Hirschfeld, calling the Sprechnoten "unaesthetic, tasteless and absurd," wrote, "There will be no shortage of people who will proclaim that the dissolution of melody must lead through Wagner to its ultimate consequence in Humperdinck's 'speech notes.' But is Richard Wagner responsible for every nonsense which the 'progressives' hang on his work? To take an *artistic* principle to its ultimate consequence is to annihilate it."[12] This remark was prophetic and essentially framed the continuing debate about pitched speech. Twenty-four years later, in a eulogizing article written after Humperdinck's death, Elsa Bienenfeld described Sprechnoten as an attempt to "dissolve Wagnerian Sprechgesang into declamation, its final consequence."[13]

The association of Humperdinck and Richard Wagner (1813–1883) was more than a subjective observation. Humperdinck was mentored by Wagner and assisted the master during the first production of *Parsifal*. A year after *Königskinder*, Humperdinck was chosen by Cosima Wagner to teach composition to her son, Siegfried. Rosmer (Bernstein-Porges) also knew Wagner and spent a great deal of her youth at Bayreuth. Her father, Heinrich Porges (1837–1900)—rumored to be an illegitimate son of Franz Liszt—was a chorus master at Bayreuth. If, as Hirschfeld opines, Wagner is not to be *blamed* for Sprechnoten, Wagner nevertheless championed an idiomatic joining of theater and music that encouraged his successors to further experimentation. The intermingling of like-minded musicians can be inferred by a letter written by Hugo Wolf (1860–1903), himself a composer with a very distinct prosody in his lieder. In an 1891 letter to his mistress, Wolf, writing from Bayreuth, noted, "I'm writing these lines at Humperdinck's. I got together with [Heinrich] Porges and [Oskar] Merz at Samet's today. They were very pleasant and communicative. I also paid a visit to Wolzogen accompanied by [Ferdinand] Jäger."[14] Among the prominent Wagnerians mentioned in this letter, Hans von Wolzogen (1848–1938), the editor of the *Bayreuther Blätter* and the scholar who coined the term *Leitmotiv*, stands out. In 1901, Wolzogen's half-brother Ernst von Wolzogen would found *Das Überbrettl*, Germany's first cabaret, which would briefly employ the young Arnold Schoenberg.

The Sprechnoten in Humperdinck's *Königskinder* is quite similar to the Sprechstimme in Schoenberg's *Gurrelieder*. In their Sprechmelodie, both composers primarily use shorter durations and a syllabic text-setting. Both composers describe a heightened speech, and both describe the desired effect as melodic. Both composers notate pitches that are consonant with the accompaniment and motivically significant. Finally, it is worth noting that both works have texts with fantasy or nonrealistic elements. *Königskinder* is a fairytale. In "Herr Gänsefuß, Frau Gänsekraut" from *Gurrelieder*, an uncharacterized "speaker"—the voice of the poet himself—narrates a redemptive wind, breathing life into a sleepy meadow.

Eduard Steuermann, Schoenberg's student in 1912 and the pianist for the premiere of *Pierrot lunaire*, dismissed the idea that Schoenberg had firsthand knowledge of Humperdinck's *Die Königskinder,* saying, "Since Schoenberg lived, so to speak, in a completely different world, it is very unlikely that he heard any Humperdinck except perhaps *Hänsel und Gretel.* And I, as Schoenberg's faithful disciple, would not have listened to such music."[15] However, it would not be entirely out of character for Schoenberg to take an interest in *Königskinder,* especially in his formative years. Under the informal tutelage of his friend and future brother-in-law, Alexander Zemlinsky (1871–1942), Schoenberg discovered the music of Wagner in the 1890s. His biographer H. H. Stuckenschmidt has estimated that between 1893 and 1896, Schoenberg saw "twenty or thirty performances of the *Ring* cycle, *Tristan, Meistersinger, Parsifal* and probably other works of Wagner as well."[16] It seems only natural that Schoenberg's concentration on the music of Wagner would promote interest in Humperdinck, a composer so obviously Wagnerian in outlook. Moreover, Schoenberg had a lifelong love of operetta and other popular entertainments that sometimes mystified his students.

Whether or not Schoenberg took an interest in *Königskinder,* it seems unlikely he could have missed the controversy about Sprechnoten. As Rudolph Stephan has noted, the critical debate that followed the premiere of *Königskinder* touched off "an extraordinarily boisterous and polemical argument questioning the validity and aesthetic worthiness of the melodrama."[17] Stephan continues, "One may well assume that the young Schoenberg had the opportunity to become acquainted with this work and was inclined towards the melodrama in the third part of the *Gurrelieder.*" Edward F. Kravitt has also speculated that Schoenberg, "who was always interested in musical controversy . . . certainly had the opportunity to hear, or to hear about the melodramatic version of *Königskinder* in Vienna, when it was performed there on May 10, 1897." [18]

Both Stephan and Kravitt reference Schoenberg's notation as evidence of *Die Königskinder's* influence. As seen in ex. 1-1, Schoenberg used a notation with x-ed noteheads in *Gurrelieder* and would use it while composing *Pierrot lunaire* and the opera *Die glückliche Hand.* (The subsequent, now familiar notation with the x on the stem was a suggestion of the editors at Universal Edition. Schoenberg adopted the new notation for the engraving of *Pierrot* and used it when completing the draft of *Die glückliche Hand.*[19]) As previously noted, melodramas typically did not use music notation for the text. In rare cases in which operas called for unpitched vocalization, a stem without a head was used.

Given Schoenberg's proprietary zeal for protecting his own ideas, it does seem curious that he did not make an effort to distance himself from Humperdinck or any other influence in the development of Sprechstimme. As noted in chapter 3, one of the reviews of *Pierrot lunaire* from the original 1912 tour directly compares the Sprechstimme of *Pierrot* with the melodrama passages in Humperdinck's *Königskinder.*[20] However, it seems quite likely that Schoenberg

Example 1-3. "Die Beiden," mm. 1–6.

had some knowledge of *Königskinder* before the composition of *Gurrelieder*: if not directly, then indirectly through other contemporaries experimenting with speech-melody. As Stephan has shown, Ludwig Thuille composed a short passage using the x-ed notehead notation in his singspiel *Lobetanz* composed in 1896, one year before *Königskinder*.[21] Schoenberg would likely have known of *Lobetanz*, because it was successful and because Alma Schindler played and admired the score when she was entertaining the clumsy courtship of Zemlinsky.[22]

Humperdinck, a shy and retiring man by nature, withered under the criticism that followed the premiere of *Königskinder*. He abandoned the idea of Sprechnoten and withdrew the melodrama, later refashioning it as an opera that premiered at the Metropolitan Opera in 1910 to great acclaim. However, speaking of Hans Pfitzner's music in 1899, Humperdinck prophetically mused, "There is certainly no doubt that with respect to the narrow union of word and tone, the melodrama is still capable of further development. Perhaps the time is not far off when external declamation is aligned in the innermost union with the accompanying music."[23] That same year, Schoenberg composed a song on Hugo von Hofmannsthal's poem "Die Beiden" ("Both"), as shown in ex. 1-3,[24] with the indication "*weniger gesungen, als deklamierend, beschreibend vorzutragen; wie von einem alten Bilde herablesend*" (less sung than declaimed, descriptive narration, like a lecture about an old painting.)[25] In the years leading up to the turn of the century, an interest in the intersection of declamation and singing was very much in the air.

★ ★ ★

Schoenberg's *Gurrelieder* is an oratorio, setting the Danish poems by Jens Peter Jacobsen (1847–1855), translated into German by Robert Franz Arnold (1872–1938). The poems are based on the legend of the medieval Danish King Waldemar and his love for the maiden Tove. The first of three parts is a series of love arias between Waldemar and Tove, telling of their love at the castle of Gurre. The last aria of the first part is sung by a wood-dove (Waldetraub) and tells of Tove's death, murdered through the plotting of Waldemar's vengeful queen Helvig. The second part is a long aria of mourning and desperation sung by Waldemar, wherein he curses God for taking Tove. In the third part, Waldemar is condemned to roam with his men at night, searching for Tove. In the last two numbers, Waldemar's wild hunt for Tove by night is compared to the wild hunt of the summer wind, which sweeps away death each morning with the regenerative power of nature.

Over the course of the poems, the narrative gives way to more conceptual verses about Waldemar's grief and subsequent transfiguration. The loosening of the narrative is subtly emphasized by a change of voice in the poems. In the first part, the poems are in the first person: Waldemar and Tove sing to each other. At the end of the first part, the personified wood-dove sings in the first person, which already signifies a shift toward less realistic and more conceptual verses. In the third part, the number of characters increases dramatically, including a chorus of Waldemar's doomed vassals. Finally, the eighth number, "Herr Gänsefuß, Frau Gänsekraut," is the voice of the poet himself, uncharacterized and disembodied. It is this text that Schoenberg sets as a melodrama with a Sprechstimme. The last few lines of the poet's text are separated to form a final number for a mixed chorus. The entrance of the speaker is shown in ex. 1-4.[26]

Example 1-4. "Herr Gänsefuß, Frau Gänsekraut," from the *Gurrelieder* Autograph.

This excerpt, which is typical of Schoenberg's writing for the speaker in *Gurrelieder*, is similar to Humperdinck's *Die Königskinder* and the Sprechstimme in *Pierrot*. Schoenberg makes very deliberate choices about the pitches. The x-ed noteheads are carefully drawn to show the exact note position on the staff. While the part of the Speaker does not have a key signature in the draft, the fair copy and every published score uses a key signature for the speaker. The accompanying lines double the pitches of the speaker, either obliquely, as in the first two measures, or exactly, as in the third measure. Moreover, the text setting is syllabic and no syllable is sustained. The prosody approximates what one would hear in normal German speech.

Schoenberg did not write a preface explaining the performance of the Sprechstimme in *Gurrelieder*. However, he did express his intentions in a letter to Alban Berg dated 14 January 1913. Berg made the piano reduction of *Gurrelieder* under Schoenberg's supervision and coached the speaker for the first performance. Later, Berg published a monograph introduction to the work.[27] Concerning the performance of the Sprechstimme, Berg wrote to Schoenberg, asking whether or not it was sufficient to achieve the closest possible approximation to Sprechmelodie. Schoenberg's reply is perplexing:

> [In the *Gurrelieder* melodrama] the notation of pitches is in no way to be taken as literally as in the *Pierrot* melodramas. Nowhere should such a song-like speech-melody develop [in *Gurrelieder*] as there. Throughout, the rhythm and the strength of tone (relative to the accompaniment) must be maintained. In some passages, in those that stand out melodically, it could be spoken *somewhat* (!!!) more musically. The pitches are only to be considered "differences of position;" that is, the relevant passages (!!! Not the individual note) are spoken higher or lower respectively. However, not the proportional intervals.[28]

Schoenberg agreed to allow Berg to reprint this portion of the letter in the *Führer*, which lends authority to these directions. However, we must remember that these directions were written months after the score of *Gurrelieder* was sent to Universal Edition for reproduction, and years after the Sprechstimme in *Gurrelieder* was first devised. In the interim, Schoenberg had composed and conducted *Pierrot lunaire*. As discussed in chapter 3, these instructions reflect a change in Schoenberg's thinking about the performance of the Sprechstimme in *Pierrot*.

What should we make of the directions found in this letter? Schoenberg clearly states that in *Gurrelieder*, the tonal work, the pitches are less important than in *Pierrot*, the post-tonal work. But the most exasperating detail is the idea that the pitches, which are carefully notated on the staff with accidentals, stand for little more than difference of position, or a basic profile of high and low without exact intervals. This detail reads like a description for an aleatoric composition: a way of writing that seems the very antithesis of Schoenberg's music and teaching.

Peter Stadlen discusses this letter in his articles, noting that Berg's question suggests that he "had at first no doubts that the part was musically unambiguous."[29] Stadlen also notes that in December 1912, four months before the premiere of *Gurrelieder* and two months after the premiere of *Pierrot*, Berg had met with disappointment in trying to engage the actor-singer Ferdinand Onno for the Speaker. Berg reports that the part was too high for Onno, from which one concludes that Berg auditioned Onno with the notated pitches.[30] Considering Berg's validation of the pitches, the disappointment with Onno, and the intervening rehearsal and premiere of *Pierrot lunaire*, Stadlen advances the following speculation:

> It is hard to avoid the impression that this radical denunciation of the pitches in *Gurrelieder* mirrors Schoenberg's disappointment when, for the first time, he was confronted with the reality of his speech-song during the 25 *Pierrot* rehearsals and the ensuing tour with his first soloist, Albertine Zehme (26 August to 8 December 1912). He must have been particularly anxious to eliminate this problem in the *Gurrelieder* since there was the danger that in a tonal work, as distinct from the atonal *Pierrot*, identifiable but wrongly reproduced pitches could sound like the wrong notes.[31]

Stadlen's speculation, while fascinating, presumes a disappointment and anxiety on Schoenberg's part about *Pierrot* and the Sprechstimme. If Schoenberg was disappointed with the *Pierrot* performances, he was likely disappointed with the Sprechstimme as performed by Albertine Zehme. However, Schoenberg's opinion of Zehme's performance was not a distanced recollection, but an ongoing concern. Just five weeks after the letter to Berg, Schoenberg conducted Zehme in a performance of *Pierrot* in Prague. Furthermore, Zehme was trying to convince Schoenberg to allow her to perform the Speaker's part in the premiere of *Gurrelieder*. Schoenberg's opinion of Zehme's suitability for *Gurrelieder*, as expressed in his correspondence from 1913, is wildly inconsistent. In a letter dated 13 February—thus one month after the previously quoted letter—Schoenberg insists that Zehme could not be the Speaker for the Vienna premiere of *Gurrelieder* because she wasn't vocally fit. However, by November, Schoenberg is recommending Zehme, on the strength of her musicianship, as the Speaker in subsequent performances to both Franz Schreker and Bruno Walter. Yet a few weeks later, Schoenberg again reverses himself after being horrified (*entsetzt*) by her rendering of the part at their first rehearsal. [32] Nevertheless, Zehme did perform the Speaker's part for the Leipzig premiere, in a concert that was underwritten by her husband's largess.

Schoenberg's experience with conducting *Pierrot* may have influenced his directions to Berg (a topic further explored in chapter 3). However, the *Gurrelieder* score belies Schoenberg's directions and prioritizes a performance with exact pitch. The notated pitches are consonant with the prevailing harmony. For example, in ex. 1-4, the Speaker's entrance on the folksong-like minor third is met with an appoggiatura in the clarinets (transposed in the score). The clarinets resolve just as the speaker continues, and the second clarinet resolves to the same D_5 as the Speaker's next gesture, while the first and third clarinets provide a G that frames the Speaker's line as an arpeggiation of a G major triad (all over an F-sharp pedal point). After a repeat of the exchange, the Speaker doubles the slightly faster woodwind line in m. 3.

Rudolf Stephan cites a similar passage from the Gurrelieder piano score, noting, "It is certain that the Sprechstimme was often conceptualized and composed as the actual part [Stimme] for melodies [Tonsatzes], and without question, assumes more importance when, at least in these passages, interpreters respect the notated pitch."[33] Stephan provides the example reproduced in ex. 1-5.

Stephan does not go on to explain the significance of the passage in ex. 1-5, but the role of the Sprechstimme is easy to see. Over a prolongation of the E major triad, every pitch of the Sprechstimme is diatonic—indeed, most are pentatonic—and the notes change to reflect the undulation between the tonic

Example 1-5. *Gurrelieder* piano-vocal score, six bars after rehearsal 88.

chord and the subdominant six-four. The Sprechstimme pitches that are not part of the triad create either recognizable dissonance resolution (the neighbor tone on the first downbeat) or form part of an extended tertian harmony (for example the F-sharp, which is found in both the Sprechstimme and the accompanying line and forms a pentatonic scale, with the often accompanying added-sixth and added-ninth chords). Finally, the Sprechstimme is clearly the Hauptstimme of this passage and stands out against the largely undifferentiated rhythms of the accompanying line. That accompanying line is repeated three times with only the solo instrument varied: a model and sequence technique. The Sprechstimme in this passage is also a simple example of Schoenberg's approach to developing thematic material. Each measure varies the descent from scale-degree six found in the first complete measure, and the fourth measure ultimately transposes the ascent up to begin on E followed by a subsequent F-sharp (third beat).

The importance of pitch in ex. 1-4 and ex. 1-5, and in many other places in the *Gurrelieder* score, suggests that pitches for the melodrama were deliberately composed, not as simple "differences of position," but rather as notes to be transformed into a spoken melody. This seems obvious from even a cursory glance at the score. The Sprechstimme is frequently doubled. As Stadlen suggested, the importance of pitch seemed obvious to Alban Berg. The only evidence that disputes the importance of pitch is Schoenberg's letter and his later statements on the Sprechstimme.

★ ★ ★

The preceding discussion introduces Schoenberg as the composer of the *Gurrelieder*, which he began composing in 1900 after completing *Verklärte Nacht*, op. 4. Despite the high level of accomplishment Schoenberg had obtained, it should be remembered that only five years earlier, he was working as a teller in a bank. While still learning the craft of composition, largely on his own, Schoenberg earned a living as best he could as a practical musician. Since he wasn't a performing musician—whatever his level of achievement on the cello, he did not have a decent instrument—conducting and teaching were the only opportunities open to him. Schoenberg largely made a meager living as the conductor of amateur choruses. His friend and mentor Zemlinsky undoubtedly helped Schoenberg find work. With Zemlinsky's help and encouragement, and Schoenberg's increased facility in composing lieder, Schoenberg secured an appointment as the music director of an important early cabaret.

The Buntes Brettl, also called the Überbrettl, was founded in Berlin by Ernst von Wolzogen (1855–1934) as the first cabaret in Germany. Wolzogen, born into a noble family that had long since lost their wealth, had established his name as a playwright. He was the librettist of Richard Strauss' second opera,

Feuersnot (1901). Cabaret had flourished in Paris since the opening of Le Chat Noir in 1881. Berlin, liberal and cosmopolitan, was demonstrably ready for cabaret: its serious theaters were under-attended while vaudeville-tinged variety shows at the Wintergarten enjoyed the patronage of an upwardly mobile middle class. In 1897, Otto Julius Bierbaum (1865–1910) published the novel *Stilpe*, in which the title character founds a German cabaret. In the novel, things go badly for Stilpe: he hangs himself on stage during a performance. However, the prospect of a German cabaret, and the arguments for such a venture, attracted considerable attention. Wolzogen, frustrated in his attempt to secure the directorship of a court theater, read *Stilpe* with great interest. Bierbaum edited *Deutsche Chansons*, a volume of cabaret-styled poems, which was published in 1900.[34] That same year, Wolzogen presented his plan for creating a German cabaret in his article, "Das Ueberbrettl."[35] After a year of raising funds, securing a house and placating the Berlin police, who served as censors, the Buntes Theater opened on 18 January 1901.

While the Überbrettl is an important chapter in the development of German cabaret, it was a relatively short-lived enterprise. Almost immediately, Wolzogen was confronted with competing constituencies: the critics, who applauded the more artistic-minded presentations, and the audience who demanded vaudevillian escapism.[36] In his writings, Wolzogen presents himself as an aristocrat, appropriating a popular art form and refitting it for a cultured clientele. Conversely, Wolzogen's actions suggest an impresario who courted a paying audience to keep his theater afloat. Indeed, the two names of the company represent this conflict: *Buntes Brettl* means *colorful* or *motley* theater: a theater of the people; *Überbrettl* or *superior theater*, speaks to Wolzogen's desire to create a Nietzschean cabaret for a well-read audience. Commerce trumped better intentions, and the financial reality of maintaining a new theater and company caused Wolzogen to program lighter and increasingly risqué fare. While the first season was a success by any measure, critics accused Wolzogen of pandering to the audience at the expense of his more lofty ambitions.

Not long after the Berlin premiere of the Überbrettl, Schoenberg, still living in Vienna, started setting poems from *Deutsche Chansons* in a cabaret style. He ultimately completed eight songs by the fall of 1901, which were later collected as the *Brettl-Lieder*. In September of the same year, the touring Überbrettl performed at the Karltheater in Vienna. In his autobiography, *Wie ich mich ums Leben brachte*, Wolzogen describes meeting Schoenberg for the first time in a scene that resembles the plot of a stage-door musical. According to Wolzogen, the musical director Oscar Straus was unable to direct the Vienna performance because it fell on Yom Kippur. Straus presented Schoenberg, who had converted to Protestantism in 1898, as a replacement, and Wolzogen hired him immediately upon hearing Schoenberg's songs.[37]

Schoenberg's contract, dated 23 December 1901, lists his duties as Kapellmeister for the Buntes Theater.[38] For a modest salary, Schoenberg was required to take part in performances in Germany and abroad, and to deliver all compositions that were appropriate for the Buntes Brettl. As it turned out, only one of Schoenberg's songs was performed. *Der Nachtwangler*, the second song of *Brettl-Lieder*, on a text by Gustav Falke, was set for the improbable combination of piccolo, trumpet, snare, and piano, and proved too challenging for the trumpeter. What Schoenberg actually did for the Überbrettl is unclear. As Stuckenschmidt notes, the contract does not enumerate conducting duties. In Wolzogen's biography, he claims Schoenberg suffered from stage fright, and that his accompanying was so "disgraceful," he had to be relieved by Waldemar Wendland, the second Kapellmeister. He concludes, "He was so ashamed of his failure, that he never let himself be seen again."[39] Wolzogen's memory is selective, and after the First World War, Wolzogen's writing takes on' an increasingly anti-Semitic tone: by 1922, the somewhat infamous Schoenberg was an easy target for hate speech. On the other hand, Schoenberg was not a pianist, and it is easy to imagine how a non-pianist might get flustered in an orchestral pit at a Viennese theater.

Ruling out performing and conducting, it is likely Schoenberg conducted rehearsals. He was certainly tapped to arrange the songs of other composers: an activity he would continue in Vienna after the dissolution of the Überbrettl. According to Peter Jelavich, Wolzogen had an expensive habit of signing artists to exclusive contracts in an effort to keep them from working with his competitors.[40] The ultimate purpose of Schoenberg's contract may have been to keep him from composing songs that could be presented in rival cabarets.

Scholars are divided about the influence of the Überbrettl on the much later creation of *Pierrot* in general and on Sprechstimme in particular. Early commentators made a connection between the Sprechstimme and cabaret performance styles. However, the image of smoky clubs and husky-voiced delivery—one thinks of Marlene Dietrich in *Der blaue Engel*—is more typical of postwar, Weimar-period cabaret.[41] Early German cabaret, performed on a proscenium stage, was a succession of songs, poems, and skits, not unlike a variety show. It sought an elite audience and struggled to elevate itself above more seedy entertainments such as *Tingeltangel*.

Pierre Boulez, who has stated unequivocally that "the Überbrettl gave Schoenberg the idea of a superior and 'intellectualized' cabaret," has found a precedent for Sprechstimme in the half-singing, half-reciting style of the French *diseuse*, a well-established staple in Paris by the 1890s.[42] Quoting André Schaeffner, Boulez noted that Albertine Zehme "was not a *chanteuse*, but a *diseuse*; she recited melodramas—in the original sense of the word—against a musical background."[43] However, Stuckenschmidt and Stadlen have both rejected a French influence on Sprechstimme, noting that early Berlin cabaret did not have the *diseuse* performing tradition. Stuckenschmidt maintained the concept of Sprechstimme was essentially formed in Schoenberg's imagination before his stint in cabaret. If Schoenberg became acquainted with *Der König-skinder* and implied a speech-song delivery for his 1899 song "Die Beiden," then Schoenberg's conception of Sprechstimme predates the creation of the Überbrettl. Moreover, as Stuckenschmidt notes, Schoenberg drafted the Sprechstimme for *Gurrelieder* before the cabaret's 1901 premiere. Nevertheless, it has already been demonstrated that Schoenberg's conception of the Sprech-stimme in the *Gurrelieder* as he composed it in 1900 is difficult to reconcile with the instructions he dictated to Berg in 1913. Chronological analysis of Schoenberg's scattered remarks and notations about Sprechstimme are, in the end, not a matter of what Schoenberg wanted but rather when he wanted it.

In a recent dissertation, Jennifer E. Goltz renews the argument for a French influence on Sprechstimme. Noting that the foremost *diseuse* of the era, Yvette Guilbert (1865–1944), had performed at the Wintergarten in Berlin as early as 1889, Goltz proposes that Sprechstimme "originates in part in the performance styles of Vienna and Munich cabarets, which were influenced heavily by Yvette Guilbert's French style."[44] Rebutting Peter Stadlen's article in particular, Goltz cites a song by James Rothstein performed at the premiere of the Überbrettl. When published, Rothstein's song "Madame Adèle" contained a text note at the bottom of the first page: "This 'deutsche Chanson'—aside from the places indicated '*parlando*'—is to be sung uniformly *on pitch* and almost always *rhythmically strict*."[45] As Goltz points out, the only parlando pas-sages are the first verse on the first page, which is in French. In her analysis, the implications of Rothstein's note indicate that "German audiences and cabaret performers alike recognized a French style of singing that had less regard for the perfect rendition of pitches and rhythms. This style was best exemplified in the performances of the *diseurs* and *diseuses* in the cabarets of Paris."[46]

Of course, Schoenberg did not attend the premiere performance of the Überbrettl. However, it's not unlikely that when Schoenberg joined the Über-brettl he found himself making similar fine distinctions between performance styles as the cabaret genre evolved in Berlin. More troubling is the implica-tion that the French style was a degradation of German singing, a fact that is amplified by the context: in Wolzogen's text, Madame Adèle is a prostitute. After her French introduction, she switches to German—with correct pitches and rhythms—exclaiming her French is only good enough for her to get by in vaudeville (*Zum Hausgebrauch fürs Varieté!*). It would seem that if the French *diseuse* style was a part of the Überbrettl, it was more likely an object of parody than a legitimate choice for performers.

The performance style at the Überbrettl, like the music that has been pub-lished, certainly had a strong affinity with Viennese operetta and Singspiel. This style was transported to Berlin by way of the composer and music director Oscar Straus (1870–1954). Wolzogen had a long-standing interest in Singspiel. As early as 1880, Wolzogen drafted a plan for the ideal Singspiel forces consisting of

> a relatively small theatre, only in which the effect of small voices could be achieved, a fully-staffed, small orchestra of at the most thirty-six musicians, and a troupe of dramatic artists, who combine the voice training one requires of a good opera singer with an actor's movement, sufficient speaking voice and above all, good humor.[47]

Despite the difference of twenty years, this description might easily have been written as a prospectus for organizing the Überbrettl. Moreover, Viennese operetta and Singspiel had a continuing influence on Schoenberg, as he continued to orchestrate works for Straus and other composers after returning to Vienna in 1902.

The composer and conductor Friedrich Cerha has speculated that the richly nuanced declamation used in the Viennese burlesque song (*Possenlied*) in particular might have been an influence.[48] Citing Schoenberg's admiration of cabaret artists such as Alexander Girardi and Fritzi Massary, Cerha describes Girardi's recorded performance of the "Rauschlied" from Edmund Eysler's *Künstlerblut* (1906), noting naturally occurring speech-melody, especially in the laughing passage. He also relates how far the declamation goes beyond the simple musical structure of the piece as notated. As would be expected, these liberties are often taken by performers to emphasize meaningful words in the text—an impromptu text-painting.

Cerha also observed that the style of declamation used for theater and poetry readings was significantly different in the early twentieth century. Citing early recordings of poetry readings by Alexander Moissi and Joseph Kainz, Cerha notes that the declamation style of the time exhibits "a much greater tessitura; a pronounced speech-melody organization; glissandi at different speeds, in part connected with ritardandi or accelerandi; in addition, the occasional lingering on the pitches of individual syllables and an ornamentation of details from the character of speech (tremolo, rolls, etc.)."[49]

Cerha's observation of the declamation style found in early twentieth-century recordings reads like a list of the problems one encounters in preparing a performance of the Sprechstimme for *Pierrot*. As singing and speaking were combining in unpredictable ways, the technique of singing was also influencing spoken presentation. The opposite also appears to be true, as singers looked to dramatic speakers for inspiration about how to make their songs more vivid. It is not difficult to reconcile Cehra's description of poetry readings with the following description of *coloring* words from Yvette Guilbert's 1919 book, *How to Sing a Song*:

Every word has its form and its color, its light and its shade. One does not for example pronounce the word *ciel* (heaven) as one pronounces the word *herbe* (grass). The words *chaud* and *froid* (hot and cold) have equal value of accent; also *beau* and *laid* (pretty and ugly), but the word *nuage* (cloud) is more ample, more majestic than the word *pluie* (rain). The word *merveilleux* (marvelous) is more accentuated than the word *splendide* (splendid). If a skilled dramatic artist has to say: *La neige couvrait la terre* (Snow covered the earth) he will pronounce the word *neige* with a long accent: *la nei-ge*, as if, musically speaking, the value was a half note (*une blanche*) for the first syllable and a quarter note (*une noire*) for the second.[50]

Guilbert writes as a performer of cabaret songs, and as such, she is used to taking extreme liberties with the printed text—the notation of the sung line. However, in genres that demand fidelity to the text, including lieder, opera, and ultimately the *Pierrot* melodramas, such liberties exceed the permissible boundaries of interpretation. Text-setting is musical prosody. The composer has already considered how the sung line should (or should not) resemble a prosaic reading of the verse. When a singer adds her interpretation of the cadences of speech to a printed melody, the singer re-composes the melody. Thus, Guilbert's suggestions, which stem from her perspective as a Parisian cabaret *diseuse*, and Cerha's observations of performances by Viennese cabaret artists, are similar in that they both represent a more distant relationship between performance and notation. Such examples are useful only in that they conjure a bygone sound world that might have influenced Schoenberg. The practice and notation of that sound world certainly could not have interested a composer who thought a great deal about musical notation.[51]

Ultimately, whether Schoenberg was influenced by German and/or French performance styles may not be relevant. Such experimentation was very much in the air. Moreover, the performance styles may not have reached Schoenberg in their purest form, but may rather have been filtered through an influence that was already synthesizing the two styles. For example, a 1920 book begins with the sentence, "I believe singing and speaking are one." The author was Albertine Zehme.

NOTES

1. We include the lieder, opp. 1, 2, 3, 6, 12, 14, and 15; the lied with chamber ensemble, op. 20; the orchestral lieder, opp. 8 and 22; the operas opp. 17 and 18; the choral work op. 13; and the melodramas with chamber ensemble, op. 21.

2. These songs, usually grouped as *Erste Lieder*, *Sieben Lieder*, and *Frühe Lieder*, are collected in *Arnold Schönberg, Sämtliche Werke, Abteilung I: Lieder und Kanons, Reihe A, Bd.*

2, Lieder mit Klavierbegleitung II, hrsg. v. Christian Martin Schmidt (unter Verwendung von Vorarbeiten von Ivan Vojtech) (Mainz-Wien: Schott-Universal Edition, 1988). For the importance of these songs, see Frisch, 1993.

3. Arnold Schoenberg, "Particell of *Gurrelieder*," Score [1901]. The Arnold Schoenberg Center, Vienna, Manuscript 60, number 2280. In the interests of space and clarity, we have moved the staff name "*Sprechen*" flush against the entrance of the speaker (eliminating an empty measure) and removed all extraneous markings (stray articulations from other systems).

4. *Die glückliche Hand*, while actually begun before *Pierrot*, will not be considered in this chapter, since contemporary scholarship has shown that Schoenberg composed much of the music after *Pierrot*.

5. German writers refer to the x-ed noteheads as *notenkruezen*, which English writers sometimes adapt as "cross noteheads."

6. Humperdink, *Die Köningskinder: Klavierauszug* (Leipzig: Max Brockhaus, [1897]), quoted in Edward F. Kravitt, "The Joining of Words and Music in Late Romantic Melodrama," *Musical Quarterly* 62/4 (1976): 577.

7. Humperdink, *Die Köningskinder: Klavierauszug* (Leipzig: Max Brockhaus, [1897]), printed in Rudolph Stephan, "Zur jungsten Geschichte des Melodrams," *Archiv für Musikwissenschaft* 17 (1960): 184.

8. Engelbert Humperdinck zum 70. Todestag (Veroffentlichung des Geschichts- und Altertumsvereins für Siegburg und den Rhein-Sieg-Kreis e.V), ed. Andrea Korte-Böger (Siegburg: Franz Schmitt, 1992), 34; quoted in Ulrich Krämer, "Zur Notation der Sprechstimme bei Schönberg," in *Schoenberg in der Sprechgesang*, eds. Heinz-Klaus Metzger and Rainer Riehn, Musik-Konzepte 112/113 (Munich: Edition Text u. Kritik, 2001), 10.

9. Korte-Böger, 75; quoted in Krämer, 9.

10. Felix Salten, *Wiener Abendpost*, May 12, 1897, 4; quoted and translated in Sandra McColl, *Music Criticism in Vienna, 1896–1897: Critically Moving Forms*, Oxford Monographs on Music (Oxford: Clarendon Press, 1996), 201.

11. Robert Hirschfeld, *Neue Musicalische Presse*, May 16, 1897, 2; quoted and translated in McColl, 217.

12. Robert Hirschfeld, *Wiener Abendpost*, May 11, 1897, 1–2; quoted and translated in McColl, 217.

13. Elsa Bienenfeld, "Feuilleton: Engelbert Humperdinck," *Neues Wiener Journal*, September 29, 1921.

14. Hugo Wolf to Melanie Köchert, 19 July 1891, in *Letters to Melanie Köchert*, ed. Franz Grasberger, English ed. and trans. Louise McClelland Urban (New York: Schirmer, 1991), 50. Oskar Merz (1830–1904) was a renowned architect. Samet's was a café in Bayreuth.

15. Schuller and Steuermann, 25.

16. Hans Heinz Stuckenschmidt, *Schoenberg: His Life, World and Work*. Translated by Humphrey Searle (New York: Schirmer, 1978), 33. Schoenberg's student, Dika Newlin, arrived at similar figures, and noted that Schoenberg knew *Tristan* so well he devised a game with fellow Wagnerians to try to find the most inner melodies in Wagner's counterpoint during a performance. See Dika Newlin, "Arnold Schoenberg's Debt to Mahler," *Chord and Discord* 2/5 (1948): 21–26.

17. Rudolph Stephan, "Zur jüngsten Geschichte des Melodrams," *Archiv für Musikwissenschaft* 17 (1960): 184.

18. Kravitt, 576.

19. As late as the spring of 1914, Schoenberg was still deliberating over the notation of a Sprechstimme. In a letter to Berg dated 20 June 1912 concerning the *Gurrelieder* piano reduction, Schoenberg writes that a notehead for half notes must be found that is distinct from the x-ed notehead for quarter notes. He then provides no fewer than ten possible noteheads to signify a half note (Brinkmann 1995, 231). At some point later, he scrawls a similar note in the printer's copy of *Pierrot* (Manuscript C, p. 9; reprinted in Brinkmann 1996, 26). In the manuscript of *Pierrot,* Schoenberg used the harmonic diamond to represent the half and whole note.

20. R. L.-S., *Münchner neueste Nachrichten,* November 7, 1912; reprinted in François Lesure, et al., ed., *Dossier de presse de 'Pierrot lunaire' d'Arnold Schönberg* (Geneva: Éditions Minkoff, 1985), 25.

21. Ludwig Thuille, Otto Julius Bierbaum, and Herm Bischoff, *Lobetanz:ein Bühnenspiel in 3 Aufzügen* (Berlin: A. Denekey Musikverlag, 1897).

22. Alma Mahler-Werfel, *Diaries 1898–1902,* ed. and trans. Antony Beaumont (Ithaca, NY: Cornell University Press, 1999), 418.

23. Otto Besch, *Englebert Humperdinck* (Leipzig: Breitkopf & Härtel, 1914), 171; quoted in Stephan, 183.

24. "Die Beiden" is discussed in this same context by Stadlen and Stuckenschmidt, but neither provides the title (Stadlen 1978, 202; Stadlen 1981, 1; and Stuckenschmidt 1978, 38).

25. Arnold Schoenberg, "Die Beiden," score, 1899, The Arnold Schoenberg Institute, Vienna, Manuscript 65, number 475.

26. *Gurrelieder,* 2280. In the interests of space and clarity, we have moved the staff name "Sprechen" flush against the entrance of the speaker (eliminating an empty measure) and removed all extraneous markings (stray articulations from other systems).

27. Alban Berg, *Arnold Schönberg Gurrelieder Führer* (Wien: Universal Edition, [ca. 1916]).

28. Berg, 93.

29. Stadlen, 1981, 4.

30. Stadlen, 1978, 205. This fact is omitted in Stadlen's 1981 English article but reappears in his later German article (Stadlen 2001, 118).

31. Stadlen, 1981, 5.

32. Schoenberg to Alban Berg, 13 February 1913; Schoenberg to Franz Schreker, 28 November 1913; Schoenberg to Bruno Walter, 18 November 1913; Schoenberg to Franz Schreker, 4 December 1912 (LC/ASC).

33. Stephan, 187.

34. Otto Julius Bierbaum, ed., *Deutsche Chansons (Brettl-lieder) von Bierbaum, Dehmel, Falke, Finckh, Heymel, Holz, Liliencron, Schröder, Wedekind, Wolzogen* (Berlin und Leipzig: Schuster & Loeffler, 1900).

35. Ernst von Wolzogen, "Das Ueberbrettl," *Voissische Zeitung,* 16 December 1900; reprinted in Wolzogen, *Ansichten und Aussichten: Ein Erntebuch; Gesammelte Studien über Musik, Literatur und Theater* (Berlin: F. Fontane & Co., 1908), 215–41.

36. Peter Jelavich, *Berlin Cabaret* (Cambridge: Harvard University Press, 1993), 38. Jelavich's second chapter, "Between Elitism and Entertainment: Wolzogen's Motley Theatre," is the principal source for much of this short summary of the Überbrettl.

37. Ernst von Wolzogen, *Wie ich mich ums Leben brachte. Erinnerungen und Erfahrungen* (Braunschweig: Georg Westermann, 1923), 216; summarized with quotations in Stuckenschmidt 1978, 49.

38. Ernst von Wolzogen to Arnold Schoenberg, 23 December 1901; reprinted in Stuckenschmidt 1978, 537.

39. Wolzogen 1923, 217. Stuckenschimdt does not include this passage, which immediately follows in Wolzogen's autobiography.

40. Jelavich, 58.

41. *Der blaue Engle,* dir. Josef von Sternberg, Berlin: Universum Film A.G., 1930.

42. Boulez 1988, 11.

43. Pierre Boulez, "A Note on Sprechgesang," liner notes for the recording; reprinted in *Notes of an Apprenticeship,* ed. Paule Thévenin, trans. Herbert Weinstock (New York: Knopf, 1968), 264.

44. Jennifer E. Goltz, "The Roots of *Pierrot lunaire* in Cabaret" (PhD diss., University of Michigan, 2005) vi.

45. James Rothstein, "Madame Adèle" (Berlin: Theaterverlag Eduard Bloch, 1901); quoted in Goltz, 124.

46. Goltz, 125.

47. Ernst von Wolzogen, "Vom deutchen Singspiel," 1880; reprinted in Wolzogen 1908.

48. Friedrich Cerha, "Zur Interpretation der Sprechstimme in Schönberg's *Pierrot lunaire,*" in *Bericht über den 1. Kongress der Internationalen Schönberg-Gesellschaft, Wien: 4–9 Juni, 1974,* ed. Rudolph Stephan (Vienna: Verlag Elisabeth Lafite, 1978), 26.

49. Cerha, 27.

50. Yvette Guilbert, *How to Sing a Song: The Art of Dramatic and Lyric Interpretation* (New York: Macmillan, 1919), 8–9.

51. Arnold Schoenberg, *Style and Idea,* ed. Leonard Stein (London: St. Martin's Press, 1975; rev. pb. ed., Berkeley, 1984). *Style and Idea* contains a section entitled "Performance and Notation."

2

The Paths to *Pierrot*

Gurrelieder and *Pierrot lunaire*, while similar in their use of a Sprechmelodie, are divided by one of the most formidable and most studied developments in music history. In the years preceding the composition of *Pierrot*, the harmonic language of Schoenberg's music became sufficiently complex that his works could no longer be contained in the framework of tonality, as it is traditionally understood. The evolution of his developmental technique led him down a path (a metaphor he favored) where tonality no longer governed the structure of his music. And that was only the first transformation. The second transformation was a shift in his musical aesthetics so profound that it essentially reversed the poles of his musical values.

While Schoenberg was still in the throes of reinventing himself, Albertine Zehme commissioned him to write *Pierrot*. Zehme was also in transition. In perhaps the least studied aspect of the creation of *Pierrot*, Zehme was trying to unite her formal training as an actress with her more recent study of singing to create a new way to present text with music. By chance, she encountered Schoenberg just as he was reconsidering the relationship between music and text. It is far beyond the scope of this chapter to minutely detail the metamorphosis of Schoenberg's musical language or the incorporation of musical praxis into Zehme's unique style of presentation. However, to fully understand the Sprechstimme in *Pierrot*, we must make our way down these paths.

★ ★ ★

Soon after the dissolution of the Überbrettl, Schoenberg returned to Vienna in the summer of 1903. There, he composed a number of works that challenged the ability of formal models, such as the sonata form, to contain increasingly chromatic music. The transition to post-tonal music is generally agreed to have happened over the two-year period of 1907–1909, and especially during the composition of the Second String Quartet, op. 10 (1907–1908); the Two Songs, op. 14 (1907–1908); and the *Fifteen Poems from "The Book of the Hanging Gardens" by Stefan George*, op. 15 (1908–1909). The first works of the post-tonal period are for the most part composed in a musical language that is wholly consistent with the music composed before 1907; they simply do not prioritize any single key as tonic.

When Schoenberg discussed this period of growth in later years, he emphasized his connection to the great tradition of music, and that connection is evident in the works of 1907 and 1908. Schoenberg's later perspective has led to an understanding of post-tonality as the logical consequent to the expanded chromaticism of late nineteenth-century music. Most of Schoenberg's writings espouse a historicist perspective: he believed it was his fate to continue the work of his predecessors. But in the years that immediately precede *Pierrot*, some of Schoenberg's letters and writings champion a bomb-throwing modernism that breaks with the past and demands an Art created of immediate, unfettered expression. Among the ways to discuss this critical era, the conflict between historicism and modernism is the most appropriate for an understanding of *Pierrot*.

The aesthetic and philosophical agendas that emerge in 1909 have analogues in Schoenberg's compositional technique. Consider four critical factors arranged along two axes, each a continuum of traditional and modernist approaches to musical construction. On one axis is the conflict between developing material using traditional procedures and creating each event as a spontaneous moment. On the other axis is the conflict between adapting historical forms and rejecting established formal models entirely. It is impossible to determine if the evolving technique in Schoenberg's music led him to reconsider his aesthetic perspective or vice-versa. What seems clear is that while Schoenberg sought to mediate these competing aesthetic outlooks, his musical language changed dramatically. Indeed, the music composed in 1909–1911 is far more revolutionary than the transition to post-tonality in 1907. In the introduction to his meticulous survey of Schoenberg's music from this era, Ethan Haimo goes even further: "Schoenberg's pre- and post-1908 music cannot be divided into two separate, distinct and different musical languages. Rather, all of Schoenberg's works from 1899–1909 are based on a single musical language."[1] Haimo explains that Schoenberg's music after 1907 is not tonal, but made with the same techniques as the music commonly regarded as tonal. In short, Haimo presents *tonal or atonal* as a false choice, and notes that the real change in musical language occurred in late 1909.

Haimo makes a powerful argument for reorganizing the commonly accepted three style periods. Where we speak of Schoenberg's transition to post-tonality, we refer only to the short steps between framing a central tonic and avoiding a tonic altogether. Schoenberg himself must have been keenly aware of this difference because he refers to it often in later lectures, even if such distinctions are framed with qualifications that tend to support Haimo's thesis. For example, consider this passage from the 1949 lecture "My Evolution":

> Coherence in classic compositions is based—broadly speaking—on the unifying qualities of such structural factors as rhythms, motifs, phrases, and the constant reference of all melodic and harmonic features to the centre of gravitation—the tonic. Renouncement of the unifying power of the tonic still leaves all the other factors in operation.[2]

The coherence defined in this passage is the coherence common to Schoenberg's music before and after his renouncement of the tonic. The music Schoenberg began composing in late 1909 renounced not only the tonic, but also the other structural factors identified in the first sentence. To appreciate the magnitude of Schoenberg's volatility in 1909, it is important to come to terms with his musical language before the period under investigation.

By 1907, Schoenberg's treatment of thematic material was the result of resolving an earlier divergence: the difference between Wagner's approach to composing-out material and Brahms' developmental technique. In the first part of his lecture, "My Evolution," Schoenberg described how the dual influences of Wagner and Brahms influenced the thematic construction in his op. 4 *Verklärte Nacht* (1899), noting that it was "based on Wagnerian 'model and sequence' above a roving harmony on the one hand, and on Brahms' technique of developing variation—as I call it—on the other."[3] Elsewhere, Schoenberg further contrasted the two practices:

> While preceding composers and even his contemporary, Johannes Brahms, repeated phrases, motives and other structural ingredients of themes only in varied forms, if possible in the form of what I call *developing variation*, Wagner, in order to make his themes suitable for memorability, had to use sequences and semi-sequences, that is, unvaried or slightly varied repetitions differing in nothing essential from first appearances, except that they are exactly transposed to other degrees. . . . Why there is a lesser merit in such procedure than in variation is obvious, because variation requires a new and special effort. But the damage of this inferior method of construction to the art of composing was considerable.[4]

The pejorative description of Wagner's model-and-sequence formulas reflects Schoenberg's resolution of the divergent influences: by the composition of the op. 7 First String Quartet (1904–1905), Schoenberg had essentially muted the remaining vestiges of Wagner's thematic approach while forging a more idiomatic approach to developing variation.[5]

One aspect of Schoenberg's treatment of thematic material is his contrapuntal development of the same motive in multiple parts. Nineteenth-century German composers had cultivated rich contrapuntal textures, especially in chamber and orchestral works. In these rich textures, there is a hierarchy of a principal voice, secondary voices, and a background or accompaniment—in German, *Haupstimme, Nebenstimmen,* and *Beglietung.* The generation before Schoenberg struggled to communicate these distinctions with their notation. While Beethoven could identify a principal voice in one of his mature string quartets with the indications *dolce, espressivo,* and *cantabile,* Richard Strauss and Gustav Mahler were often forced to communicate fine distinctions with differences in dynamics and increasingly inadequate expressions. A conductor might be asked to distinguish the difference between *molto espressivo* woodwinds marked *forte* and a (merely) *espressivo* horn marked *fortissimo.*

The contrapuntal design of Schoenberg's music became sufficiently complex, that he was eventually moved to identify the Hauptstimme in his music. Beginning with the last of the op. 16 *Five Pieces for Orchestra* (1909), Schoenberg marks the Hauptstimme with a bracket, which eventually becomes the familiar H- and N- symbols for *Hauptstimme* and *Nebenstimme.*[6] This practical notation solution is an outward manifestation of a textural richness so busy it strains classification as homophonic.

In his *Harmonielehre,* Schoenberg insisted that melody and harmony were not separate processes but merely aspects of a unified whole. He later said, "[T]he accompanying harmony came to my mind in a quasi melodic manner, like broken chords. A melodic line, a voice part, or even a melody derives from horizontal projections of tonal relations. A chord results similarly from projections in the vertical direction."[7] Schoenberg's creative process was sufficiently unified to transcend the distinctions between melody and accompaniment. In a short analysis of Schoenberg's op. 7 First String Quartet, Anton Webern said, "It is amazing how he builds an accompaniment figure out of the smallest part of a motive, how he introduces the themes, how he conceives of the connections between the individual main sections. And it is all done thematically! There is, so to say, no note in this work that doesn't become thematic. This is unprecedented. Most likely this is still a connection to Johannes Brahms."[8]

The contrapuntal development of thematic material concerns music at its smallest level—the note-to-note details of composition. Schoenberg was simultaneously concerned with the largest level of musical design—the form. As noted, the sextet *Verklärte Nacht* resembles Wagner in its treatment of thematic material. The sextet is also Wagnerian in its idiomatic approach to form. Indeed, the form has been variously identified as a free fantasia, a rondo, and varying types of sonata forms.[9] However, in the next group of works, Schoenberg actively—and audibly—confronts the traditional movement structure of the sonata. The three instrumental works that follow *Verklärte Nacht* are the op. 4 symphonic poem *Pelleas und Melisande* (1902–1903), the aforementioned First String Quartet and the op. 9 Chamber Symphony. These three works comprise three different approaches to the same idea—the combination of the four movements of a sonata (or symphony) into a single movement that simultaneously maps to a sonata form. In each of these works, Schoenberg moves further away from the formal designs characteristic of Wagner. *Pelleas* is a combination of traditional forms, but it is also a tone poem, based on the play by Maurice Maeterlinck. The First String Quartet is similarly based on a loose, secret program, only revealed in 1986, but unlike *Pelleas*, it is in distinct, but conjoined movements.[10] The Chamber Symphony, while dramatic, has no known program, and like the First Quartet is in conjoined movements. The next two instrumental works are the op. 10 Second String Quartet (1907–1908) and the first movement of the op. 38 Second Chamber Symphony (1906–1908; completed in 1939). These two works continue the trend toward more traditional forms in that they eschew the four-move-ments-in-one design for four smaller movements in the manner of a Classical sonata. Walter Frisch has noted that these two works function as complements to their previous works in the same genre (the First Quartet and Chamber Symphony) both in their formal design and in what he calls "a more lyrical idiom and a less cluttered texture."[11]

By 1907 Schoenberg was fully possessed of a musical language that was both highly idiomatic and strongly rooted in the Classical tradition, by way of Brahms. He had not only minimized the Wagnerian aspects of thematic development, but also the Wagnerian rhapsodic approach to large-scale form. Moreover, Schoenberg's connection to the past was undoubtedly emphasized by his teaching, which dealt almost exclusively with masterpieces from the common practice period. Indeed, when signing a copy of his First String Quartet for his student Karl Horwitz, Schoenberg inscribed: "Don't strive to learn *anything* from this; rather try to learn from Mozart, Beethoven, and Brahms!"[12] However, these core musical values were challenged in the years preceding *Pierrot*.

Joseph Auner has presented a model for understanding the conflict that emerged in 1909.[13] Schoenberg's 1946 essay "Heart and Brain in Music" challenges the simplistic notion that inspiration and intuition come from the heart and are thus somehow superior to contemplation and organization, which are said to come from the brain. In short, Schoenberg argues that it is hard to separate these two creative wellsprings because inspiration requires cerebral work to realize, while cerebral work can yield sudden inspiration. Auner parallels this later perspective with the period of conflict forty years earlier and notes, "[T]he intensity with which Schoenberg in 1946 argued for the interdependence of inspiration and intellect was matched by his insistence on their incompatibility in the years leading up to the First World War."[14]

In the critical period before the composition of *Pierrot*, the cerebral aspects, or *brain*, of Schoenberg's music included the development of thematic material and the approach to traditional forms as previously addressed. However, by 1909, Schoenberg's letters and writings reveal a sudden interest in the opposite of everything he had accomplished in his music—the intuitive aspect or *heart*. The extent to which Schoenberg's values seem to have changed can be judged in the often-quoted passage, from a 1909 letter to Ferrucio Busoni that Schoenberg arranged like a prose poem:

> I strive for: complete liberation from all forms
> from all symbols
> of cohesion and
> of logic.
> Thus:
> away with 'motivic working out'.
> Away with harmony as
> cement or bricks of a building.
> Harmony is *expression*
> and nothing else.
> Then:
> Away with Pathos!
> Away with protracted ten-ton scores, from erected or constructed
> towers, rocks and other massive claptrap.
> My music must be
> *brief.*
> Concise! In two notes: not built, but '*expressed*'!!
> And the results I wish for:
> no stylized and sterile protracted emotion.
> People are not like that:
> it is *impossible* for a person to have only *one* sensation at a time.
> One has *thousands* simultaneously. And these thousands can no
> more readily be added together than an apple and a pear. They go
> their own ways.
> And this variegation, this multifariousness, this *illogicality* which
> our senses demonstrate, the illogicality presented by their interactions,
> set forth by some mounting rush of blood, by some reaction of the
> senses or the nerves, this I should like to have in my music.
> It should be an expression of feeling, as our feelings, which bring
> us in contact with our subconscious, really are, and no false
> child of feelings and "conscious logic."[15]

The extreme positions taken in this letter are consistent with similar sentiments in a number of letters to Kandinsky and Busoni. However, they cannot be accepted without qualification. For example, this excerpt comes from a letter in which Schoenberg was expressing irritation with Busoni: the letter begins, "Above all, you have wronged me." Busoni, a brilliant pianist, had criticized Schoenberg's writing for the piano in the Piano Pieces, op. 11, nos. 1 and 2. Thus, it was a debate, and even though it was a polite and collegial debate, Schoenberg was not one to concede ground in a debate, even if his argument eventually strayed into hyperbole.

In a larger context, as Auner notes, many of Schoenberg's radical statements from this period are contradictory. For example, in the next letter Schoenberg writes to Busoni, he says, "I do not believe in putting *new wine* into old bottles." In the context of the letter, the metaphor suggests that when the language of music changes, it must be recast in new forms and genres. However, three paragraphs later, Schoenberg writes, "Yes indeed, when a new art seeks and finds new means of expression, almost all earlier techniques go hang: seemingly, at any rate; for actually they are retained; but in a different way. (To discuss this would lead me too far.)"[16]

Despite Schoenberg's occasionally inconsistent statements, there is no question that his music changes dramatically in August 1909. Having written two of the op. 11 Three Piano Pieces and four of the op. 16 Five Pieces for Orchestra, Schoenberg completes those works with final movements that are models of athematic composition showing little of the motivic development and traditional form that can be detected in the earlier movements. And having turned the corner, Schoenberg continues in this gestural style with the op. 17 short opera *Erwartung* (1909), most of the op. 19 Six Little Piano Pieces (1911), and the op. 20 song "Herzgewächse."

In order to both dramatize the change in Schoenberg's musical language and to keep our focus on vocal music, we will consider two songs. "Ich darf nicht dankend" is the first of the op. 14 Two Songs (1907). Schoenberg identified the op. 14 songs as the "first step" in the direction of renouncing a tonal center.[17] Example 2-1 presents the first five measures. The example shows the development of a motive saturating the texture. The three-note motive in the piano right hand, m. 2, is immediately adopted by the voice and composed out to the end of the phrase. However, before the appearance of the motive in m. 2, it is anticipated by a variant in the left hand at the end of the first measure. Considering that the basic shape of the motive is undergoing variation, it is easy to find other motivic variants. In addition to the anticipation of the motive at the end of m. 1, it is also anticipated by the two chords in the right hand, m. 1. The soprano notes G-sharp and G-natural form an inversion of the first two notes of the motive from m. 2: it is the short step of the motive without the leap that follows. However, the two soprano notes assume greater importance as the phrase proceeds, returning in m. 3 transposed down a half-step in the right hand (anticipating m. 4 in the soprano) and, most significantly, at the end of the phrase in the soprano with the drop down to an A_3—the same A in the same octave that is a common tone to both chords in m. 1. At the same time, the chord in the left hand of m. 5 comprises elements from the two chords in m. 2: it contains the augmented fourth of the first chord—composed of the only two pitches it shares with m. 1—and the minor seventh of the second chord.[18]

The rest of "Ich darf nicht dankend" continues in the manner of the excerpt in ex. 2-1. The song is essentially a two-part form, which matches the two verses of the poem. In a device that he will use often for the Pierrot melodramas, at the end of the first verse, following two connecting bars, Schoenberg presents a varied reprise of the beginning, which continues as a second section with still further development.

As a "first step" in post-tonality, there is still much about this passage and the song that continues the techniques found in Schoenberg's more traditionally tonal music. The key signature implies a focus on a particular diatonic collection, and the last measure contains octave Bs in the bass, under a B minor triad. Moreover, the conspicuous use of bass octaves in the second section is a vestige of nineteenth-century piano writing that will soon be excised from his language.[19] And while the passage is highly chromatic and only vaguely centered (the low C-sharps and leading E-sharps suggest F-sharp minor), it is only a little more dissonant than Beethoven's op. 131 String Quartet in C-sharp minor—a work this passage resembles both in the entrance of the motive in the left hand, m. 1, and the fugato-like spacing of that motive in the first, third, and fifth measure.[20]

Example 2-1. "Ich darf nicht dankend," mm. 1–5.

Despite identification of "Ich darf nicht dankend" as an incipient post-tonal work, in most respects it is consistent with the motivic development and formal designs that Schoenberg cultivated in the early years of the twentieth century. To demonstrate the extent to which Schoenberg departed from such logical organization, consider the op. 20 song "Herzgewächse" (1911), written for "high" soprano, celesta, harmonium, and harp.

"Herzgewäsche" is perhaps the least analyzed work that Schoenberg composed in the period under investigation.[21] It is easy to understand why. In what must be one of the first references to "Herzgewächse" in print outside Germany, an anonymous wit described it in the *Musical Times* by noting, "Anyone can invent the accompaniment by playing any chords at any moment below the vocal line. . . . Care must be taken to avoid any agreement between the intervals."[22] The sarcasm in this statement masks the writer's frustration in seeking the coherence in the song, and especially the kind of thematic and harmonic coherence that Schoenberg expressly avoided. Allen Forte has shown that the passage in ex. 2-2 reveals an intricate structuring of pitch-class sets, and that the entire song comprises only nineteen pitch-class sets and their complements.[23] However, the surface of the music is not available to the kind of analysis that was possible, even obvious, for "Ich darf nicht dankend." Each instrument, including the soprano, seems to proceed with its own idioms.

The instrumentation of "Herzgewächse" was likely chosen to support the text—the bright and glassy timbres matching the "blue glass of tired melancholy" from the first line of the poem. However, the possibilities and limitations of the instruments in and of themselves figure prominently in the composition. In the 18 August 1909 letter to Busoni, Schoenberg briefly summarizes his

Example 2-2.   "Herzgewächse," mm. 1–4.

view on the relationship between composition and instrumentation: "Composition is the dominant factor; one takes the instrument into account. Not the contrary."[24] This is consistent with Schoenberg's other writings on instrumentation, in which he argues that instrumental timbre is not an end, but a means to an end—the clarity of compositional design.[25] He further predicts that only the most versatile instruments, instruments with large ranges and uniform dynamics, will endure, whereas instruments that exist merely to provide novel colors will eventually disappear from the orchestra. "Herzgewächse" was written for publication in *Der blaue Reiter*, an almanac of paintings and essays organized by Wassily Kandinsky and Franz Marc. Flush with his enthusiasm for painting and the synesthesic relationship between color and timbre, Schoenberg scored "Herzgewächse" for colorful instruments despite their limitations. The harp can only produce seven pitches at any given time, which presents challenges for a composer who is avoiding the tonicizing effect of a diatonic collection. The celesta sounds an octave higher than written, but its bell-like spectrum makes it difficult to determine the actual register. The harmonium, the only instrument in the ensemble that can sustain notes, has an expansive range but lacks the intensity of the other instruments. Finally, the soprano is duly challenged by the tessitura of "Herzgewächse," which ranges from low G-sharp$_3$ to high F$_6$. Far from illuminating an underlying compositional design, the instrumentation of "Herzgewächse" is the most salient aspect of this song.

"Herzgewächse" is perhaps the last complete composition to use the gestural, athematic language that Schoenberg adopted in 1909. Just as Schoenberg eventually emerged from the spell of Wagner's idioms and returned to a compositional technique more closely aligned with Brahms, so too the fever of modernism eventually broke and Schoenberg returned once more to his pre-1909 musical values—if somewhat altered for the experience. Schoenberg acknowledged the extremity of the 1909–1912 period in 1946:

> Usually when changes of style occur in the arts, a tendency can be observed to overemphasize the difference between the new and the old. Advice to followers is given in the form of exaggerated rules, originating from a distinct trend "*epater le bourgeois*," that is, "to amaze mediocrity." ... Intoxicated by the enthusiasm of having freed music from the shackles of tonality, I had thought to find further liberty of expression. In fact, I myself and my pupils Anton von Webern and Alban Berg, and even Alois Hába believed that now music could renounce motivic features and remain coherent and comprehensible nevertheless.[26]

Even before the composition of "Herzgewächse" there is some evidence that Schoenberg was vacillating between the extremity of his new musical language and the idioms cultivated before 1909. Haimo has noted that the fourth of the op. 19 Six Little Piano Pieces is in three phrases, in which the third phrase begins with a varied reprise of the first phrase.[27] Perhaps the most instructive case of Schoenberg's return to his original music values is the op. 18 opera, *Die glücklische Hand*. This opera, the focus of Auner's research, was begun in 1910 at the very height of Schoenberg's enthusiasm for modernism and begins in a musical language that resembles *Erwartung*. However, when Schoenberg returned to *Die glücklische Hand* in late 1912, Auner notes that Schoenberg "depended increasingly on thematic and motivic development, imitative counterpoint, and a clearly defined form based on large- and small-scale repetition."[28] While the crisis wasn't completely solved, clearly, the corner had been turned. During the first half of 1912, Schoenberg had essentially worked out a way to return to his former musical values.

During the first half of 1912, Schoenberg composed *Pierrot lunaire*.

★ ★ ★

Among the many things that set *Pierrot* apart from Schoenberg's previous works is that it was composed on commission to be performed by the commissioner. This fact, in itself, was troubling to Schoenberg. At a time when he wrote about composing as the result of an inner need, *Pierrot* was clearly the result of an external stimulus. Moreover, *Pierrot* was an opportunity to make money. Schoenberg was clearly conflicted about how the prospect of financial gain squared with his more idealistically pure motivations. On the other hand, the fact that *Pierrot* was commissioned was also liberating. It gave him an opportunity to set aside *Die glücklische Hand*, on which work had stalled. It also allowed him to compose with a degree of distance from the material. But the most interesting thing about *Pierrot* may have been the commissioner herself. In Zehme, he found, at least initially, a colleague with similar ideas about the joining of words and music.

Albertine Zehme, neé Aman (1857–1946), was born in Vienna.[29] She trained as an actress and made her way through a regional theater in Oldenberg until her appointment at the Leipzig Stadttheater. While acting in Leipzig, she caught the eye of Dr. Felix Zehme (1849–1924). Dr. Zehme was an attorney from a cultured family. Albertine claimed a noble lineage and said she had been born "in the shadow of the Stephansdom," but Dr. Zehme's family unsuccessfully opposed the marriage.[30] Albertine Zehme's contract with the Stadttheater ended with her nuptials, but she remained devoted to cultural pursuits, opening her home to writers and artists.

In 1891, she went to Bayreuth to study singing. There, she studied the Brünhilde parts in *Der Ring des Nibelungen*, among other roles, with Cosima Wagner and Julius Kniese. On her return to Leipzig, she organized lieder recitals with mixed results. An 1895 recital of lieder by Franz Liszt at the Hôtel de Prasse was reviewed in the *Musicalisches Wochenblatt*. In a decidedly guarded tone reflecting the "private character" of the event, the reviewer notes that she managed "Lasst mich ruhen" and "Die Fischerstochter" with a fine mezzo soprano voice and disposition. However, some of the songs required "greater artistic abilities than Frau Zehme seems to possess."[31] Dr. Rudolf Mothes, a contemporary attorney in Leipzig, remembered Zehme's recital of Hugo Wolf's lieder in the great hall of the Buchhändlerbörse, which he had been persuaded to attend by a friend who was a critic for the *Leipziger Tageblattes*. "As the audience began to move, slowly and calmly but inexorably toward the doors, they were locked. As I recall, despite her various relationships with the city's literary circles, Frau Albertine Zehme received no more favorable press."[32] Despite the reviews, Zehme appears to have learned a lesson about captive audiences: the program for her 1911 recital of the Pierrot poems ends with the line, "During the recitations, the doors to the hall will remain locked."[33]

Many sources about *Pierrot* describe Zehme as an actress, which slights the mixture of singing and speaking throughout her career. It is significant that as early as 1894, while Zehme was still giving lieder recitals, she had already begun to make appearances as a reciter. The Leipzig correspondent for the *Musikalisches Wochenblatt* describes a recital of Martin Krause's piano studio. A long sentence that lists each student and his pieces, concludes, "[T]he spirited recitation of Frau Dr. Zehme followed."[34] Krause and Zehme must have been acquaintances: she performed there more than once. This is notable because Krause—a student of Liszt—taught at the Stern Conservatory from 1896 to 1911; he was there when Schoenberg taught harmony at the Stern Conservatory in 1902.

Things changed considerably for the Zehmes at the turn of the century when Dr. Zehme entered the litigation of a notorious divorce. Friedrich August, the Crown Prince of Saxony, had become estranged from his wife, Luise of Tuscany. The popular Luise had embroiled the Saxon crown in a scandal when, pregnant with her seventh child, she left the prince in 1902 for her children's French tutor, widely believed to be the father. The divorce was particularly difficult. As members of the Imperial House of Austria, the prince and princess were beyond the jurisdiction of any court. On the other hand, they were married as Catholics and the Vatican would not consent to a divorce or grant an annulment. The King of Saxony eventually convened a tribunal that crafted a civil divorce, which was finalized in February 1903. In her autobiography, Luise disputed the legality of her divorce: a religious marriage that was not a civil marriage ended with a civil divorce but not an annulment.[35]

Dr. Zehme continued to represent Luise in lingering issues against her ex-husband, who ascended to the throne in 1904. In a vivid scene from her autobiography, Luise claims to have been betrayed by her lawyer (certainly Zehme) when she attempted to surprise her children with Christmas presents. However, Zehme continued to represent her interests. [36] The case made Zehme's career and fortune.

Comfortably established, Albertine Zehme made a slow return to the stage. She carefully chose roles, particularly in Ibsen's plays, to perform at the Leipziger Schauspielhaus. According to Mothes, it was widely said at the time that Felix Zehme underwrote the costs of engaging famous actors for plays in which his wife appeared. Moreover, Mothes notes, "As I remember, we did not go the Schauspielhaus to see Mrs. Albertine Zehme's interpretation of Ibsen's roles for women. Instead, we went because of the famous guests from abroad."[37]

A brief glimpse of life at the Zehmes' home, the Villa Albertine in Gautzch (now Markkleeberg) near Leipzig, can be found in the letters of American dancer Isadora Duncan (1877–1927). Duncan had established a school in Berlin, and the students performed at the Zehmes' home. In 1906, Duncan became pregnant with the child of English theater designer Craig Gordon, the son of English actress Ellen Terry. Spurned by Berlin society, she stayed at Villa Albertine for several weeks. While Duncan was grateful for the safety and isolation of Villa Albertine, she found the Zehmes occasionally meddlesome but mostly indifferent hosts. (Much later, Schoenberg would describe Albertine Zehme as "not an overwhelmingly generous hostess," when his family stayed in Gautzch in 1913.[38]) Duncan's letters allude to Dr. Zehme's continuing interest and patronage of the theater; he offered to found a society to host Craig Gordon in a new enterprise in Berlin. Albertine Zehme is said to be commuting between her home and an unspecified engagement in Berlin; Duncan says only that she "will play in Berlin from July 15 to Aug 1."[39] Finally, the letters suggest the extent of the Zehmes' integration in a wider European cultural life. Duncan refers to her friend, the Italian actress Eleanor Duse. Duse was also connected to the Zehmes through Robert von Mendelssohn and his wife, the former Giulietta Gordigiani, who referred Duncan to the Zehmes. Both Mendelssohns were prominent amateur musicians. Robert Mendelssohn, whose father was the cousin of Felix Mendelssohn, had known Clara Schumann and Johannes Brahms. In such company, the Zehmes had broad access to the most prominent musicians and actors in Europe.

Salka Viertel (born Salomea Steuermann, 1889–1978) was the sister of Eduard Steuermann (1892–1964), the pianist who would later coach Zehme on the Sprechstimme of *Pierrot*. An accomplished actress herself, Viertel would later summarize Zehme as she appeared in 1912: "Married to a wealthy man, her children grown up and the boredom of a middle class existence upon her, she had decided to have a fling at an artistic career, and, dressed as Pierrot, she toured Germany reciting the moody, delicate poems."[40] Viertel certainly over-states the case. However, from the few sources available, an image of Albertine Zehme emerges as a frustrated performer putting her family ahead of her career and finding herself eclipsed by her successful husband, who was courting the company of more successful artists.

At some point near the end of the decade, Zehme's interest in the relationship between sound and poetry intensifies. She corresponded with Richard Dehmel about the differences between the declamation of actors and poets and invited him to performances of her readings.[41] In 1910, the poet and impresario Max Burkhard sent her the following poem, rendered loosely:

> It spins forth, a mysterious swell, from word to tone, from tone to word. Only a few are summoned to unravel this puzzling needlepoint and to secure other joys with the solution. You are so favored! You pass it on! To please strangers, on whom life has never smiled, your full hands scatter roses, plucked from your flowering tree—our art![42]

Around the same time, Zehme became fascinated with the Pierrot poems in Otto Erich Hartleben's translation, first published in 1893. It is possible Zehme knew Hartleben; Hartleben stayed in Leipzig in the winter of 1886–1887 studying law, which may have put him in contact with Dr. Zehme. In Leipzig, Hartleben met his future wife, Selma Hesse. Formerly a waitress, Selma became well-known in literary circles in Leipzig and Berlin, where she was called "Moppchen" ("little mop").[43] Zehme could possibly have known her, either from her own salad days as an actress or her later association with writers. When Schoenberg could not obtain a copy of Hartleben's translations, Zehme appealed directly to Selma Hartleben, to no avail.[44]

In a program for a concert on 4 March 1911 at the Choralion-Sall—where Schoenberg's *Pierrot* would premiere eighteen months later—Zehme gave a recital that she described as "[p]oetic experiences in tone."[45] The music for this performance was selected from a cycle of songs by the composer Otto Vrieslander (1880–1950). Vrieslander, today better known for his later writings on Heinrich Schenker, had set 46 of the 50 Pierrot poems to music in 1903.[46] Zehme selected the songs/texts from Vrieslander's collection of 46 and arranged them in three cycles with a short pause between each cycle. It is unclear if Vrieslander had any direct involvement with Zehme's performance. It is also unclear how Zehme performed the text. The Vrieslander songs are conventional songs with piano accompaniment. However, the program includes a short text by Albertine Zehme, under the title, "Why I Must Speak These Songs."[47]

The text begins with a theatrical conceit: a newborn's first cry is his first experience in tone. As the infant grows, so does his ability to vary his sounds.

"Thus timbre [*Tonfarbe*] and pitch [*Tonhöhe*] remain in a close relationship with an assortment of desires."[48] A mother can recognize what her child wants despite the fact that the child's tone-language (*Tonsprache*) bears little relation to language. This observation engenders her thesis: we are so biased toward the literal meaning of words, we have lost the ability to take meaning from vocal sounds.

> In daily life, the ear is not the interpreter; rather we have become accustomed to take what we would know or communicate from the sense of the word.
>
> Over the course of years, the head assumes more and more of the work of the ear, ever more completely . . .
>
> *I* want to restore the ear to its position in life. Meaning should be conveyed not only by the words we speak; the sounds should also participate in relating the inner experience. To make that possible, we must have unrestricted freedom of tone [*Tonfreiheit*]. Emotional expression should not be denied any of the thousands of oscillations. I demand not free-thinking, but freedom of tone!
>
> The singing voice, bound in otherworldly chastity, fixed in its ascetic bondage as an ideal, exquisite instrument—even a strong exhale dulls its inaccessible beauty—is not suitable for intense emotional outbursts.
>
> Life can no longer be played out with only beautiful sounds. The final, deepest happiness, the final deepest sorrow, sounds in our breast as a noiseless, unheard scream that threatens to burst forth or erupt like a stream of flaming lava over our lips. For the expression of these final things, it seems nearly cruel to me to allow the singing voice the manual labor of performing realistically, from which it must emerge scattered, frayed and broken.
>
> To communicate, our poets and our composers need both singing as well as the spoken tone [*Sprachton*].[49]

Zehme's brief text is remarkably similar to concurrent writings by Schoenberg. Like many of Schoenberg's contemporary statements, Zehme's emphasis is on direct expression and inner experience. Similarly, there is a critique of older techniques and genres. Where Schoenberg disparages motivic development and traditional form, Zehme denigrates singing as a voice "bound in otherworldly chastity" and "fixed in its ascetic bondage." But most significantly, Zehme's language anticipates ideas in Schoenberg's essay, "The Relationship to the Text."

Written in January 1912, and mailed for publication in *Der blaue Reiter Almanac* just before learning of the *Pierrot* commission, this essay is a remarkable exploration of the relationships, and especially the differences, between words and music. The first part of the essay is a broad consideration of attempts to translate the experience of music into words. As such, Schoenberg approvingly quotes Arthur Schopenhauer as saying, "The composer reveals the inmost essence of the world and utters the most found wisdom in a language *which his reason does not understand.*" Schoenberg then critiques efforts to translate the inmost essence, as found in music, into the abstraction of language. He notes that in Wagner's programs for the Beethoven symphonies, Wagner received the essence by listening to the music and was stimulated to translate that essence into the material of another art—the words of poetry. However, he opines that a misunderstanding of Wagner's effort had misled too many musicians and critics to focus too narrowly on a verbal interpretation of music. The most celebrated passage from the essay is about text-setting, here quoted in full:

> A few years ago I was deeply ashamed when I discovered in several Schubert songs, well-known to me, that I had absolutely no idea what was going on in the poems on which they were based. But when I had read the poems it became clear to me that I had gained absolutely nothing for the understanding of the songs thereby, since the poems did not make it necessary for me to change my conception of the musical interpretation in the slightest degree. On the contrary it appeared that, without knowing the poem, I had grasped the content, the real content, perhaps even more profoundly than if I had clung to the surface of the mere thoughts expressed in words. For me, even more decisive than this experience was the fact that, inspired by the sound of the first words of the text, I had composed many of my songs straight through to the end without troubling myself in the slightest about the continuation of the poetic events, without even grasping them in the ecstasy of composing, and that only days later I thought of looking back to see just what was the real poetic content of my song. It then turned out, to my greatest astonishment, that I had never done greater justice to the poet than when, guided by my first direct contact with the sound of the beginning, I divined everything that obviously had to follow this first sound with inevitability.[50]

In this passage, Schoenberg unwittingly fills a need that Zehme identifies. She lamented that people are too biased toward the literal meaning of words to the exclusion of the sound of words. Schoenberg describes setting text primarily on the basis of the sounds—and not the meaning—of the first few words of text. Schoenberg's idea is substantially more elaborated, as befits the difference between an essay and a program note. He goes on to advance a theory of organicism wherein each part contains the image and inner meaning of the whole.

While often cited, Schoenberg's essay contains comparatively little about text-setting. Moreover, what Schoenberg does reveal about his working method has been challenged by a number of scholars. Carl Dahlhaus argues that Schoenberg's statement about being led by the first sounds of the first words "turns out to be all the more revealing in the context of the history of ideas on account of the fact that an analysis of the George Songs [op. 15] proves it to be blatantly untrue."[51] Dahlhaus asserts that Schoenberg's aesthetic philosophy is singularly directed toward instrumental music. Karl H. Wörner has made a similar argument. In many of Schoenberg's later articles, which, as noted in chapter 2, tend to put his career in the historicist context of continuing the great German tradition, Schoenberg lists his influences and what he learned from their example. It is interesting that in these retrospectives, Schoenberg never mentions text-setting, prosody, or song. Wörner suggests Schoenberg's practice of relating music and words may have developed through an unselfconscious imitation of models.[52] Jonathan Dunsby argues similarly and concludes that Schoenberg "had no special theoretical concerns about setting words: this was compositional work he took in stride."[53] Nevertheless, Schoenberg continued insisting his text-setting was largely guided by his impressions of the sound of the words. In a 1931 response to a questionnaire, Schoenberg listed five stages of composing a song. In the first stage, Schoenberg refers to an "unnameable sense of a sounding and moving space, of a form with characteristic relationships." In the second phase, Schoenberg spoke of "translating the poem into everyday music."[54] And his American student, Dika Newlin, recounted a composition lesson from 1939 in which Schoenberg reiterated his statements from "The Relationship to the Text," seemingly without reference to the source. As she recalled, "[H]e says that his usual procedure has always been to repeat the poem over and over again until he gets a definite sensation of the rises and falls of the speech melody, which he then applies to the vocal melody. (He didn't say, but I take it this is the germ of the idea of *Sprechgesang*.)"[55]

Schoenberg's statements about text-setting may be entirely sincere and accurate, while simultaneously speaking to an aspect of the poem he cannot describe. For example, as discussed in chapter 4, Schoenberg looked to poetry to provide form for his post-tonal music. One might assume that the form of such music would model the narrative implicit in the poem—a higher-level form of word-painting. But even word-painting is a concept that Schoenberg thoroughly reexamined. In his 1931 lecture about the Orchestral Songs, op. 22, Schoenberg wrote:

> My music, however, took representational words into account in the same way as abstract ones: it furthered the immediate, vivid rendering of the whole and of its parts, according to the measure of their meaning within the whole. Now, if a performer speaks of a passionate sea in a different tone of voice than he might use for a calm sea, my music does nothing else than to provide him with the opportunity to do so, and to support him. The music will not be as agitated as the sea, but it will be *differently* so, as, indeed, the performer will be. Even a painting does not reproduce its whole subject

matter; it merely states a motionless condition. Likewise, a word describes an object and its state; a film reproduces it without color, and a color film would reproduce it without organic life. Only music, however, can bestow this last gift, and that is why music may impose a limit on its capacity to imitate—by *placing* the object and its being *before the mind's* eye, through performance.[56]

Thus, Schoenberg's relationship to word-painting is not unlike a painter's relationship to his model: the object is not to render the meaning through mimicry, but rather to present the artist's impression of the object. This idea is also implicit in "The Relationship to the Text," in which Schoenberg concludes, "[I]n all music composed to poetry, the exactitude of the reproduction of the events is as irrelevant to the artistic value as is the resemblance of a portrait to its model." On this point especially, Schoenberg and Zehme—who wore a Pierrot costume at the premiere—had far different ideas. However, in identifying the sound of words as more important to their meaning, Schoenberg and Zehme agreed on an uncommon idea. And it was certainly this shared conviction about the immediate force of sound over meaning that led to the quote of Novalis, prominently placed on the second page of the program:

> Narratives can be conceived with associations but without coherence, like dreams—poems, which are merely euphonious, filled with beautiful words, but also without sense and cohesion, at most only a few intelligible lines, like fragments from the most disparate things. This true poetry can have at most only an allegorical sense in general and an indirect result like music.[57]

NOTES

1. Ethan Haimo, *Schoenberg's Transformation of Musical Language* (Cambridge: Cambridge University Press, 2006), 7.

2. Arnold Schoenberg, "My Evolution," in *Style and Idea*, ed. Leonard Stein (London: St. Martin's Press, 1975; rev. pb. ed., Berkeley, 1984), 87. Hereafter, the anthology will be abbreviated *Style and Idea*, without editor or publishing details.

3. "My Evolution," *Style and Idea*, 80.

4. "Criteria for the Evaluation of Music," *Style and Idea*, 129.

5. For a more nuanced discussion of developing variation and early Schoenberg, see Walter Frisch, "Brahms, Developing Variation, and the Schoenberg Critical Tradition," *19th-Century Music* 5/3 (1982): 215–32 and *The Early Works of Arnold Schoenberg, 1903–1908* (Berkeley: University of California Press, 1993).

6. Schoenberg provides a compelling explanation of these symbols in his preface to his *Die vereinfachte Studier- und Dirigier-Partitur* [of Vier Lieder für Gesang und Orchester op. 22] (Vienna: Universal Edition, 1919).

7. "My Evolution," *Style and Idea*, 87.

8. Anton Webern, "Schoenberg's Music," trans. Barbara Z. Schoenberg, in *Schoenberg and His World*, ed. Walter Frisch, 195–261 (Princeton: Princeton University Press, 1999), 217. Originally published in *Arnold Schönberg* (Munich: R. Piper & Co., 1912).

9. The literature on the form of *Verklärte Nacht* is summarized and examined in Frisch 1993, 112–16.

10. "Schönberg's 'Very Definite—But Private' Program zum Streichquartett Opus 7," in *Bericht über den 2. Kongreß der Internationalen Schönberg-Gesellschaft*, ed. Rudolf Stephan and Sigrid Wiesmann (Vienna: Eilsabeth Lafite, 1986), 230–34.

11. Frisch 1993, 249.

12. Karl Horwitz, "[The Teacher]," trans. Barbara Z. Schoenberg, in *Schoenberg and His World*, ed. Walter Frisch, 195–261 (Princeton: Princeton University Press, 1999), 256. Originally published in *Arnold Schönberg* (Munich: R. Piper & Co., 1912).

13. Joseph Auner, "'Heart and Brain in Music': The Genesis of Schoenberg's *Die glückliche Hand*," in *Constructive Dissonance: Arnold Schoenberg and the Transformations of Twentieth-Century Culture*, ed. Juliane Brand and Christopher Hailey (Berkeley: University of California Press, 1997), 112–25.

14. Auner 1997, 113.

15. *Ferrucio Busoni: Selected Letters*, trans. and ed. Antony Beaumont (New York: Columbia University Press, 1987), 389. Hereafter "Busoni/Beaumont."

16. Busoni/Beaumont, 392–93.

17. "My Evolution," *Style and Idea*, 86.

18. For slightly different analytical approaches to this passage, see: Bryan R. Simms, *The Atonal Music of Arnold Schoenberg, 1908–1923* (New York: Oxford University Press, 2000), 34–35, where the semitone in m. 1 is emphasized as the generating unit; and Haimo 2006, 236–40, where the chords in m. 1 are designated motive 'a' and the motive in the left hand is designated motive 'b.'

19. In the letters to Busoni quoted earlier in the chapter, Schoenberg defends his writing for the piano by distancing himself from a nineteenth-century pianism, which Schoenberg later came to believe was an attempt to transfer an orchestral sound to the piano. For a fine later summary of the Second Viennese School's approach to the piano, see Eduard Steuermann, "*Die Eignung des Klaviers für moderne Musik*," *Musikblätter des Anbruch* 9 (1927): 367–68; trans. Richard Cantwell, David Porter, and Clara Steuermann as "The Appropriateness of the Piano for Modern Music," in *The Not Quite Innocent Bystander: Writings of Edward Steuermann*, ed. Clara Steuermann, David Porter, and Gunther Schuller (Lincoln: University of Nebraska Press, 1989).

20. Frisch has noted a similarity between Beethoven's famous op. 131 subject and the first subject of a double fugue that Schoenberg sketched for an incomplete string quartet in 1901–1904; Frisch notes that Schoenberg later acknowledged op. 131 as a formal model for his op. 7 First String Quartet (Frisch 1993, 185–86).

21. As of summer 2007, the periodical index JSTOR listed only fifteen articles that contained the word *Herzgewächsen*, and of them, only two were primarily concerned with Schoenberg's op. 20.

22. "The Vocalist of the Future," *Musical Times*, March 1, 1913, 165.

23. Allen Forte, "Sets and Non-Sets in Schoenberg's Atonal Music," *Perspectives of New Music* 11/1 (1972): 43.

24. Busoni/Beaumont, 389.

25. For example, "The Future of Orchestral Instruments," *Style and Idea*, 322–26; "Instrumentation," *Style and Idea*, 330–36.

26. "My Evolution," *Style and Idea*, 87–88.

27. Haimo 2006, 351.

28. Auner 1997, 122.

29. Some sources give Albertine Zehme's maiden name as Satran.

30. Andreas Höhn, "Im Dienst der Krone und der Kunst: Albertine und Felix Zehme," *Leipziger Blätter* 39 (2001): 39.

31. "nN," "Leipzig," *Musikalisches Wochenblatt*, November 28, 1895, [4]; reprinted in *Musikalisches Wochenblatt:Sechsundzwanzigster Jahrgang*, ed. E. W. Fritzsch (Leipzig:Verlag E. W. Fritzsch, 1895), 624.

32. Rudolf Mothes, "Lebenserinnerungen," n.d. Archiv der Stadt Leipzig, Leipzig, Teil C, 11 at http://www.quelle-optimal.de/mothes.html (accessed on July 23, 2007).

33. Brinkmann 1996, 306.

34. "F," *Der Musikalisches Wochenblatt*, July 12, 1894, [6]; reprinted in *Musikalisches Wochenblatt:Fünfundzwanzigster Jahrgang*, ed. E. W. Fritzsch (Leipzig:Verlag E. W. Fritzsch, 1894), 356.

35. Luisa of Tuscany [Louise Antoinette Marie], *My Own Story* (New York: G.P. Putnam's sons, 1911), 285.

36. Luisa, 336–38. Some sources claim Luise's relationship with composer Enrico Toselli prompted her divorce. However, the divorce was imposed by fiat in 1903, long before her 1907 marriage to Toselli.

37. Mothes, 11.

38. Alban Berg and Arnold Schoenberg, *The Berg-Schoenberg Correspondence: Selected Letters*, ed. Juliane Brand, Christopher Hailey, and Donald Harris (New York: W. W. Norton & Company, 1987), 184.

39. Isadora Duncan to Craig Gordon [June 1906], The Craig-Duncan Collection, New York: New York Public Library. The letters are summarized in "*Your Isadora*": *The Love Story of Isadora Duncan & Gordon Craig*, ed. Francis Steegmuller (New York: Random House, 1974), 127–28.

40. Salka Viertel, *The Kindness of Strangers* (New York: Holt, Rinehart, and Winston, 1969), 57.

41. Two letters survive: Richard Dehmel to Albertine Zehme, 31 August 1906; Richard Dehmel to Albertine Zehme, 14 November 1910 (Stadtgeschichtliches Museum Leipzig).

42. Max Burkhard to Albertine Zehme, 24 May 1910 (Stadtgeschichtliches Museum Leipzig).

43. Alfred von Klement, *Die Bücher von Otto Erich Hartleben: eine Bibliographie, mit der bisher unveröffentlichten Fassung der Selbstbiographie des Dichters* (Salò: Halkyonische Akademie für unangewandte Wissenschaften, 1951), 44.

44. Albertine Zehme to Arnold Schoenberg, 10 March, 1912; reprinted in Brinkmann 1995, 226. Albertine Zehme to Arnold Schoenberg, 12 March, 1912; reprinted in Brinkmann 1995, 228.

45. Brinkmann 1995, 306.

46. Otto Vrieslander, *Pierrot lunaire: 46 Dichtungen nach Albert Giraud* (Munich: Henrich Levy, 1904). Vrieslander would go on to set the remaining four poems to complete the cycle, published in 1911. However, one of the poems he set appears to be inauthentic. See "Translator's Note" in *Albert Giraud's Pierrot lunaire*, trans. and ed. Gregory C. Richter (Kirksville, MO: Truman State University Press, 2001), xxiii.

47. *Warum ich diese Lieder sprechen muss.* Brinkmann 1996, 307.

48. Brinkmann 1996, 308.

49. Brinkmann 1996, 308.

50. "The Relationship to the Text," *Style and Idea*, 144.

51. Carl Dahlhaus, *Schoenberg and the New Music: Essays*, trans. Derrick Puffett and Alfred Clayton (Cambridge: Cambridge University Press, 1987), 85.

52. Karl H. Wörner, "Arnold Schoenberg and the Theater," trans. Willis Wager, *Musical Quarterly* 48/4 (1962): 446.

53. Dunsby 1992, 204, 69.

54. Arnold Schoenberg, "Self Analysis," Appendix 1 to Willi Reich, *Schoenberg: A Critical Biography*, trans. Leo Black (New York: Praeger, 1981), 236.

55. Newlin 1978, 68.

56. Arnold Schoenberg, "Analysis of the Four Orchestral Songs Opus 22," trans. Claudio Spies, *Perspectives of New Music* 3/2 (1965): 3.

57. Program, 2. The quote comes from Novalis' second "Fragments," of 1798. Novalis, *Sämmtliche Werke*, vol. 3, ed. Carl Meissner, (Florence und Leipzig: Eug. Diederichs, 1898), 37.

3

The Sprechstimme in *Pierrot lunaire*

$\mathcal{A}$lbertine Zehme, having made the transition from acting and singing lieder to performing melodramas, sought a composer to create a work that would feature her unique style of declamation. Arnold Schoenberg, who had begun structuring his post-tonal compositions around textual narratives and also the sounds of the words constituting selected texts, was uniquely positioned to fulfill her request. This chapter details the commissioning, creation, early performance, and publication of *Pierrot lunaire* with a particular emphasis on how the Sprechstimme as conceived in early 1912 may have been quite different from what is described in the preface to the score, published in 1914. The chapter continues with an analysis of the preface and a history of Schoenberg's later thinking about the *Pierrot* Sprechstimme.

★ ★ ★

The existing documents reveal a somewhat dramatic commissioning process. Schoenberg was informed of the commission by Emil Gutmann, a concert producer. Gutmann, who had produced the premiere of Mahler's Eighth Symphony, acted as Schoenberg's emissary; he would ultimately produce the premiere. Zehme was, of course, represented by her husband, whose firm drafted the contract.

Much has been suggested about Schoenberg's state of mind during the commission process, which can be considered from his letters and his intermittent attempt at keeping a diary. When Schoenberg first described the project, the second sentence he wrote was "Promises a high fee (1000 Marks)." However, he follows that with, "Have read the preface, looked at the poems, am enthusiastic."[1] More significantly, when the negotiations faltered in mid-Feb-

43

ruary, Schoenberg's reaction reflects the continuing turbulence of his aesthetic worldview:

> Quite unpleasant since I was really counting very much on that money. Yet at the same time I feel somewhat relieved, because I had felt quite depressed about having to compose something I felt not actually compelled to do. It seems as if my fate were to keep me from even the most minor artistic sin. Since, the one time I do not have the courage to decline a sum of money offered to me and which I need sorely, nothing comes out of the negotiations. This way I will always remain clean and will only have committed a sin in my thoughts. Is that not bad enough[?].[2]

As late as 19 August, with the composition completed and on the eve of rehearsals, Schoenberg's description of *Pierrot* in a letter to Kandinsky is so dismissive as to almost constitute a sheepish disavowal of the whole project: "Perhaps the subject, the contents (Giraud's *Pierrot lunaire*) is not dear to the heart. But the form may be. In any case, it is remarkable for me as a prefatory study to another work . . ."[3]

The Pierrot poems were certainly dear to Zehme's heart, but she was just as enthusiastic about the form, or genre, the work would take. She saw the project as nothing less than a culmination of her "poetic experiences in tone," and took great pains to explain her vision to Schoenberg. The first direct contact between them was Zehme's letter of 26 January. After introductory pleasantries, she writes, "I have a special recitation-style [*Vortragstil*] based on my own system: trained in vocal- and expressive-possibilities, and I am eager to make you acquainted with the affective [*seelischen*] instrument on which you will hang your talents."[4] As is typical of Zehme, she uses the German word *Vortrag*, which is roughly equivalent to the English word *recital*. As such, a *Vortrag* could imply both a lecture and a performance. For example, in early twentieth-century usage, *Klaviervortrag* translates "piano recital" while *Mahler-Vortrag* translates "Lecture on Mahler" (such as the lecture Schoenberg gave five days before the premiere of *Pierrot*). Thus, there is always some ambiguity in Zehme's statements: her *Vortragstil* likely refers to a manner of reciting, but could also refer to a manner of performance that would include techniques that are more characteristically musical.

On 3 February, Schoenberg and Zehme met at a performance of Schoenberg's works in Berlin. They retired to Zehme's Berlin residence with Emil Gutmann and presumably discussed their expectations. Schoenberg wrote in his diary:

> She was very enthusiastic about my pieces and that seemed rather genuine to me. She is very pleasant. Reminds me to some degree of Mildenburg (the aloofness) and to some degree of Gutheil (the cordiality, modesty); in other words, of people I like. What she said was very interesting to me. But I will pose different problems for her than the music of Vriesland[er]. Bad!"[5]

Schoenberg's intermittent diary is an extraordinary source because it shows a vulnerability and personal introspection that is not communicated in his correspondence and papers. Given his ambivalence about the project, this passage might be read as if Schoenberg was trying to convince himself to take the commission. However, in the context of his other diary entries, his assessment of Zehme seems candid. As such, it is significant that he judges Zehme's interest in his music authentic, and he must have been deeply touched to find in her a sympathetic listener. This point is also accentuated in a letter from Zehme the next day in which she claims to be still intoxicated (*berauscht*), presumably from their discussion. In her excited state, she writes, in language resembling "O alter Duft," that Schoenberg's music reveals "a fairytale land, in which all my longings would be stilled."[6] Days later, Schoenberg writes in his diary that he had spoken to her and found her "already very enthusiastic about my compositions."[7]

It is also notable that in documenting his first impression of Zehme, he associates her with two of the most famous singers of the era. Anna von Mildenburg (1872–1947) was a Wagnerian soprano and the protégé and one-time lover of Gustav Mahler. Marie Gutheil-Schoder (1874–1935), another Mahler protégé, would premiere a number of Schoenberg's works, including the Second String Quartet and *Erwartung*. Schoenberg had a variety of professional relationships with formidable women. In addition to teaching many women, he collaborated with medical student Marie Pappenheim, who wrote the libretto for *Erwartung*, and maintained the sponsorship and friendship of the mercurial Alma Mahler. Of all the women in Schoenberg's life, he associates Zehme with two singers but identifies personal characteristics as his basis for comparison. That they were both singers is either a subconscious association or so obvious to Schoenberg as to not merit mention.

Finally, perhaps the most remarkable statement in Schoenberg's diary entry is that he was interested in what Zehme said. Personal reminisces of Schoenberg tend to characterize him as more of a talker than a listener in every situation. Alma Mahler's memoirs recount evenings of shoptalk at which Schoenberg spoke freely, and not always cordially, with Gustav Mahler, then perhaps the most domineering personality in Viennese musical life.[8] Similarly, Salka Viertel describes Sunday outings in 1912 at the Schoenbergs' Berlin home at which "Schoenberg dominated the conversation, while his awed pupils listened and rarely said anything. An inspired teacher, he was interested in everything, and everything seemed to give him new ideas."[9] Clearly, Schoenberg heard something from the "aloof" and "modest" Zehme that sparked his imagination.

It was surely at or soon after the 3 February meeting with Zehme that Schoenberg began to formulate a heightened conception of Sprechmelodie. As noted in chapter 1, he had used a speaking part in *Gurrelieder*, but he had not heard it performed. In fact, it is reasonable to assume that Schoenberg had become disenchanted with the Sprechmelodie concept. With the exception of *Gurrelieder* and the still earlier prefatory note to the song "Die Beiden," there are no letters or papers of any kind written before 1912 that suggest Schoenberg gave the matter further thought. Moreover, he did not use anything even resembling the Sprechstimme notation in all the lieder composed after *Gurrelieder* or in the opera *Erwartung*, op. 17. Schoenberg had begun a second opera, *Die glücklische Hand*, op. 18, which would make extensive use of Sprechmelodie; indeed, a chorus of twelve singers intones in harmonic Sprechmelodie. However, if we accept Joseph Auner's composition chronology of *Die glückliche Hand*, none of the sections with Sprechmelodie were composed until July 1912, after the completion of *Pierrot*.[10] Indeed, there is even evidence to suggest that he was hesitant to use Sprechmelodie. At the first use of Sprechmelodie in *Die glückliche Hand*, manuscript 2445, corresponding to mm. 214–16 of the score, the x-ed noteheads appear to have been added on top of regular noteheads. This page probably dates from late 1912, and the notation of the Sprechstimme is consistent with contemporary sketches from the op. 22 orchestral lieder. The final form of the *Pierrot* Sprechstimme notation wasn't adopted until late in 1913.[11] Thus, the placement of the x-ed noteheads over the oval noteheads seems to be a change of heart and not an experimental notation.

If Schoenberg had doubts about the viability of Sprechmelodie, what prompted a reexamination of the concept? As noted, Schoenberg initially understood that the project was to be melodramas for Zehme to recite/perform (*vortragt*). Surely it must have been his faith in Zehme's musical abilities, a faith that she buttressed in a number of extant letters. On 13 February, she writes about how "intimately music is bound with all that I was saying" at their last meeting. She urges Schoenberg: "Go as far as possible—I will follow, understanding—feeling—creating. Have confidence in my affinities and my listening and intellectual acculturation."[12] As if to further underscore the point, she takes her case to Gutmann, no doubt during some phase of the negotiations. It was then that Gutmann relayed her wishes to Schoenberg, as quoted in the introduction, that she was a trained musical interpreter, not a mere speaking machine.[13] And it was just at this moment that the negotiations broke down, presumably over Schoenberg's counteroffer, which, with Gutmann's commission, constituted a fifty percent escalation of the total fees. Money and performing rights occasioned this disagreement, but both Zehmes had been and would continue to be generous patrons of the arts. Is it also possible that the Zehmes' recalcitrance was due in some part to a disagreement over the artistic direction of the project? Over Albertine Zehme feeling herself treated as a mere speaking machine?

Whatever happened in the endgame of the negotiation, after signing the contract, Zehme continued to press her case. She declares herself completely at Schoenberg's disposal, and while offering to go so far as to speak (*sprech*) for Schoenberg whatever he imagined, she also notes that after hearing Schoenberg's First String Quartet, her musical imagination is further inflamed: "I hear things in my inner ear that only became fully conscious through your Quartet."[14] This is likely the last thing Schoenberg read from Zehme before he composed "Gebet an Pierrot" on 12 March.

The first day of composition is documented by one of the most remarkable and most-often quoted entries in Schoenberg's diary. He began by noting on the morning of 12 March he was "very much in the mood to compose." This struck him as something of a surprise. His first six months in Berlin had been a time of establishing himself as a composition teacher, arranging concerts, and supervising the final stages of the publication of *Harmonielehre* and *Pelleas und Melisande*, op. 5. However, the diary entry reveals a more interesting and personal reason for what he considered the possibility that he might not ever compose again. He expressed frank concern about his relationship to his students, writing: "The persistence with which my students nip at my heels, intending to surpass what I offer, puts me in danger of becoming their imitator, and keeps me from calmly building on [the stage] that I have just reached." Given the few new students he had in Berlin and his low regard for their prior training, also noted in the diary, he must certainly have been thinking of Webern, who was living in Berlin and was in constant contact with the Schoenbergs. The entry goes on to reveal that Schoenberg didn't feel as young, and that he misses the aggressive qualities of his creative personality. He concluded by optimistically considering, "Maybe this will change for the better since I am now composing once more anyway.... Now as I suddenly see the earlier possibilities for unrest again, I almost have a yearning for them. Or are they here again [already]?"[15]

Schoenberg's candid entry is a glimpse at the composer's anxiety about his place in contemporary music at the onset of composing *Pierrot*. In early 1912, Schoenberg was still trying to sort out his aesthetic bearings in relation to his music before 1909 and his more recent music—a struggle that was largely a matter of orienting himself between Busoni and Kandinsky, the two recurring correspondents in his most-quoted letters from this period. However, the 12 March diary entry seems to suggest that his struggle took on an even closer interpersonal dimension as he tried to preserve a self-image as relevant, original, and ever the master of students who still greeted and referred to him with formal address.

In this state of mind, Schoenberg composed "Gebet," and described it in the same diary entry, which he continues the following day:

Yesterday, (12th) I wrote the first of the *Pierrot lunaire* melodramas. I believe it turned out very well. This provides much stimulation. And I am, I sense it, definitely moving towards a new way of expression. The sounds here are truly become an animalistically immediate expression of sensual and psychological emotions. Almost as if everything were transmitted directly, I am anxious [to see] how this is going to continue. But, by the way, I do know what is causing it: Spring!!! Always my best time . . .[16]

Zehme's response is typically enthusiastic: her every letter praises Schoenberg with the flowery prose idioms of her era. But there is also the enthusiasm of victory in her exhortations: "Yes, completely as I *imagined*! You work all the ideals of artistic imagining into tones. It is wonderful, I cannot say more. I am completely encircled in the expressive harmony . . ." But having achieved a more musically pertinent role in the score, she also sounds a note of caution when asking to have Steuermann sent to her.[17]

From the preceding examination of the sources, a picture emerges of Schoenberg at the start of composing *Pierrot*. Already vacillating between aesthetic ideals, he is presented with the commission. The commission promises desperately needed money to sustain the Schoenbergs: a fact that is troubling in the abstract, but also perhaps just as liberating in that it gives him a sense of distance from the material and results. The commission comes from a performer, Zehme, who seems to share his independently determined belief that the meaning of words is wrongly prioritized, often at the expense of the sound of words. Schoenberg compares her personality to two of the more formidable singers of his era. Zehme, who had heard a reasonable sample of Schoenberg's recent music, encourages Schoenberg to trust her musicianship and to all but envelop her role into the discourse of his music. And she presses her case in letters, in personal meetings, in contract negotiations, and in an unknown number of telephone conversations. (In the first letter after receiving "Gebet," Zehme, presumably satisfied that Schoenberg is composing, promises not to disturb him by phone.) Finally, in the last hours before beginning, Schoenberg questions his own relevance and doubts his ability to keep pace with a school of composers that he himself engendered. "Gebet" seems to have soothed these concerns.

★ ★ ★

Among the animalistic sounds in "Gebet," the Sprechstimme is the most salient and continuous part of the texture. Unlike the Sprechmelodie part in *Gurrelieder*, Schoenberg was immediately compelled to explain the Sprechstimme of *Pierrot*. There are, in fact, three extant sets of written instructions regarding the Sprechstimme in *Pierrot lunaire*, each associated with a different source. The first instruction is the single sentence he wrote on the first day of composition. This is found in the autograph manuscript (source B), was added to the fair copy, and was errantly engraved in the final score.[18] Schoenberg composed *Pierrot* with a different order in mind (a topic resumed in chapter 4). As he completed each melodrama, he copied it. When he had a few melodramas copied, he sent a package of melodramas to Eduard Steuermann to rehearse with Zehme. Later, these packages were collected and assembled in the final order. The copied manuscript was prepared for Universal Edition to engrave in early 1913, and has since been called the *Stichvorlage*, or printer's copy (Source C). After sending it to Universal, he wrote a second set of instructions on the title page of the score. Later, the second set was crossed out with big strokes. When the score was published in early 1914 (Source D), the third set of instructions, the familiar preface, was added. It is unclear when he wrote the third set of instructions, but in the interval between when Universal received the score and when they published Pierrot, the notation of the Sprechstimme was finalized. With each set of instructions, Schoenberg added more directives, but there is no indication that the added details better reflect his original conception of the sound. Thus, while this third set of instructions is well known and has been often parsed, the first instruction may be much closer to what Schoenberg imagined and what actually developed during the rehearsal and premiere.

The first instruction—the single sentence—appears at the bottom of the page on which Schoenberg composed "Gebet an Pierrot." It reads, "*Die Rezitation hat die Tonhöhe andeutungsweise zu bringen*," or "The recitation has to effect the pitch as if by suggestion." In contrast to the later instructions that dominate discussions about the *Pierrot* Sprechstimme, in this first instruction there is nothing to suggest the pitch is varied in any way, and there is no reference to moving between pitches by rising or falling. There is also nothing said about the rhythm: the care with which the rhythm is notated in the Sprechstimme should make it perfectly obvious that the rhythm is to be followed.

The noun *Andeutung* is a word that can be used to mean an allusion or reference: something that is communicated in an indirect way. As an adverb, it can be found in nineteenth-century writing about painting and stage directions to suggest something that is present but not focal. The idea that the pitch could be projected in an indistinct manner is analogous to Schoenberg's famous passage about *Klangfarbenmelodie* at the end of his *Harmonielehre*. There, he noted that musical sounds were composed of pitch, color, and volume, but that only pitch had been cultivated for musical purposes. Concerning the relationship of pitch to timbre, Schoenberg wrote:

> The distinction between tone color and pitch, as it is usually expressed, I cannot accept without reservations. I think the tone becomes perceptible by virtue of tone color, of which one dimension is pitch. Tone color is, thus, the main topic, pitch a subdivision. Pitch is nothing else but tone color measured in one direction.[19]

Schoenberg's passage continues to speculate on the possibility of music based on the organization of timbre. *Klangfarbenmelodie* has come to connote a musical passage in which timbre is the leading constructive element: Schoen-berg's Orchestral Piece op. 16, no. 3, is usually cited, along with most of We-bern's orchestral works, as models of the technique. However, as Alfred Cramer has argued, Schoenberg's general usage of the word *Klang*, as well as his later writings, strongly suggests that *Klangfarbenmelodie* referred to the succession of *combinations* of timbres—not merely changes in instrumentation. Cramer also noted that the burgeoning understanding of phonetics and timbre provided a model relationship of pitch and timbre as they combined in vowels. The next logical step is to note, as Cramer does, that Sprechmelodie is "itself a type of *Klangfarbenmelodie* . . . as an attempted merging of music with language."[20]

Given Schoenberg's speculation, written only a year before the com-position of *Pierrot*, that timbre precedes pitch in the immediate perception of a musical sound, his instruction to present the pitch in an indirect way is entirely sensible. Schoenberg wanted the Sprechstimme to sound primarily as the timbre of speech. The pitch was to be present, but only as a secondary consideration, in the ears of the listener. Sprechmelodie is speech: measured in another direction, the speech is pitched.

Zehme's initial understanding of the Sprechstimme was based on this first instruction, which she received a few days after it was composed. Presumably, this note was part of what made "Gebet" precisely as she imagined. The short note may have been clarified verbally. Despite Zehme's promise not to disturb Schoenberg, we know that Schoenberg and Zehme conversed by telephone to discuss the instrumentation of the ensemble.[21] It is possible Schoenberg said more about how to perform the Sprechstimme. Alternatively, Schoenberg may have relayed further instructions through Eduard Steuermann, who began working with Zehme almost immediately.

What we can learn of the rehearsal process comes primarily from the writings of Eduard Steuermann, his sister Salka Viertel, and the extant letters Zehme sent to Schoenberg. Steuermann remembered that

> every few days the 8 o'clock mail would bring me manuscript pages of a new piece of the work. I would feverishly try it out on the piano and rush to the studio of Mrs. Zehme with the rather difficult task of studying it with her. She was an intelligent and artistic woman, but by profession an actress and only as musical as the well-bred, German ladies of the time. I still remember that sometimes, in despair of ever making her feel the exact dif-ference between three-part and two-part rhythm, I would ask her to dance a few bars of a waltz, then a polka, alternating in ever shorter intervals to try finally the first bars of the "Dandy."[22]

Salka Viertel, who was living with her brother at the time, essentially reiter-ated these details in her memoir, adding the description of Zehme quoted in chapter 2 and concluding Frau Zehme had to "study with Edward the intricate rhythms, the pitch and the inflections of the precisely devised speaking part. She was not very musical. . . . However, her 'capacity for taking pains' was infinite, although I do not claim that in her case it was a sign of genius."[23]

As previously noted, Zehme was perhaps not as well-bred as her station suggested to Steuermann and his sister, and whatever musical training she received in her youth was certainly augmented with more recent study. However, Steuermann's assessment of Zehme's musicianship is consistent with the published reviews of Zehme's lieder recitals. It is interesting that in discussing Zehme's musical deficiencies, Steuermann speaks immediately to the issue of rhythm. "Der Dandy" presents especially acute rhythmic problems for the recitation. As discussed in chapter 5, the recitation, frequently written in quarter-note triplets, superimposes a six-four meter over the marked cut-time meter: it receives little metrical confirmation from the piano, clarinet, and piccolo. Finally, "Der Dandy" was the second melodrama Schoenberg composed. We know from Zehme's letters, discussed below, that Steuermann and Zehme learned the melodramas in the order they were completed. Therefore, it seems Steuermann's vivid anecdote about dancing the rhythms comes from a memory of the early rehearsal process.

Both Steuermann and Viertel wrote their memoirs 50 years after the premiere of *Pierrot*. In the two extant letters from 1912, Steuermann notes only that Zehme was finding the music "maddeningly" difficult.[24] On the other hand, we have Zehme's account of her coachings with Steuermann preserved in her contemporary letters with Schoenberg.

After five weeks of letters that concern only business matters, Zehme's letter of 2 May alludes to her coachings with Steuermann. Zehme asks Schoenberg to send the completed melodramas as soon as possible so that she and Steuermann can keep pace. At that point, ten of the melodramas had been completed. Perhaps accentuating the urgency of her request, she notes, "I learn it completely: rhythmically, pitches flat-out memorized [*Tonhöhe glatt auswendig*]." Two days later, she added, "We work very intensively. . . . I hope that I am preparing to your expectation. We keep strict rhythm and pitch positions [*Tonlage*] and their movement within the phrases. I hope that I can manage the somewhat higher passages."[25] These two letters both prioritize her commitment to learning the rhythms, which, coupled with Steuermann's statement, identifies rhythm as a persistent concern in the rehearsal process. Pitch seems no less important, or else there would be no need to memorize them. However, in the second letter, she uses the word *Tonlage*, which is a word typically used to mean *tessitura*, an association emphasized by her concern about the high notes. Moreover, the qualification to keep the *Tonlage* as it moves in the phrase is a curious choice of words.[26] This phrase may suggest a variable approach to the notation whereby the intervals are maintained, but the actual pitches are not fixed. Such an interpretation is consistent with Schoenberg's January 1913 letter to Berg and much later remarks by Schoenberg, Steuermann, and Erwin Stein, discussed below. One final note of interest is her request from 12 June: "I would be very happy if at some point Steuermann and I may perform [*vortragen*] for your assessment the other set, which we did not attempt for you last time."[27] This request establishes that Schoenberg was not relying entirely on Steuermann, but was also intermittently evaluating their progress.

★ ★ ★

Another window into the early performance practice of the *Pierrot* Sprechstimme is provided by the reviews of the premiere and first tour. In significant contrast to the substantial attention given to the Sprechstimme in subsequent writing about *Pierrot*, consideration of the Sprechstimme forms only a small part of the reviews of the first performances. Indeed, the Sprechstimme in *Pierrot* generated nothing like the controversy that followed the premiere of *Die Königskinder* fifteen years earlier. Some of the most negative reviews scarcely mention the Sprechstimme, aside from a few cursory lines about the poems. This fact is extraordinary when one considers that Zehme was the only visible performer, appearing alone in front of scrims that concealed the players. In retrospect, the concealment of the players seems vaguely analogous to the physical arrangement of the Bayreuth Festspielhaus, built to Wagner's specification that the orchestra be concealed beneath the stage. However, the arrangement at the Festspielhaus successfully directs the audience's attention on the singers contending with Wagner's massive orchestra. The effect of concealing the players in the Choralion-Saal was ultimately opaque: reviewers seemed to look and listen past Zehme to the instrumental quartet and its unseen conductor. In part, this reflects the critical attitude toward Schoenberg's music. Many of the reviews read like a colloquy on the appropriateness of post-tonal music. The most prevailing issues are the preponderance of dissonance and the textural density, often judged to be an example of counterpoint taken beyond the bounds of some standard of musicality.

Much of the writing about Zehme's performance addressed her theatrical movements and *Pierrot* costume. The reviewer for *Musical America* spoke immediately to the issue of gender, quoting snickering audience members wondering aloud if Zehme was a man or woman. He continued, "To enhance the effect this 'speaking voice' was dressed in a white *Pierrot* costume with her hair done in the reform style. In fact, there was reform in everything about her appearance, her half-frightened entry, her movements, her poses (usually including a bend at the knee) and her unlovely features."[28] Dr. Elsa Bienenfeld's description in the *Neues Wiener Journal* was equally abrasive: "[O]ne saw a crumpled, meager figure, in a white, black-rimmed Pierrot costume in workshop style, [with] weathered features grotesquely distorted under yellow hair."[29] On the other hand, James Huneker, in a much-quoted review, describes Zehme as "a lady of pleasing appearance in a mollified Pierrot costume."[30]

The most dismissive review of Zehme's vocal performance was written by Hermann Starcke, the *Allgemeine Musik Zeitung*'s Dresden correspondent. Starcke ends a terse column, in which he objects to having to cover the performance at all, with the sentence, "Mrs. Albertine Zehme is virtually impossible as a speaker [*Sprecherin*] of these very beautiful poems by Giraud, even with modest pretensions of the listeners."[31] While Starcke's disapproval of the music seems genuine, it is notable that Starcke wrote in Dresden, the seat of the Saxon Crown, which had only a few years earlier been embarrassed by the future king's ex-wife, who was represented by Dr. Zehme. An equally summarial judgment takes an opposite position: The reviewer for the *Neue Donau-Post* wrote, "The highest recognition is to be credited to all of the performers, particularly to Mrs. Albertine Zehme, who spoke [*sprach*] the verses with the coordination of her complete vocal and intellectual abilities."

One of the most insightful reviews was written by Siegmund Pisling for the *National Zeitung*. Pisling noted the similarity between the melodrama passages in Humperdinck's *Die Königskinder* and the Sprechstimme in *Pierrot*. In one of the few reviews to use the word *Sprechstimme*, he suggested *Pierrot* was a "modification of '*gebundenen* melodramas' wherein the rough pitch placement [*ungefähren Tonstufen*] of the Sprechstimme and its rhythms, possibly also its dynamics, become detached from what the composer has written."[32] Similarly, Elsa Bienenfeld described the writing as "perhaps an expression of the extreme consequence of what could be wrenched from the principle of Wagnerian Sprechgesang."[33]

Several reviews discussed the Sprechstimme in the context of textural density. The reviewer in the *Regensburger Neuste Nachrichten* wrote, "Each instrument, absolutely detached from relationships to the remaining instruments, spins forth an idea that concerns itself precious little with the *what* and *how* of other ideas: and also the Sprechgesang—not recitative, not melodrama, perhaps a mixture of the two—likewise assumes the position of an unfettered solo, so that we confront here perhaps the most independent counterpoint imaginable."[34] Similarly, a Dr. K., writing for the *Münchener Zeitung*, also spoke to the density of texture when he observed, "Zehme's presentation [*Vortrag*] was . . . singing [*Singen*] that was undoubtedly incomprehensible, even in the first row."[35] The most detailed description of Zehme's performance comes from Elsa Bienenfeld:

[one] heard a voice, presently screeching—presently lingering and sugary in hysterical cooing and raving—words, of which the high and low syllables, with furious ecstasies on each vowel, plunged as if from precipitous heights

into an abyss. Can it be possible that Schoenberg, who appeared beside this reciter [*Rezitatorin*] on the podium, considers this kind of interpretation appropriate? I do not ascribe this to even his well-known love of paradoxes. . . . The *Sprechton* in *Pirrot* [*sic*] *lunaire* runs singsong up and down in a long row of intervals, the instrumental parts clinging to the rhythm and pitch, as far as one can speak of rhythm and pitch relationships at all in this manner of music.[36]

Bienenfeld's review must be read in the context of her relationship with Schoenberg. Like Anton Webern, Elsa Bienenfeld (1877–1942) studied privately with Schoenberg while completing her Ph.D. at the University of Vienna under Guido Adler. She also taught alongside Schoenberg and Zemlinsky at the Schwarzwald School in Vienna. Bienenfeld remained on cordial terms with both Schoenberg and his wife, Mathilde. It's unlikely her familiarity with Schoenberg skewed her objectivity, but it did give her special insight into Schoenberg's music. Moreover, that insight was likely buttressed by her occasional discussions with Schoenberg. For example, Bienenfeld wrote to Schoenberg in late October 1912 to ask how she could acquire a copy of the *Pierrot* score, in anticipation of her review of the Vienna performance in early November.[37] Schoenberg's answer is unknown, but aside from the manuscript and copies, there was no score to acquire: in Stravinsky's famous account of attending a performance of *Pierrot*, he remembered following the performance with Schoenberg's score.[38] However, since Schoenberg traveled to Vienna to conduct the 2 November performance at the Bösendorfer-Saal and give his Mahler lecture, it seems possible Schoenberg and Bienenfeld met, if only briefly. Schoenberg was accompanied by Mathilde and made arrangements to visit friends and associates.

Considering the sources about the rehearsal process and the reviews, one can make reasonably assured assumptions about Zehme's performance. For example, it seems likely Zehme executed the rhythms of the Sprechstimme as best as she could. She had memorized the part under Steuermann's tutelage and had the entire summer to practice on her own. Furthermore, as suggested below, she likely had the help of another voice teacher. However, her rhythmic accuracy must have been somewhat compromised by the physicality of her dramatic performance, as noted in the reviews. Since she was spatially removed from the ensemble, separated by scrims, and wearing a costume, she must have had some difficulty following the conductor.

Memorization almost certainly aided the correct presentation of pitches. While both Schoenberg and Steuermann refer to her prior experience with the music of Otto Vrieslander, Zehme had sung more chromatic music; she had sung the lieder of Liszt. On the other hand, Zehme's preface to her 1911 recital indicates that she felt somewhat limited by the twelve tempered pitches of western music. That fact is made more interesting by Schoenberg's own curiosity about microtones, as he had considered them in his critique of the writings of Busoni.[39]

Therefore, it is not impossible that Zehme may have shaded—or outright disregarded—some of the pitches. Pisling's review raises the issue of imprecise pitches by referring to "approximate pitch placement [*ungefähren Tonstufen*]." However, the reviewer talks about this phenomenon in the context of Humperdinck's Sprechnoten, and Humperdinck's discontent with the pitch aspect of the performances of *Die Königskinder* was already well known. Moreover, Pisling qualifies his observation by noting he had not examined the score to *Pierrot*: he was thus ultimately unsure of the fidelity of Zehme's performance.

Underlying the early writing about the Sprechstimme is the unstated difference between the sound of the voice and the sound of instruments. While the *Pierrot* ensemble is heterogeneous—there is little similarity between the timbre of the strings, piano, flute, and clarinet—the rich timbre of the voice always predominates. Schoenberg's overwhelmingly syllabic text-setting tends to emphasize the predominance of the voice. There is a preponderance of consonants in the German language. Moreover, German is rich in phonemes that group particularly noisy consonants: *ch*, *sch*, *scht*, *szts*, etc. Each consonant and consonant grouping adds a different transient attack to the vowel. Thus, the human voice that presents German text is a highly variable instrument. Compared to the number of attacks possible on even the violin, the human voice is a veritable percussion orchestra. The difference between the voice and the instruments was further exaggerated by the placement of Zehme in front of scrims that concealed the instruments and undoubtedly dulled their resonance.

The difference between voice and instruments informs the reviews of *Pierrot*, regardless of the reviewer's opinion of the work or the performance of the Sprechstimme. When Elsa Bienenfeld notes that people who are unfamiliar with Schoenberg's music may find that the parts of *Pierrot* blend together as uniform unfamiliar noises (*gleichförmig fremdartige Geräusche*), she is speaking of the instrumental writing; her strong condemnation of Zehme is found in a different part of the article and is presumably quite unrelated. Similarly, the sympathetic reviewer for the *Neue Donau-Post* who praised Zehme's performance wrote, "[W]ith all the often unnatural and violent appearances in the leading of the individual instrumental parts [*einzelnen instrumentalen Stimmen*] and also the Sprechstimme, we are still able to hear a strong force of musical language from the whole." Here again, the wording suggests a need to keep the instruments separate from the Sprechstimme instead of simply writing about the leading of individual parts (*Führung der einzelnen Stimmen*), which would include the instruments and Sprechstimme.

Ultimately, the first reviewers accepted the Sprechstimme a priori. Some reviewers, like Bienenfeld, criticized Zehme's performance. Some reviewers noted the precedents of the Sprechstimme and even discussed the combination of singing and speaking. But no reviewer identified the Sprechstimme as the principal concern of the work. The performance of the Sprechstimme only becomes a central concern of reviewers after the start of the 1921 tour—that is to say, after the publication of the study score with its preface about the performance of the Sprechstimme.

★ ★ ★

The second set of instructions for the performance of the Sprechstimme is Schoenberg's aborted first attempt to write the preface. Schoenberg wrote this on the same large piece of staff paper he used to draft the title page for the printer's copy (Source C), and begins without a heading (e.g., *Vorwart*). This first draft of the preface resembles the final version in many respects, but the writing about the Sprechstimme is only two-thirds the length of the corresponding passage in the final version. Given the placement at the bottom of the title page, it is reasonable to surmise that Schoenberg began writing and found that he had more to say about the topic than he expected.

Die in der Sprechstimme durch Noten angegebene Melodie ist (bis auf ~~die~~ einigeeinzelne besonders bezeichnete Ausnahmen) <u>nicht</u> zum Singen bestimmt. ~~Dagegen soll~~ Trotzdem ist es Aufgabe des Ausführenden des <u>Rhythmus absolut genau</u> wiederzugeben, die vorgezeichnete Melodie aber, was die tonhöhen anbelangt um eine <u>Sprechmelodie</u> umzuwandeln, in dem die Tonhöhen ~~zu~~ untereinander stets das im vorgezeichneten [*sic*] Verhältnis einhalten. Der unterschiedes zwischen ~~dem~~ Singen Gesangs- und ~~dem~~ Sprechen Sprechen- ton [*sic*] ist ~~dabei~~ folgender ~~maßen zu fixieren~~: Der Gesangton hält die Tönhöhe unabänderlich fest, der Sprechton gibt sie an, verläßt sie aber sofort wieder durch Steigen oder Fallen.

The melody indicated by notes in the Sprechstimme (except for ~~the~~ individual particularly designated exceptions) is <u>not</u> intended for singing. ~~On the contrary~~ Nevertheless it is the task of the performer to completely represent the <u>rhythm absolutely precisely</u>, but transform the notated melody which concerns the pitches, into a <u>Sprechmelodie</u>, in which the pitches always adhere to the notated relationships among themselves. The difference between ~~the~~ singing sung tone and ~~the~~ speaking spoken tone is ~~thereby specified~~ as following: the singing tone holds the pitch unwaveringly; the speaking tone indicates it but immediately leaves it again through rising or falling.

The most significant difference between the drafts is the third phrase of the second sentence, in which Schoenberg explains that the performer should adhere to the relationships among the pitches as notated. The word *Verhältnis* (relationship), used in proximity with *tonhöhen* (pitch), almost certainly speaks to intervals.[40] Thus, the passage seems to indicate that the intervals, in particular, are to be observed and are presumably prioritized over the actual pitches. As such, the explanation of the Sprechstimme pitches in this version of the preface is remarkably similar to Schoenberg's explanation of the Speaker's part in *Gurrelieder* in his 14 January 1913 letter to Alban Berg, quoted in chapter 1. In that letter, Schoenberg indicated that the pitches should be only understood as differences of position (*Lagenunterschiede*). The word *Lagenunterschiede* fuses the word *Unterschiede* (difference) with *Lage*, a word usually used in connection with register or tessitura. As such, Schoenberg's wording in the letter to Berg recalls Zehme's letter of 5 May 1912, quoted above, in which she claims to keep pitch positions—pitch ranges (*Tonlage*), actually—and their movement within the phrases. A final possible reference to such an interpretation of the Sprechstimme notation is the previously quoted review by Siegmund Pisling. When Pisling spoke of the rough pitch placement, he may have been referring to a variable approach to the notation. However, as previously noted, Pisling had no access to the score, and speaks in the context of Humperdinck's Sprechnoten, which were certainly intended to be pitch-specific.

The idea that one should perform the Sprechstimme with the intervals rendered exactly (or inexactly) as written without tethering the intervals to the written notes is fraught with difficulties. Consider any short passage from the Sprechstimme. If one accepts that the intervals are to be preserved but that the actual notes are fungible, then a performance of that passage could theoretically be transposed to any of twelve pitch levels in each of the octaves available to the performer. (In fact, the number of performers could be increased to include men, who could simply transpose the passages down into a more comfortable tessitura.) However, that total number of transpositions would also include the unison transposition—the performance of the passage exactly as notated. Nothing in the description of fixed intervals and varying pitches discourages the performer from rendering the passage as notated. Indeed, the performer would likely prioritize a performance of the passage as notated, because, aside from the obvious satisfaction of rendering the score as written, she will find correspondences of pitch and motivic shape in the surrounding texture. In essence, every possible transposition that is not the unison transposition becomes a kind of ossia—an option the performer may or may not take. However, unlike a notated ossia, a transposition of a passage in *Pierrot* could utterly destroy the stylistic integrity of the passage, creating unisons and other unintended consonances that randomly prioritize tonal hierarchies. And all these considerations apply to only one hypothetical passage among hundreds of measures in the score. Presumably, a performer would need to work through similar issues in each passage to find a transposition that seems consistent with the style of the work. But ultimately, the style of the work does not favor literal transpositions. Schoenberg's technique of motivic development prioritizes the shape of the motive over the intervals between the notes. To adapt a passage from the Sprechstimme for a specific performer, it would be far more like Schoenberg's compositional technique to render new pitches in the notated shape. But there again, there is always the possibility that in rendering the shape, the new pitches will create unintended consequences. If a passage were rendered with indefinite pitches—notes between the notes, or some of the "thousands of possible oscillations" of which Zehme wrote in her 1911 preface—the problem of unintended correspondences and agreements would be solved, only to reveal other problems. One wonders how many fin de siècle musicians could manage to keep even approximate intervals on pitches offset from the pitches of the accompanying ensemble. Moreover, a microtonal tuning of the Sprechstimme will cause it to be unduly prioritized for the listener. The alternate tuning will make the Sprechstimme brighter and ultimately louder; it won't blend with instruments playing in a consistent tuning. Short of amplification or vibrato, what would call more attention to the Sprechstimme than having it tuned only with itself?

Performances of the Sprechstimme that deviate from the notated pitches, share one thing in common: they tend to call more attention to the pitches. Perhaps the random pitches sound louder because the performer feels liberated. Perhaps the random pitches sound louder because they accidentally allude to other sounding pitches. Or perhaps their indefinite tuning rings wrong against the tempered pitches of the ensemble. Far from indicating the pitch in an indirect way, many variable-pitch performances sound self-conscious and mannerist. Perhaps some of these difficulties contributed to Schoenberg's decision to remove the possibility of fixed intervals with variable pitch from the final draft of the preface. On the other hand, the idea returns almost immediately in his continued work on *Die glücklische Hand*, and, as noted below, is applied to *Pierrot* again in the 1920s.

In the final draft of the preface, which was published in the first edition of the score, the performer is advised to observe the notated pitches.

VORWORT.

Die in der Sprechstimme durch Noten angegebene Melodie ist (bis auf einigeeinzelne besonders bezeichnete Ausnahmen) nicht zum Singen bestimmt. Der Ausführende hat die Aufgabe, sie unter guter Berücksichtigung der vorgezeichneten Tonhöhen in eine Sprechmelodie umzuwandeln. Das geschieht, indem er

PREFACE

The melody indicated by notes in the Sprechstimme (except for individual particularly designated exceptions) is not intended for singing. The performer has the task, with good consideration of the marked pitches to convert it into a speech melody. That happens, by:

I. den Rhythmus haarscharf so ein-
hält, als ob er sänge, d. h. mit nicht
mehr Freiheit, als er sich bei einer
Gesangsmelodie gestatten dürfte;

I. keeping the rhythm razor sharp as
in singing: i.e., with no more liberty,
than one might permit oneself with a
melody that is sung;

II. sich des Unterschieds zwischen
Gesangston und *Sprechton* genau be-
wusst wird: der Gesangston hält die
Tonhöhe unabänderlich fest, der
Sprechton gibt sie zwar an, verlässt
sie aber durch Fallen oder Steigen
sofort wieder. Der Ausführende muss
sich aber sehr davor hüten, in eine
»singende« Sprechweise zu verfallen.
Das ist absolut nicht gemeint. Es
wird zwar keineswegs ein realistisch-
natürliches Sprechen angestrebt. Im
Gegenteil, der Unterschied zwischen
gewöhnlichem und einem Sprechen,
das in einer musikalischen Form mit-
wirkt, soll deutlich werden. Aber es
darf auch nie an Gesang erinnern.

II. becoming precisely aware of
the difference between the *singing
tone* and the *speaking tone*: the singing tone holds the pitch unwaveringly, the speaking tone indicates
the pitch but immediately leaves it
again by falling or rising. The performer must however be on guard
not to fall into a "singsong" manner
of speaking. That is absolutely not
intended. Realistic-natural speech
is by no means the aim. To the
contrary, the difference between ordinary speech and a speech that
participates in a musical form must
be distinct. But it may also never
remind one of singing.

Common to both drafts of the preface is Schoenberg's explanation of the difference between the speaking tone (*Sprechton*) and the singing tone (*Gesangton*).
Schoenberg uses the German word *Ton* with about the same ambiguity as the
English *tone*; it is not as precise as *pitch* or *Tonhöhe*. *Ton* suggests the general
impression of the sound, which would include elements of pitch, timbre, and a
general, idiomatic impression—the *sound* of speaking, the *sound* of singing.

However, in further explaining the difference between the sound of
speaking and singing, Schoenberg immediately refers to the role of pitch
(*Tonhöhe*). He notes that in the sound of singing, pitch is steady, whereas in the
sound of speaking, the pitch is given but then left immediately by either rising
or falling. This is the most problematic aspect of the instructions: Schoenberg
does not provide a set of guidelines for how the pitch should be approached,
held, and left. It is generally presumed that the pitch should be left in the direction of the next pitch, but the only authoritative source for that inference is
the 1940 recording, which is problematic in a number of ways discussed below,
not the least of which is that the reciter does not always follow the profile of
the written notes. In fact, Schoenberg does not even say that the pitch should

be left by rising or falling; he says simply that the performer *should be aware* of such a distinction and leaves the performer to assume that such information will figure into the correct interpretation.

Peter Stadlen, speaking directly to the issue of glissandi in Sprechmelodie, has argued that performers who follow these directions too literally will ultimately fail to achieve an amalgam of singing and speaking. Working with a phoneticist, Stadlen explained that while syllables do begin with definite frequencies, the initial frequency is not necessarily privileged.[41] In any given syllable, the vowel is crucial both to understanding and sustaining the syllable. However, a vowel is usually begun, or concluded, or begun *and* concluded with consonants. Consonants are equally important for meaning and have an appreciable effect on the vowel, in that they stop the air, force the air through the nose, or behave in the manner of vowels. The German language is rich in consonants, and they play a significant role in complicating a delivery of Sprechmelodie that relies on constant glissandi.

Consider the entrance of the Sprechstimme in "Serenade," presented in ex. 3-1. Simply put, the text is a mouthful. Only the relatively insignificant word *auf* presents a syllable in which the vowel—and thus the pitch—can be established *immediately* and left through rising or falling. In every other syllable, the vowels are prefigured by consonants, which range from the relatively quick, plosive *b* in *bogen* to the more complicated combination of the plosive *k* and the liquid *r* (which, in German, amounts to a trill in the back of the throat) in *kratzt*. Moreover, most of the syllables have final consonants that either interrupt the airflow, as in the *t* of *mit*, or further burden the articulation of the next syllable, as in the *s* in *groteskem*. At this relatively slow tempo, these syllables are manageable, but the onset of a glissando will be delayed because the vowels, which give the pitch, will be delayed. The word *kratzt* and the first syllable of *Pierrot* in m. 17 represent how the delayed onset of the glissando factors into the performance. At Schoenberg's slowest tempo, 120 beats per minute, each beat lasts 0.5 seconds, and each note of an eighth-note triplet lasts just over 0.16 seconds. Thus, the reciter has about 0.16 seconds to voice the *k,* trill the

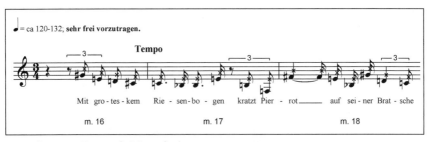

Example 3-1.   "Serenade" Sprechstimme, mm. 16–18.

r, sound the B-natural on the vowel, and glissando down six semitones to the F. Then, the clock is reset, and in the next 0.16 seconds, the reciter must finish the previous word with the consonant-complex *tzt*, stop the airflow for the *P* of *Pierrot*, voice two vowels on the low F, and glissando up thirteen semitones to F-sharp$_4$. For the first syllable of *seiner* in m. 17, the sixteenth-note allows only 0.125 seconds for a similar set of tasks. Obviously, these problems are exacerbated at a faster tempo.

Consider the rise and fall of pitch in connection with the familiar effects of glissando and portamento. Technically, the difference between glissando and portamento is that a glissando only uses the actual tempered pitches that exist on an instrument while the portamento uses all frequencies between a starting and ending pitch. In practice, by the turn of the twentieth century, glissando had become synonymous with portamento. Schoenberg uses the word *glissando* in his score note about a famous passage for trombones in his op. 5 *Pelleas und Melisande* in which the effect is clearly a portamento.[42] The word *portamento* is typically reserved for un-notated, less-distinct glides in expressive string passages that require changes of hand position. Schoenberg uses both devices in *Pierrot*.[43]

In late nineteenth-century music, the notation of glissando (i.e., portamento) string passages was rhythmically imprecise. A famous glissando, just before the reprise of the principal theme in the Adagietto of Mahler's Fifth Symphony, is shown in ex. 3-2. The non-string player could be excused for thinking the glissando lasts for the entire half note when, in fact, the actual glissando happens at the very end of the second beat. This can be confirmed in a number of recordings, including the early recordings by conductors who heard Mahler conduct his Fifth Symphony. Thus, there is a difference between what the notation suggests and what the tradition of performance practice records.

Schoenberg, a cellist who boasted that he "never wrote a single note for a string instrument without trying it out," may have been troubled by the difference between how glissandi were notated and how they were actually played.[44] Consider the glissando in the violin part in m. 37 of "Mondestrunken," shown in ex. 3-3. When Schoenberg was composing, he used a curious notation for the glissando, writing a dotted-half note that sounded the entire duration of a measure, but including stems to indicate the

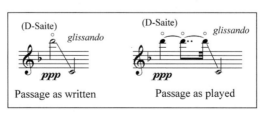

Example 3-2.   Mahler, "Adagietto" from Symphony No. 5, Violins 1, m. 72.

relative positions of the glissando during the last eighth-note of the measure; the glissando corresponds to the scalar passage in the flute on the same last eighth-note. A short time later, Schoenberg copied the manuscript and used a more conventional notation for the glissando, albeit with a short break in the middle of the glissando's wavy line. The original publication of the score and parts had the wavy line spanning the entire measure. However, on the recording Schoenberg conducted in 1939, violinist Rudolf Kolisch plays this glissando on the last quarter note of the measure, as Schoenberg approximately notated it in the manuscript. In later publications, the wavy line was changed to begin midway through the measure, corresponding again with the passage in the flute.[45]

The performance practice of glissando is more germane to a correct interpretation of Sprechstimme than the notation of glissando. The correct performance of glissando emphasizes the departure and arrival pitches and willfully minimizes the duration of the glissando: put another way, in most contexts, the notated pitches are emphasized over the sliding effect. Similarly, the correct interpretation of Sprechstimme is to emphasize the pitch and minimize the effects of "falling or rising." Naturally, the idea of Sprechstimme does not entirely map onto the idea of glissando. In the instructions, Schoenberg actually indicates that the pitch should be given and left immediately (*sofort*), although that may be a rhetorical negation of the description of the singing

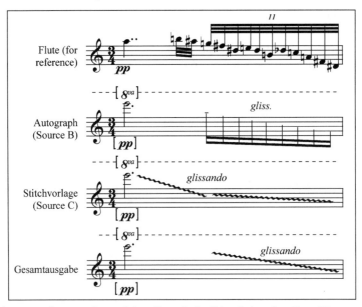

Example 3-3.   Three versions of the glissando in "Mondestrunken," m. 37.

sound, which holds the pitch unwaveringly (*fest*). Moreover, Schoenberg does not reference glissando in his preface and does not use the customary glissando line between all pitches in the Sprechstimme. Finally, Schoenberg does in fact use glissando, properly marked, as an effect in the Sprechstimme part (for example, "Rote Messe," mm. 11–12; "Gebet an Pierrot," mm. 9–10). If Schoenberg could request a glissando of the reciter that exceeds the "falling or rising" from the pitch, it then follows that the falling or rising that is part of Sprechstimme must be modest in comparison.

Rising and falling pitches, described by Schoenberg in the second preface, are not chronicled in the reviews of the first tour. While Bienenfeld speaks of dramatic highs and lows, she does so in the context of other extremities. Moreover, there are dramatic glissandi in the score, notably in "Die Kreuze." A constant wavering portamento, which has become a feature of some *Pierrot* interpretations, would likely have been an extremely unusual phenomenon in 1912. Reviewers often confessed—or complained—that they could not tell the difference between correct notes from wrong notes. But even the least-musical critic would have noted pronounced and continuous glissandi between notes. That glissando does not inform the early critical record speaks in part to the fact, noted above, that the Sprechstimme was not the most pressing concern. It also suggests that Zehme's glissandi were understated.

Schoenberg completes the paragraph with a final set of constraints. The realization cannot be "singsong," but also must not be realistic-natural speech; it must not be ordinary speech but cannot remind the listener of singing. These final sentences have received the least attention in commentary about Sprechmelodie. However, they speak more immediately to the difficulty in realizing Schoenberg's directions.

In attempting to clarify Schoenberg's definition of developing variation, Carl Dahlhaus remarked that when confronted with concepts that are difficult to explain or understand, one should seek to understand what makes the concept difficult to express in words. In the case of developing variation, Dahlhaus argued that the two terms *developing* and *variation* are ultimately more opposing than complimentary.[46] As Michael Cherlin has detailed, dialectical opposition is central to Schoenberg's writing and musical thought.[47] The conceit of opposing forces shapes his fundamental view of the world. Dialectical opposition also informs the directions in the *Pierrot* preface. In every aspect, Schoenberg attempts to characterize the delivery of the Sprechstimme as a dialect between singing and speaking, framed by a series of narrow antipodes:

- Regarding rhythm, Sprechmelodie is like singing and unlike speaking.
- Regarding the stability of pitch, Sprechmelodie is like speaking and unlike singing.

- Regarding the category "naturalness," Sprechmelodie is unlike speaking and like singing.
- Regarding the category "singsong-like," Sprechmelodie is unlike singing and like speaking.

Thus, Schoenberg defines Sprechmelodie by including some qualities that apply and excluding the other qualities that do not apply. However, Schoenberg's definition ignores *quantities*; his rhetorical frame is so rigidly fixed on binaries that it seems to proceed on the assumption that a thing is either *this* or *that*: there is no middle course. The definition assumes each particular aspect of the voice production is either "precisely" like singing or like speaking. On the other hand, the binary choices for each particular aspect fail to define Sprechmelodie as a total. Even if each one of Schoenberg's binary conditions can be resolved, the final equation results in only one type of voice production that is composed of likenesses to singing and likenesses to speaking. How can it be *not-singsong*, like speaking, and *not-realistic*, like singing, without being somewhere between *not-singsong* and *not-realistic* and thus somewhere between singing and speaking? The parts of Sprechmelodie do not allow for a middle ground or compromise; the whole of Sprechmelodie is a compromise—a middle ground between singing and speaking.

Naturally, Schoenberg was not constructing a logical argument but was rather intuitively fashioning a definition of an abstract concept. However, the word choices for each sentence leave no room for mediation. The wording is precise and the tone is confident, if not actually domineering. Moreover, his own analysis of musical concepts typically involves a similar linguistic deconstruction. For example, he objected to the expression *linear counterpoint* because it stressed joining points in a line and contrasting points simultaneously. He objected to the expression *non-harmonic tone* on the grounds that any simultaneity creates a harmony. He similarly objected to *atonality* because any combination of tones is a tonality.[48] The word *Sprechmelodie* does not belong in this list because, as one imagines Schoenberg's clarification, all *speech* has *melody*. It follows that *Sprechstimme* is equally valid because one part of the texture can be used for speaking. However, the logic that obtains for the words is not reflected in his definition of the concept. One can imagine a theoretical parallel—Schoenberg fussily demanding how a vocality that involves some degree of pitch, glissando, and strictly observed rhythms, while participating in the creation of musical form but avoiding the manifestation of natural speech, could possibly *never* remind the listener of singing.

Another issue that lurks in Schoenberg's formulation of Sprechmelodie is the difference between singing and speaking as it was understood in the early twentieth century. A cursory glance at singing treatises from the turn of the century reveals the commonly held position that the differences between singing and speaking are not differences of kind, but rather differences of degree. Even if, as is likely, Schoenberg worried little about singing treatises, he should very well have intuited this fact from the varying means of vocal production around him. As chapter 1 establishes, he had worked in a cabaret and was almost certainly aware of the well-documented debate about Humperdinck's *Der Königskinder.* Beyond both of these admittedly narrow precedents towers the example of Richard Wagner. All of European musical life wrestled with the consequences of Wagner's Sprechgesang—the style of recitative Wagner employed for his late operas. As noted below, Albertine Zehme's critique of Wagner's theories, as they were applied after his death, was central to her search for a new technique. Wagner's thesis in *Opera and Drama* hinges on his argument that true melody exists at the threshold of word-speech and tone-speech. Wagner's argument is sufficiently fine as to consider words at the phonetic level and, contemporarily drawing on the same sources as Helmholtz, to relate the sound of vowels to instrumental timbre. In the 1871 essay "The Destiny of Opera," a terse summation of the third part of *Opera and Drama,* Wagner writes that in the modern Artwork:

> [The boundary between spoken theater and music] would be found at the exact point in that Artwork where Song is thrusting toward the spoken Word. By this we in no sense imply an absolutely lowly sphere, but a sphere entirely different, distinct in kind; and we may gain an instant notion of this difference, if we call to mind certain instinctive transgressions on the part of our best dramatic singers, when in the full flow of song they have felt driven to literally *speak* a crucial word.[49]

The implication is clear: the appearance of the spoken word is not a sudden change, or even a choice. Rather, the spoken word arrives as a result of increasing the intensity in an effort to capture the true essence of the meaning. The boundary is fluid: singing gives way to speaking.

Here then is the root of the difficulty in understanding Schoenberg's description of Sprechmelodie: Schoenberg's description of the parts of Sprechstimme is dialectical while the whole is compound. The distinction between singing and speaking, as commonly held during the composition of *Pierrot,* is not a distinction of kind, but a distinction of degree. The degrees of singing and speaking that compose Sprechmelodie cannot be adequately communicated by setting singing and speaking in opposition.

★ ★ ★

While drafting and revising the preface to *Pierrot,* Schoenberg was in regular contact with Zehme for the final stages of the tour. In May of 1913, Zehme became Schoenberg's landlord when the Schoenberg family lived on the second floor of the house she used during her Berlin sojourns. As previously detailed, Zehme relentlessly proselytized for her idiomatic style of delivery. She had arrived at her style largely by intuition, but she was thoroughly trained in the theater and had studied singing with Cosima Wagner. However, Zehme had another, more immediate influence on her vocality during the creation of *Pierrot*, which has so far not appeared in the literature about Sprechmelodie.

Zehme's 1920 book, *The Fundamentals of Artistic Speaking and Singing*, is dedicated to "King Clark" and consists of her summation of the "Clark Method."[50] Frank King Clark (1868–1914) studied in Chicago under William Neidlinger.[51] He went to Paris in 1901, and his success was such that he was eventually made *Officier d'académie*. In a 1907 travel guide, Clark is listed as a "successful and well-known teacher" of "singing and voice production," among many other teachers who are listed only for singing lessons.[52] It would appear that in addition to his achievement as a singing teacher, he taught elocution or diction. According to Zheme, Clark was a répétiteur at Bayreuth for several years as a successor to Julius Kniese (1848–1905). In 1910, he moved to Berlin, which remained his home until his death in 1914. Zehme also reports that she was one of Clark's many students during his last several years in Berlin.[53] The combination of singing and speaking studies would certainly appeal to Zehme and help shape her declamation style. Absent any other sources, it is impossible to establish exactly when Zehme studied with Clark. (She studied at Bayreuth in 1891 when Clark was still in America.) However, even a conservative interpretation of several (*mehrere*) years would put Zehme in Clark's studio during the creation of *Pierrot*. Clark lived until October of 1914 and at the very least could certainly have seen one of the Berlin performances.

Zehme's book is a voice method based on the teachings of Clark as she applied them in her own studio. After a brief forward, Zehme begins: "I put forward that speaking and singing are one. All that is said to be necessary for developing the singing voice holds for both."[54] She provides a brief history of all that she finds wrong with the teaching of voice, as she encountered it in the prior training of her own students. In Zehme's view, Richard Wagner's emphasis on clear diction was distorted by his followers. Because the German language is rich in consonants, German singing teachers began teaching would-be Wagnerian singers to enunciate with exaggerated consonants, which distorts the vowel and ruins the voice. Zehme labels this group of teachers, largely associated with Bayreuth, a "consonant cult," and says of their training, "One reveled in hissing, exploding, humming and nasal noises, which I must reject as a characteristic sound. One believed that the sharper *s*, *k*, *l*, *m*, *n*, and *r* burst forth with amassed air, the more zealously one served clarity. Accordingly, vocal ruin became an inescapable certainty."[55]

Zehme credits "the American King Clark" for finding a way to unite the clarity of the vowels, which prevailed in Italian voice instruction, with the consonants that are necessary for intelligibility in German. She emphasizes three principles of Clark's method: much-needed relief (*Entlastung*) to the larynx, dissolving the consonant into the vowel without blocking the airflow or marring the sound of the vowel, and systematic breathing from the diaphragm. Easing the burden on the larynx is particularly emphasized, which is consistent with Zehme's concern about damaging the voice. As she notes, "Power and clarity are not produced by over-exertion or over-enunciated consonants but rather from systematic training about vowels."[56]

The core of Zehme's short book is the explication of the Clark method, which is contrasted with other singing methods. Many of the asides speak to related singing issues, and it includes a section with exercises engraved on staves. However, the last fifth of the book, drawn from her "experiences in art and life," speaks to a number of other issues, ranging from stage fright to memorization. In this section she briefly discusses melodrama and Sprechmelodie, which she calls *Sprachmelodie*, subtly shifting the emphasis from the material (speech, words) to the voice.

The subsection on Sprechmelodie contrasts the recitation of poetry with acting and the recitation of melodrama. Zehme stresses that even the recitation of poetry requires musical treatment. She notes however, that spoken language, "freer sister, or silhouette, of strict vocal music," provides more opportunities for dramatic expression than singing. As an example of freer expression, she quotes Schoenberg's preface to *Pierrot* and remarks that it "yields a finer and more delicate shade of speaking tones, compared to musical [tones]. Between absolute pitches there are many frequencies which the reciter can use without compunction for melodrama, as well as unadorned poetry."[57]

Zehme's remarks here must be understood in the context of her argument. She invokes Schoenberg's preface as an example of freer expression. She is surely not describing the performance of *Pierrot* when she immediately continues to remark of a melodrama reciter:

> No dread about pitch scares him, no system of noteheads and lines subordinates him—no singing-judge [*Merker*] stirs—free, absolutely free, he lets his speech rhythms be heard. Language, melody and rhythm offer an inexhaustible richness of expressive means for the recitation of poetry. One must find the characteristic note for the expression of each emotion and nuance. The recitation of poetry and melodrama without musical training is unthinkable. ... [T]he artist who wants to recite poetry and melodrama must be able to find and sustain the fundamental harmony [*Grundakkord*] that provides the mood for each individual poem.[58]

It is inconceivable that she would describe a performance of *Pierrot* as "absolutely free" with regard to the rhythm, especially since rhythm seems to have been the most difficult part of her rehearsal process with Steuermann. However, later in the same subsection, she adds one last interesting remark that does speak to performing *Pierrot*. Characterizing the preface as Schoenberg's warning that *Pierrot* is "wholly particular to a singing manner of speaking," she explains that it "requires a stretching [*Dehnen*] of the word, so the pitch is to be immediately abandoned [*verlassen*] and the voice is adapted to the music in the manner of *Sprachmelodie* [*sic*]."[59] This "stretching" that causes the pitch to be abandoned must surely speak to Schoenberg's description of the voice leaving the speaking tone through rising and falling.

It is unfortunate that Zehme relied so heavily on the preface and did not discuss the rehearsal process and tour. Nevertheless, the few remarks that speak directly to *Pierrot* reiterate her commitment to the notes between notes that she first wrote about in her 1911 program note. However, these intermediary notes seem to be anchored to the (written) pitches, which she relates are only immediately abandoned, as indicated in the preface; they are not disregarded altogether. Finally, Zehme's discussion of the Clark Method proves Zehme to have been knowledgeable about—if not actually equipped with—a vocal technique adequate to the demands of performing *Pierrot*.

★ ★ ★

Schoenberg lived thirty-seven years beyond the 1914 publication of *Pierrot lunaire*. In the years that followed, he used Sprechmelodie in a number of works in varying ways, ranging from the similar use in *Die glückliche Hand*, op. 18, to the dramatically different use in *A Survivor from Warsaw*, op. 46, from 1947. In *Die glückliche Hand*, the ambiguity about pitch is greatly exacerbated. As previously noted, the passages for *Die glückliche Hand* that use Sprechmelodie were almost certainly composed after the completion of *Pierrot*. In his sketches, Schoenberg used a score note not unlike the one he used when composing "Gebet an Pierrot": the notes in the Sprechstimme were to be "spoken at exactly the prescribed time and sustained as indicated; the pitch is to be realized approximately through speech."[60] However, the Sprechstimme is written for three speakers who create three-note chords. In those passages, he writes, "The three-note chords are meant to indicate that the passages in question are to be spoken on pitches that lie within the corresponding registers of the singers."[61] Thus, Schoenberg creates a performing potentiality in which the Sprechmelodie chords are harmonically aligned in the part, but only randomly aligned with the rest of the parts of the texture. By the time he wrote *A Survivor from Warsaw*, his notation of the Sprechstimme borders on the absurd; he uses only a single line but indicates sharps and flats (as shown in ex. 3-4). Essentially, the notation of Sprechstimme in the later works returns to the sterile reduction of the nineteenth-century melodrama but also adds an unexplained chromatic apparatus that anticipates indeterminacy.

Schoenberg's later use of Sprechmelodie is only marginally useful for evaluating the Sprechstimme of *Pierrot.* However, these scores model how Schoenberg's thinking about Sprechmelodie changed over time and parallel later statements about the performance of *Pierrot.* Peter Stadlen collected and analyzed these statements in three articles; they need be only summarized here.

When *Pierrot* was revived in 1921 in conjunction with the Society for Private Musical Performances, Schoenberg's associate and former student Erwin Stein (1885–1958) conducted a new group of musicians (except for Eduard Steuermann, who returned as pianist) and coached a new vocalist. Erika Wagner (1890–1974), perhaps better known as *Stiedry-Wagner* after her marriage to Fritz Stiedry, was selected for *Pierrot* after a number of difficulties with the soprano Marie Gutheil-Schoder. As Stiedry-Wagner wrote in 1924, she came to the attention of the society through Alban Berg's sister Smaragda, who introduced Stiedry-Wagner to Schoenberg's early lieder. Like Zehme, Stiedry-Wagner was also primarily an actress and she recalled, "The combination actress/singer struck them as fortunate on the basis that *Pierrot* is certainly a speaking part [*Sprechpartie*], the speaking of which rests on an enormous physical effort; on the other hand, what strikes one most if not the requisite musicianship?"[62]

While the new ensemble toured, Darius Milhaud assembled a number of performances with Marya Freund (1876–1966) performing the Sprechstimme in Giraud's original French. Alma Mahler, aware of both tours, had both ensembles perform the work in her home on 28 February 1923. Schoenberg conducted the German performance with Stiedry-Wagner, and Milhaud conducted Freund in the French version. Peter Stadlen describes this evening as a pivotal moment in Schoenberg's subsequent characterization of the *Pierrot* Sprechstimme. According to Stadlen, "Schoenberg came down on the side of the predominantly spoken delivery of the actress Erika Wagner-Stiedry [*sic*]

Example 3-4. *A Survivor from Warsaw* **Sprechstimme, mm. 22–24.**

and decided against the predominantly sung interpretation—later censured in several letters—by Marya Freund."[63]

For much of the two decades following the 1921 revival, Erwin Stein became a proxy for all matters pertaining to *Pierrot*. He made the piano-vocal score under Schoenberg's guidance, which was published in 1923. Moreover, he wrote an article concerning the performance of the *Pierrot* Sprechstimme.[64] From Stein's article, presumably written with Schoenberg's imprimatur and later praised in a letter from Schoenberg,[65] one learns that "dropping and raising of the voice should not link the intervals in the way of a portamento," except where indicated; one should avoid "an undue anticipation of a succeeding consonant, even if this is a sounded one"; and "the colouring and gliding of a long vowel has to sound like a short vowel in slow motion."[66] Moreover, Stein's article returns to the idea that the pitches can be adjusted to fit the reciter's range. According to Stein, the reciter is "free not only to transpose his part according to the type of his speaking voice and regardless of the other instruments, but also to narrow down his intervals so as to accommodate them within his individual (speaking) compass and tessitura."[67] It would seem that Stein went even further than Schoenberg dared in his second version of the *Pierrot* preface or his notes about *Die glücklische Hand*, but in fact Schoenberg's contemporary perspective on the *Pierrot* Sprechstimme was quite similar. In a 1923 letter to Josef Rufer, Schoenberg wrote, "The pitches in the *Pierrot* depend on the range of the voice. They are good to consider but not to be kept strictly. One can divide the range of the voice into as many parts, when half-tones are used; perhaps then each distance is only one 3/4-tone." Moreover, the issue of preserving the interval relationships is also swept aside when Schoenberg continues, "But this need not be carried out pedantically because the pitches have no harmonic relationships [*harmonischen Verhältnisse*]."[68] This remarkable statement amounts to a dramatic revision of the score. But more extraordinary by far is Peter Stadlen's personal recollection of performing *Pierrot* with Erwin Stein. Stadlen, a pianist who had studied with Anton Webern, summarized Stein's writing on Sprechmelodie and dryly added, "None of this was evident when I took the piano part in the *Pierrot* performances that Stein conducted in England in 1942. On the contrary, he tried his utmost during rehearsals to get the speaker, Hedli Anderson, to render the pitches correctly."[69] And in his review of Schoenberg's final statements on the *Pierrot* Sprechstimme, Stadlen concludes, "Schoenberg was prepared to accept any pitches whatsoever, with the sole exception of those which he had actually composed."[70]

Recent scholarship has shown that Stein's beliefs about the performance of the Sprechstimme changed as a direct result of Schoenberg's recording and Schoenberg's subsequent anxiety about the results. In the fall of 1940,

Schoenberg was invited to record *Pierrot* for CBS. As far as can be determined, Schoenberg had last conducted *Pierrot lunaire* in Europe in 1927. In that Paris performance, he conducted Marya Freund, who performed the recitation in French (which is annotated above the Sprechstimme in Schoenberg's copy of the score, source D2). In a frequently cited letter, Schoenberg stated he had about two weeks to assemble the players and rehearse for the recording.[71] Erika Stiedry-Wagner, Eduard Steuermann, and violinist Rudolf Kolisch were immediately collected for the recording, thus establishing continuity with the 1921 performances in Vienna. Cellist Stefan Auber, flautist Leonard Posella, and clarinetist Kalman Block were hastily added to complete the quintet. Dika Newlin, then a precocious graduate student studying with Schoenberg, describes a chaotic period leading up to the recording:

> To be brief about that, it has all the earmarks of a recording that will never be made. Schoenberg gets mad and won't direct rehearsals, leaving that to Kolisch; Kolisch gets mad, I don't know why; [Anthony] Linden leaves town for a few days, thus balling things up immeasurably, and he isn't a very good flute-player, anyway (everybody else wanted to have Ary van Leeuwen, but Schoenberg wouldn't have him); Kalman Bloch has never tootled a bass-clarinet in his life; no parts are to be had, and the players are having to play from miniature scores until such time as parts can be copied ([Leonard] Stein and I are going to get to work at that right away); all the full-sized scores in the U.S. seem to be out of commission in one way or another (Steuermann's is back in N.Y., and can't be found; mine's still at the bindery in Lansing, etc. etc.); Schoenberg wants the recording made before school starts, and Erika Wagner'll be in town any day now, but it couldn't possibly be done before two weeks; then it would be too late because Kolisch and Steuermann will have gone back to N.Y. to participate in the performance under Klemperer! Schoenberg is mad about that because he doesn't think Klemperer is sympathetic to his works; Schoenberg is mad at Kolisch because he gave Kolisch the choice of taking the cost of recording or the royalties and K. chose cost (doubting, and I suppose rightly, that the royalties would be worth taking). Did you ever hear of such a mixup in your life?[72]

Salka Viertel provides a more sympathetic recollection of a rehearsal that was attended by the "literary and musical elite," including Bruno Walter, Otto Klemperer, and Thomas Mann, declaring, "It was an almost unopposed success for everyone concerned."[73] But even if Viertel's memory is somewhat more favorable, one wonders how much work could be done, rehearsing *Pierrot* in such company.

The recording itself is a document that is almost as controversial as the preface. While it has always been an essential source for musicologists, it has rarely, if ever, been cited as evidence that correctly informs a performance. However, that may change in the near future. Recently, the test pressings of the recording along with a live performance broadcast in 1940 were unearthed by Avior Byron, who has meticulously analyzed them in two articles, and a third co-written with Matthias Pasdzierny.[74]

As Byron detailed in his analysis, Stiedry-Wagner's pitch is consistently a third or a fourth below the notated pitch. In general, she is closest to the score at the beginning and end of phrases. In many passages, her pitches are consistent in four recorded takes but different from what is notated. Byron attributed the differences between the score and the performance to both a difference in approach between Schoenberg's coaching in 1940 and what she may have learned with Erwin Stein in 1921. He also suggests that Stiedry-Wagner made deliberate changes to enhance her reading of the text, which Byron notes is contrary to what Schoenberg wrote in the preface.[75] Another aspect of Stiedry-Wagner's performance, outside the scope of Byron's article, is her dramatic and often emphasized glissandi between pitches, which Pierre Boulez has called "irritating."[76]

Despite Schoenberg's obvious haste to assemble and rehearse the players, he apparently planned to have Stiedry-Wagner rework her interpretation of the Sprechmelodie. In the same letter that expresses his concern about the narrow time frame, Schoenberg writes to Stiedry-Wagner:

> We must also refresh the Sprechstimme thoroughly—at the least, because I aim this time to see whether I can tease-out the light, ironical-satiric tone in which this piece was originally conceived. Furthermore, times and attitudes have changed, so what at the time perhaps appeared to us as Wagnerian, or at the worst, Tchaikovskian, today suggests Puccini, Lehar and the like.[77]

Since there is no extant recording from Stiedry-Wagner's performances from the 1920s, there is no way to judge how—indeed, *if*—the Sprechstimme is refreshed. The identification with Tchaikovsky, Puccini, and Lehar vaguely conjures a singsong delivery that would emphasize pitch, albeit not necessarily the correct pitches. Such a performance would seem to be at odds with the preface. Ultimately, this statement is ambiguous, especially with regard to pitch. More interesting by far is the letter Schoenberg sent to Erwin Stein dated 25 December 1941.

> Do you know that, in September 1940, I conducted a recording of it for Columbia, with Kolisch, Steuermann and Mrs. Stiedry [?] These records have only been released two months ago, and I doubt, whethe[r] you know them. They are to a great part quite good, though Mrs. Stiedry is never in pitch and several pieces are not very well recorded. I can say, most was played better than recorded. Nothing is better recorded than played.[78]

Byron and Pasdzierny have demonstrated that this letter prompted the sharp change in Stein's approach to Sprechmelodie. When Stein held the vocalist Hedli Anderson to the notated pitches in *Pierrot*, he was responding to Schoenberg's critique of Stiedry-Wagner's accuracy. However, Byron and Pasdzierny argue that Schoenberg's concern about the Sprechstimme pitches did not signal a revision of his conception of Sprechmelodie, but rather reflected his anxiety about the archival nature of the recording. Because Stiedry-Wagner's pitches are so obviously different from the score, Byron and Pasdzierny suggest Schoenberg feared "that now and in the future, people would be able to check whether Stiedry-Wagner was adhering to the notated pitch."[79] Their argument is not significantly different from Peter Stadlen's suggestion that Schoenberg wanted to deemphasize the pitches in the melodrama at the end of *Gurrelieder* because, given the tonal musical language, "identifiable but wrongly reproduced pitches could sound like wrong notes."[80]

Hearing the work on record afforded Schoenberg the opportunity to listen with his full attention as opposed to simultaneously conducting the work or checking the preparedness of the ensemble. The recording of *Pierrot* may very well have been one of the few performances he heard, with the exception of hearing Stein rehearse Stiedry-Wagner and hearing Milhaud conduct Marya Freund at Alma Mahler's house. Moreover, the record allowed for repeated listening. If it may be theorized that Schoenberg was suddenly concerned that the pitch accuracy could be compared to the score, it may be also theorized that Schoenberg was for the first time suddenly confronted with Stiedry-Wagner's vast divergence from, if not intermittent disregard of, the score. While it may seem ludicrous to suggest that Schoenberg had been conducting the work for over 25 years without considering the pitch so carefully, the non-singing vocality used for *Pierrot* actually does project the pitch "in an indirect way"; the fact of the voice and the rhythm of the Sprechstimme are more immediately apparent. Moreover, as Byron and Pasdzierny also cite, Schoenberg was embarrassed by the fact that during one of the early rehearsals for *Pierrot* in 1912, the clarinetist used an A clarinet for the B-flat clarinet part in "Der Mondfleck," which resulted in the subject of one of the fugues entering a half-step below what is actually notated. Schoenberg hastily justified this fact in an entry in his diary, noting, "[I]t is not proven that I didn't indeed notice it (in parts) anyway and simply did not have the courage to criticize such a thing, since one would not really seriously consider the possibility that a person would play a whole piece one half-step lower, but [instead] assumes that one heard wrong."[81]

Another aspect of the recording that directed Schoenberg's attention to the pitch is the balance of Stiedry-Wagner with the rest of the ensemble. Stiedry-Wagner recalled:

[Schoenberg] was very stubborn in some cases and he was afraid my voice (on the recording of *Pierrot lunaire*) would be too loud and the music would be a little bit too soft. And he said to me, "Go away, go away from the microphone." I said "No, Mr. Schoenberg. That is no good. I know. I did a lot of things at the radio and I know how my voice sounds." There were no tapes of course, then. It was on wax and you couldn't play it back. You couldn't hear what you were doing. And so, I had really a temper with him, and I said, "No, you won't hear me." And he said, "No, I know it's better." And so on, so on. And we nearly didn't finish it. And, later on, he said, "Oh, you were right. I was stubborn." So my voice on the recordings is too soft—much, much, sometimes much too soft. He was very sad then but it was too late and we couldn't do it again.[82]

But the violinist on the recording, Rudolf Kolisch, Schoenberg's brother-in-law, remembered that "the *Sprechstimme* turned out to be too prominent on the recording."[83] If Kolisch's recollection reflects Schoenberg's opinion, then the louder Sprechstimme on the recording certainly confronted Schoenberg with the reality of Stiedry-Wagner's performance in ways that live performances had not.

Byron and Pasdzierny conclude that Schoenberg's sudden anxiety about pitch, resulting from his listening to the recording, ultimately subsided and he returned to the conception of Sprechmelodie represented by Stiedry-Wagner's performance. Certainly, Schoenberg's last few statements on the subject support the fact that he resumed talking about the *Pierrot* Sprechstimme in a manner consistent with his statements from the 1920s. Just as in 1923, Schoenberg claimed that the pitches in the *Pierrot* Sprechstimme lack harmonic relationships, and in his last year, Schoenberg apparently expressed concerns that the notated pitches did not fit the music.[84] However, one may again apply Stadlen's framework to this argument: just as Schoenberg's statements from the 1920s seem to distance Schoenberg from confusion about the pitches in performances of the *Pierrot* Sprechstimme, his statements from the 1940s and 1950s distance him from the same confusion resulting from the discrepancies between the score and the recording.

★ ★ ★

This chapter analyzes statements and events over a span of thirty-seven years. By way of conclusion, some summation is in order.

Arnold Schoenberg was interested in the theories of Albertine Zehme. She was committed to a declamation style that united her training as an actress with her more recent activities as a singer of lieder. Schoenberg found an analogue in Zehme's idiomatic delivery to the delivery he had devised for the melodrama in *Gurrelieder*. During the period between their first contact and the signing of the *Pierrot* contract, Zehme encouraged Schoenberg to make full use of her abilities and especially implored him to capitalize on her musician-ship. Whether or not Schoenberg and Zehme really understood each other is ultimately unknowable. However, when Zehme received the first completed melodrama, she replied that it completely met her expectations.

During the composition process, Zehme's name fades from the extant relevant sources about *Pierrot*. Excepting some references to the rehearsals, her own letters were increasingly concerned with matters of business. The reviews tended to address the composition as a whole and minimize her role. At the same time, Schoenberg took full ownership of the Sprechmelo-die concept. In a series of performance directions, his emphasis changed from 1) directing the performer to render the pitch "in an indirect way" to 2) directing the performer to preserve the intervals to 3) directing the per-former to render the pitch in a way that conforms to his idiomatic model of speaking, in which the pitch is sounded and immediately left "through rising or falling."

In the early 1920s, Erika Stiedry-Wagner began a tour of *Pierrot* under the baton of Erwin Stein. Stein's letters and articles, as well as Schoenberg's contemporary statements, return to the conception of Sprechmelodie that was originally stated in the first draft of the preface but excised from the final draft. The conception of the *Pierrot* Sprechstimme that was clarified (if not formed) in the early 1920s is documented by Stiedry-Wagner's performance on the 1940 recording, conducted by Schoenberg. Subsequent performances and recordings vary widely with regard to the relationship between the pitches as notated in the Sprechstimme and as rendered by the performer as Sprech-melodie.

The scholarship that addresses the *Pierrot* Sprechstimme can be broadly partitioned into three schools of thought.

Some scholars have argued that the notated pitches in the *Pier-rot* Sprechstimme are ultimately guidelines, representing imprecise pitch movement in suggested pitch contours. Schoenberg's American students, who worked with Schoenberg while he was radically reworking the Spre-chmelodie concept for his later works, have generally taken this position. For example, Boulez has written that Schoenberg's teaching assistant Leon-ard Stein confided:

> Schoenberg was infinitely more interested in *expression* than in the *intervals* (it is true that the notation of the *Ode to Napoleon* is very simple as com-pared with that of *Pierrot lunaire*); wanting to show the interpreter how to speak the text, he himself recited various passages, deviating considerably from his notation. Leonard Stein also confirmed to me that the deviations from the musical text in Erika Wagner-Stiedry's [*sic*] performance did not disturb Schoenberg at all.[85]

Avior Byron's recent work on the test pressings of Schoenberg's *Pierrot* recording is similar to this view, albeit elegantly reformulated. Byron's previous work largely focused on Schoenberg's activities as a performer and conductor. Consideration of Schoenberg's performance activities inevitably reveals that Schoenberg prized the direct musical expression of sentiment and feeling, and would sacrifice a degree of technique and fidelity to the literal text of a score to achieve direct expression. Regarding *Pierrot*, Byron argues that Schoenberg's view of Sprechmelodie remained fairly consistent because his notation of the Sprechstimme was always intended to cede a certain amount of liberty to a performer seeking direct expression of the textual and musical ideas.

A second school of thought holds that Schoenberg's later statements, including even the preface, are inconsistent with the score and ultimately insoluble. From this perspective, Schoenberg's recording is held in low regard either because the circumstances surrounding the recording precluded a satisfactory result or because he had simply changed his conception of Sprechmelodie long before the recording was made. Boulez's writings on Sprechmelodie have consistently supported this view. Most recently, he wrote, "[T]he conception arises, in my view, from an erroneous analysis. For over three quarters of a century a satisfactory solution to the problem posed in *Pierrot lunaire* has still not been found. Only lame solutions have emerged, referring to one factor more than another, preferring one mode of delivery over another."[86]

While arguing that Schoenberg's statements are inconsistent is conceptually antithetical to arguing that Schoenberg consistently did not want (only) the notated pitches, both arguments may in fact cause the same result—a performance with varying degrees of similarity to the notated pitches. Boulez himself has conducted several recordings that vary widely with regard to the Sprechstimme pitches.

A third school of thought advances that the score is internally consistent but marred by Schoenberg's subsequent statements. Often citing specific events in the score—for example, the canons in "Parodie" and the doubling in "O alter Duft," both discussed in part 2—this school tends toward a conception of Sprechmelodie that is faithful to the notated pitches. This perspective must, of course, embrace the second school of thought: Schoenberg originally wanted *indirect* pitch, but failing to get that, deemphasized pitch in his later statements and performances, starting with the preface. Finally, at an abstract level, this school of thought also subsumes the first school of thought as well, in that a degree of freedom in interpreting the Sprechstimme would include the freedom to perform it exactly as written and originally described on 12 March 1912.

NOTES

1. Arnold Schoenberg, "Attempt at a Diary," trans. Anita Luginbühl, *Journal of the Arnold Schoenberg Institute* IX/1 (1986), 7–52. (Henceforth "Schoenberg/Luginbühl.")

2. Schoenberg/Luginbühl, 30.

3. Arnold Schoenberg to Wassily Kandinsky, 19 August 1912; reprinted in Brinkmann 1995, 238.

4. Albertine Zehme to Arnold Schoenberg, 26 January 1912; reprinted in Brinkmann 1995, 225.

5. Schoenberg/Luginbühl, 22.

6. Albertine Zehme to Arnold Schoenberg, 5 February 1912; reprinted in Brinkmann 1995, 225.

7. Schoenberg/Luginbühl, 26.

8. Alma Mahler, *Gustav Mahler: Memories and Letters*, 3rd ed. further enlarged, ed. Donald Mitchell, trans. Basil Creighton (Seattle: University of Washington Press, 1975), 84&c.

9. Viertel, 58.

10. For the chronology see chapter 2 of Auner, 1997. A concise version can be found in Joseph H. Auner, "In Schoenberg's Workshop: Aggregates and Referential Collections in *Die glückliche Hand*," *Music Theory Spectrum* 18/1 (1996): 77–105.

11. Auner 1991, 128–32.

12. Zehme to Schoenberg, 13 February 1912; Brinkmann 1995, 226.

13. Emil Gutmann to Schoenberg, 24 February 1912; Brinkmann 1995, 226.

14. Zehme to Schoenberg, 10 March 1912, Brinkman 1995, 226.

15. Schoenberg/Luginbühl, 39–40.

16. Schoenberg/Luginbühl, 40–41.

17. Albertine Zehme to Arnold Schoenberg, [13–14] March 1912; reprinted in Brinkmann 1995, 228.

18. See chapter 6, note 3.

19. Arnold Schoenberg, *Harmonielehre* [Theory of Harmony], trans. Roy C. Carter (Berkeley: University of California Press, 1978), 422.

20. Alfred Cramer, "Schoenberg's 'Klangfarbenmelodie': A Harmony Principle of Early Atonality," *Music Theory Spectrum* 24/1 (Spring 2002): 16.

21. Schuller and Steuermann, 24.

22. Eduard Steuermann, "*Pierrot lunaire* in Retrospect," *Juilliard News Bulletin* 1 (1963); reprinted in Brinkmann 1995, 243–44.

23. Viertel, 57.

24. Eduard Steuermann to Arnold Schoenberg; Brinkmann 1995, 234.

25. Zehme to Schoenberg, 2 May 1912 and 5 May 1912; Brinkmann 1995, 229.

26. Zehme does not use the word *Tonlage* in her 1920 book; she does use *Höhenlage*, *Mittellage*, and *Tieflage* to refer to register.

27. Zehme to Schoenberg, 12 June 1912; Brinkmann 1995, 230.

28. "Der Wanderer," "What Is Arnold Schönberg?" *Musical America*, November 16, 1912; reprinted in Lesure, 16.

29. Elsa Bienenfeld, *Neues Wiener Journal*, November 10, 1912; reprinted in Lesure, 58.

30. James Huneker, "Schoenberg, Musical Anarchist Who Has Upset Europe...," *New York Times*, January 19, 1913; reprinted in Lesure, 19.

31. Hermann Starcke, *Allgemeine Musik Zeitung*, Novemenber 29, 1912; reprinted in Lesure, 39.

32. Seigmund Pisling, *National Zeitung*, December 7, 1912; reprinted in Lesure, 17.

33. Bienenfeld, 58.

34. DS, *Regensburger Neuste Nachrichten*, 6 April 1914; reprinted in Lesure, 39

35. Dr. K., *Münchener Zeitung*, 7 November 1912, reprinted in Lesure, 26.

36. Bienenfeld, 58 and 59.

37. Elsa Bienenfeld to Arnold Schoenberg, 22 October 1912 (LC/ASC).

38. Igor Stravinsky and Robert Craft, *Dialogues and a Diary* (London: Faber, 1968), 104–5.

39. See Schoenberg's annotations to his copy of Busoni's treatise, reprinted *Ferruccio Busoni: Entwurf einer neuen Ästhetik der Tonkunst. Faksimile einer Ausgabe von 1916 mit den handschriftlichen Anmerkungen von Arnold Schönberg. Im Anhang Transkription der Anmerkungen und Nachwort von H. H. Stuckenschmidt* ([Frankfurt am Main]: Insel Verlag, 1974).

40. *Meyers Konversationslexikon* begins its definition of Intervall with "in der Musik das Verhältnis zweier Töne in Bezug auf ihre Tonhöhe . . ." Regarding the importance of *Meyers Konversationslexikon*, see p. 174, note 1.

41. Stadlen 1981, 2–3.

42. Just before rehearsal 31, Schoenberg writes, "[T]he [trombone] slide is moved through all positions, but in such a way that the chromatic intervals as well as the quarter tones, eighth tones, and smaller tones in between are distinctly audible, as in a glissando for strings." Arnold Schoenberg, *"Five Orchestral Pieces" and "Pelleas und Melisande" in Full Score* (New York: Dover Publications, 1994), 49.

43. In addition to the glissandi we discuss, "Mondestrunken," m. 37, one finds arco and pizzicato glissandi for the cello in "Madonna," mm. 18–24. Portamento is not designated, but may be inferred from a number of string passages that recall changes of hand position, especially when Schoenberg calls for large leaps to be taken on a single string, as in mm. 15–21 of the violin part in "Mondestrunken."

44. Schuller and Steuermann, 30.

45. The provenance of this revision to the glissando line is unclear. The original 1914 Universal Edition score has the glissando line spanning the entire measure. In Schoenberg's two copies of the score and his copy of the parts (sources D1, D2, and E1), the glissando is shown from dotted half-note to the bar line without annotation or correction. Later reprints, presumably from the same plates with light corrections, have a shorter glissando line beginning midway through the measure to coincide with the tuplet in the flute. Brinkmann chose the shorter line for the *Gesamtausgaben*, rather uncharacteristically without comment. The Dover Publication of the score expressly states that it is a reproduction of the 1914 publication, but the glissando line is placed in the middle of the measure.

46. Carl Dahlhaus, "What Is 'Developing Variation'?" in *Schoenberg and the New Music*: Essays, trans. Derrick Puffett and Alfred Clayton (Cambridge: Cambridge University Press, 1987), 128.

47. Michael Cherlin, "Dialectical Opposition in Schoenberg's Music and Thought," *Music Theory Spectrum* 22/2 (2000): 157–76.

48. All cited, with commentary, in Cherlin, 170.

49. Richard Wagner, "The Destiny of Opera," in *Richard Wagner's Prose Works,* vol. 5, *Actors and Singers,* trans. William Ashton Ellis (London: Kegan Paul, Trench, Trüber & Co. 1896), 153.

50. *Die Grundlagen des künstlerischen Sprechens und Singens* (Leipzig: Verlag Carl Merseburger, 1920). The copy examined by the authors has a sticker announcing the publisher as "Friedrich Hofmeister, Leipzig," but Merseburger's imprint is clearly visible below.

51. Oscar Thompson and Nicolas Slonimsky, eds. *The International Cyclopedia of Music and Musicians*, 5th ed. (New York: Dodd, Mead, 1949), 343.

52. Elizabeth Otis Williams, *Sojourning, Shopping & Studying in Paris; A Handbook Particularly for Women* (Chicago: A.C. McClurg & Co, 1907) 96.

53. Zehme 1920, 10. Curiously, she reports he died in 1915, but 1914 is given in every other source.

54. Zehme 1920, 7.

55. Zehme 1920, 8.

56. Zehme 1920, 26.

57. Zehme 1920, 33.

58. Zehme 1920, 33.

59. Zehme 1920, 34.

60. Stadlen 1981, 3.

61. Quoted in Stadlen 1981, 5.

62. Erika Wagner, "Treffen mit Schönberg anläßlich der Aufführung des *Pierrot lunaire*," *Pult und Taktstock* 7–8 (1924): 284.

63. Stadlen 1981, 6.

64. Erwin Stein, "Die Behandlung der Sprechstimme in *Pierrot lunaire*," *Pult und Taktstock* 4 (1927): 45–49; reprinted in Hans Keller's translation in Stein's *Orpheus in New Guises* (London: Rockliff, 1953), 86–89. Stein also wrote "Vom Melodram," *Musikblätter des Anbruch* 10 (1928): 370–72.

65. Schoenberg calls it a "most excellent article, full of clarity, wisdom and understanding." Schoenberg to Erwin Stein, 19 May, 1927 (ASC).

66. Stein 1927, 87–88.

67. Stein 1927, 88.

68. Schoenberg to Josef Rufer, 8 July 1923; Brinkmann 1995, 300.

69. Stadlen 1981, 7.

70. Stadlen 1981, 8.

71. Schoenberg to Fritz Stiedry and Erika Stiedry-Wagner, 31 August 1940 (LC/ASC).

72. Newlin 1978, 243.

73. Viertel, 260.

74. Avior Byron, "*Pierrot lunaire* in Studio and in Broadcast: Sprechstimme, Tempo and Character," *Journal of the Society for Musicology in Ireland* 2 (2006–7): 69–91; "The Test Pressings of Schoenberg Conducting *Pierrot lunaire*: Sprechstimme Reconsidered," *Music Theory Online* 12/1 (2006); Avior Byron and Matthias Pasdzierny, "Sprechstimme

Reconsidered Once Again: '. . . though Mrs. Stiedry is never in pitch,'" *Music Theory Online* 13/2 (2007).

75. Byron 2006, 3.1–3.9; 2.11.

76. Boulez 1968, 264.

77. Schoenberg to Fritz Stiedry [and Erika Stiedry-Wagner], 31 August 1940 (LC/ASC).

78. Schoenberg to Erwin Stein, 25 December 1941 (LC/ASC); quoted in Byron and Pasdzierny, [2].

79. Byron and Pasdzierny, [16].

80. Stadlen 1981, 5.

81. Schoenberg/Luginbühl, 41.

82. Joan Allen Smith, "Schoenberg's Way," *Perspectives of New Music* 18/1–2 (1979): 277.

83. Smith, 279.

84. Reported in Stadlen 1981, 8.

85. Boulez 1964, 265. Schoenberg's last amanuensis, Richard Hoffmann, made similar statements in lectures at the Peabody Institute of the Johns Hopkins University, Baltimore, MD, 28–29 March 2005.

86. Pierre Boulez, "Timbre and Composition—Timbre and Language," trans. R. Robertson, *Contemporary Music Review* 2 (1987): 166.

4

An Overview of Compositional Materials

𝒯he present authors are committed to a performance of the *Pierrot lunaire* Sprechstimme that is faithful to the notated pitches. The notes of the Sprechstimme can be transformed into pitched speaking. A fully supported tone, without vibrato, will give the impression of speech, just as a stage whisper gives the impression of an actual whisper. Unlike the sung tone, the timbre of this blunt tone will be more immediate than the pitch. The impression of speech will also be heightened with modest dynamic tapering of each syllable. The tapering should coincide with the unstressed glide between pitches. Preparations should always proceed from speaking the part in rhythm to speaking the part in rhythm with pitch. The performer must conceptualize the work as heightened speech, and never as degraded singing. The range of the Sprechstimme, as well as some passages that involve long durations or larger leaps, will naturally require solutions particular to each voice. Most performers will find it advantageous to apply modest vibrato to notes above G-sharp$_5$. On the other hand, vibrato should not be used as a means to make the Sprechstimme salient against the busier instrumental textures. The injudicious use of vibrato is the leading cause of performances that are remarked to be "too much like singing." If there is one thing on which all listeners, performers, and scholars can agree, it is that the Sprechstimme should not be sung. However, a rendering of the Sprechstimme as pitched speech has become increasingly common in performances and recordings.

That future musicians, scholars, and listeners would someday reach consensus about the performance of the *Pierrot* Sprechstimme may be too much to hope for (if it is in fact desirable). However, it is to be expected and should indeed be demanded that every interpretation of *Pierrot* be informed by a musical understanding of the score. Schoenberg frequently turned to a small number of trusted performers for his works. In part, these performers were already sympathetic to his musical style. But the real value they brought to a performance of his work was their keen understanding of his compositional rhetoric, and their eagerness to look beyond their own parts to take the full measure of the score. This chapter briefly summarizes details of the text, including the immediate context of the Pierrot character, the structure of the poems, the narrative suggested by Giraud's collection, and the heightened narrative created by Schoenberg's selection of twenty-one poems from the original collection of fifty. The chapter continues with aspects of Schoenberg's score, including the instrumentation, the form, the order of composition, and the motivic design. These details should aid in an analysis of *Pierrot* as they indeed aid in the analysis presented in part 2.

THE PIERROT CHARACTER AND GIRAUD'S TEXT: STRUCTURE AND NARRATIVE

Pierrot is a stock character in the Commedia dell'Arte, a form of Italian improvisational theater that dates back to the fifteenth century. Called *Pedrolino* in Italian, Pierrot is a *zanni* or servant. In the early seventeenth century, Pierrot was popularized by the French mime Jean-Gaspard Deburau (1796–1846). Deburau's development of the character stripped away the physical slapstick and emphasized a capacity for a rich inner life and emotional understanding. By the nineteenth century, the Pierrot character came to personify the condition of the artist.[1]

Albert Giraud, born Albert Kayenbergh (1860–1929) was a Belgian poet and littérateur, who had been a concert pianist in his youth. *Pierrot lunaire: Rondels bergamasques* (1894) is the first of three works by Giraud that feature the famous clown. He wrote *Pierrot* during a struggle between rival factions of Belgian poets.[2]

Giraud wrote criticism for *La Jeune Belgique* ("The Young Belgian"), a literary review that served as an organ for a movement of the same name. The Young Belgians were inspired by an assortment of mid-nineteenth-century poets collectively called the Parnassians. The Parnassians, in turn, were a reaction to what they deemed the sentimentality and maudlin theatricality of Romanticism. The Young Belgians were aesthetes who projected a foppish and distant critical stance. They emphasized art for art's sake and dismissed attempts to use poetry as a pretext for social good or personal confession. Finally, they sought to achieve a disaffected craftsmanship and a control of classical models of form, and they evaluated all other poetry by these measures.

A contemporary journal, *L'Art Modern*, was initially aligned with the Young Belgians. However, *L'Art Modern* increasingly advocated socially responsible poetry and useful art. The term *Art nouveau* originated in the pages of *L'Art Modern* a decade before it was used to describe the decorative arts. A struggle ensued between the writers at *L'Art Modern* and the Young Belgians; at one point, Giraud actually fought a duel with Edmond Picard, the editor of *L'Art Modern*. (Neither was hurt.) In 1886, the feud took an unexpected turn. That year, Jean Moréas published a manifesto on Symbolism.[3] Symbolism and Parnassianism—and by extension, the Young Belgians—shared common precursors and objectives. Nevertheless, the editor of *La Jeune Belgique* attacked Moréas and the symbolist poets for prioritizing images and abstraction over craftsmanship and form. The editor of *L'Art Modern*, sensing an opportunity, embraced Symbolism, ironically attaching his socially conscious colleagues to a morally ambiguous poetic movement.

The most acute and divisive acts of this literary struggle occurred in 1885, around the time Giraud attacked writers of free verse for disregarding poetic form. By 1889, Giraud had assumed the editorship of *La Jeune Belgique*, and found himself embroiled in an argument that he didn't begin and advocating an antagonistic position that did not accurately reflect his own more nuanced view of Symbolism. In contrast to the fashionable allure of Symbolism, Giraud's defense of Parnassian ideals seemed antiquated.

Pierrot lunaire was published in 1884, before the escalation of this debate. In essence, *Pierrot* is Giraud's extended flirtation with Symbolism. As Robert Vilain notes, the rondels are "an exploration of the tempting idea that Symbolism could be seen as a development of Parnassianism, always provided that it was kept firmly insulated against Decadence."[4] Pierrot, like the Young Belgians, is a dandy, who cultivates poetry for no other reason than for the sake of poetry. True to his Parnassian ideals, Giraud wrote *Pierrot lunaire* as a collection of rondels—a poetic form derived from the medieval *rondeau*. On the other hand, the imagery in the Pierrot rondels, as well as certain details of the dreamlike narrative they merely suggest, aligns with the Symbolists' rejection of objective reality.

Théodore de Banville (1823–1891), whom Giraud admired, is credited for popularizing the modern derivation of the rondel with his "Rondels composés à la manière de Charles d'Orléans" (1875). Other notable essays in the form include the collections by Maurice Rollinat (1846–1903), especially "Dans les brandes" (1877) and Les Névroses (1883). Like Giraud, Rollinat was a pianist; he often appeared at Le Chat Noir, performing his poems to his own accompaniment.

The rondel, as it came to be established in the nineteenth century, was written in the *octosyllabe* meter. Most English poetic meters count metrical feet.

The foot is a unit of accented and unaccented syllables. The *octosyllabe* is written for exactly eight syllables. The last syllable of the verse must be accented to emphasize the rhyme scheme, but the internal ordering of accents is left to the discretion of the poet.

The *Pierrot* rondels alternate two rhymes among thirteen verses arranged in three stanzas. The first and second stanzas have four verses and the last stanza has five verses for a total of thirteen verses in all. This simple pattern of two rhymes also embeds a refrain. The first two verses of the poem return as the seventh and eighth verses. Moreover, the first verse returns again as the last verse. The rhyme scheme of the rondel may be mapped as follows in figure 4-1.

Literary critic Henri Morier has noted that the two verses that form the refrain must be dependent but syntactically detachable.[5] Nevertheless, the return of the first verse at the end of the poem tends to suggest the second, even if it is not stated.

The text refrain imposes a narrative template. The first stanza is expository; a characteristic image is stated in the first two verses, and verses three and four elaborate on the image. The second stanza allows for only two new verses before returning to the refrain in verses seven and eight. The third stanza is not only the one line longer, but by returning to only one of the two verses of the text refrain, the third stanza has twice as many nonrefrain verses as either the first or the second. Thus, the third stanza is the logical place in the structure for rising action and conflict resolution. In many rondels, adherence to the narrative template results in two parts superimposed over the three verses—description and characterization in the first two stanzas and resolution or commentary in the third stanza.

Otto Erich Hartleben (1864–1905) wrote plays and poetry, founded societies with colleagues, and contributed to literary magazines. It is unclear why Hartleben decided to translate *Pierrot*. However, it was clearly a creative enterprise and took the better part of six years to complete. Hartleben's translations are idiomatic renditions of the poems. He retained the basic rondel structure, but discarded the rhyme scheme. The meter is essentially the same, but the accents are more pronounced in German. Most significantly, Hartleben streamlined the imagery. He cut references to other writers, composers, and

Stanza:	First Stanza				Second Stanza				Third Stanza				
Verse:	1	2	3	4	5	7	6	8	9	10	11	12	13
Rhyme:	A	B	b	a	a	b	A	B	a	b	b	a	A
Refrain:													

Figure 4-1.   **The rondel rhyme scheme.**

painters. Giraud's furtive attempts at Symbolist imagery are greatly amplified by Hartelben. Indeed, as early as 1895, the German cultural critic Max Nordau, a detractor of Symbolism, denounced on principle Hartelben's translation of the "so-called 'poetry' of the Belgian Symbolist, Albert Giraud." It's unlikely that any contemporary French critic would have described Giraud as a Symbolist.[6]

After hearing an early performance of Schoenberg's *Pierrot*, Ferrucio Busoni wrote to Egon Petri, "It is unforgivable that the poems have not remained in their original French, which certainly comes closer to the 'esprit' of their content. This longing for the native hills of Bergamo doesn't 'sound' in German."[7] A similar sentiment is expressed by the reviewer for the *Münchner neueste Nachrichten*, who opines that Hartleben's translation is by definition a distortion of Giraud and that Schoenberg's setting amplifies that distortion.[8]

Until recently, it was generally accepted that Hartleben's translation had improved Giraud's original poems. The pianist and musicologist Charles Rosen, who completed a Ph.D. in French literature, dismissed Giraud as a "justly forgotten poet," and Willi Reich praised Hartleben's translation as "significantly deepening the content of the work."[9] The musicologist Susan Youens argued that Hartleben's translation "utterly transforms Giraud's poetry for the better—immeasurably better."[10] However, Giraud's poetry has been the subject of recent critical reevaluation and a more balanced view of the source and translation has emerged.[11]

In chapters 5 through 7, we have translated the poems with a view toward keeping the content of each line intact. It is hoped that the translation will make it possible for the performer to locate each idea in the original German without reference to translating dictionaries. Following each poem, a short discussion notes any passages that Hartleben significantly altered with reference to Giraud's original text. In her correspondence, Zehme refers to a possible version of the poems in their original language. Schoenberg knew of several performances in French, including at least one he personally heard featuring Marya Freund at the home of Alma Mahler. In 1927 he conducted a performance in Paris with Marya Freund performing in the original French. However, despite the fact that he copied the original French above the Sprechstimme in his published score (Source D2), it is unlikely that Schoenberg made a study of the poems in their original language. Nevertheless, we refer to the French text in an effort to shed light on the meaning of the poems.

In our translations, we have made no attempt to craft an English version suitable for performance. After his emigration to the United States, Schoenberg took an active interest in arranging a recording of the work in English. Schoenberg had hoped to make his own recording in English, but CBS wanted to release a recording in the original German version. In 1942 he tried to convince Erwin Stein to record an English version in England.[12] The jazz singer

Cleo Laine recorded an English version of *Pierrot* in 1974, and more recently, Lucy Shelton recorded and toured with an English version.[13] Andrew Porter has reviewed a number of English translations of *Pierrot* and has made his own performance translation, which is included in Dunsby's *Pierrot lunaire*.[14]

Hartleben dedicated 27 of his translations to friends, colleagues, and personal heroes, identified below the title of the poem. The copy of the text from which Schoenberg chose the poems (Source Ab) indicates the dedicatees. Of the 21 poems Schoenberg selected, 16 have dedicatees. Thus, Schoenberg chose poems with dedicatees at a significantly higher rate than he chose poems without dedicatees. Moreover, of the five poems he chose without dedicatees, four—"Der Dandy," "Raub," "Galgenlied," and "Gemeinheit"—are some of the most comedic poems in the cycle and take the lightest tone in their musical setting. The fifth, "Parodie," is not as obviously comedic but is rendered in a droll musical treatment somewhat similar to that of "Der Mondfleck," which does have a dedicatee and immediately follows. It would be too extreme to insist on a causal relationship between Hartleben's dedications and Schoenberg's selection of poems. However, since the dedications do seem to factor into the selection of poems and the structure of the whole, we have included and identified the dedicatees for each poem.

SELECTION OF TEXT

Giraud's situation and state of mind in 1883 is uncannily similar to Schoenberg's aesthetic and musical crisis on the eve of composing Pierrot. Schoenberg's essentially traditional view of musical development—a vague analog to Parnassianism in music—was challenged by the liberating promise posed by a new aesthetic. Schoenberg's Kandinskian moment, 1909–1912, is similar to Giraud's flirtation with Symbolism.

It is unlikely that Schoenberg gave much thought to the details of Giraud's life and work. However, it seems clear that he identified aspects of the Pierrot character that were analogous to the struggle of an artist in transition. Zehme's advocacy and interpretation of the poems must have supported such an interpretation as well: she certainly thought of herself as a misunderstood artist and identified with the Pierrot character. From these elements, Schoenberg fashioned a loose narrative. Susan Youens described Schoenberg's *Pierrot* plot as "the narration of an artist's rejection of and reconciliation with the past, of the spiritual violence that comes from the attempt to obliterate tradition and therefore to deny who one is."[15]

Following the example of Zehme's 1911 recital, Schoenberg's treatment casts the work in three cycles. In her review, Elsa Bienenfeld noted that the first and the third cycles were calmer than the middle section, which contained "blood, gallows, black monsters and the like."[16] Subsequent analysis, particularly the work of Susan Youens, has contended that the first section presents Pierrot as a poet bathed in the moonlight, which is the wellspring of his poetry. Over the course of the first seven poems, the mood darkens considerably. By the end of the first section, the narrator describes the moon as sickly and consumptive. The middle section begins with the gruesome image of giant black butterflies obscuring the sky—and thus the moon. With the exception of some comic relief and gallows humor, the second section is pervasively dark and leads to the terror of "Enthauptung" and "Die Kreuze," Pierrot's nadir and the climax of the work. The final section brightens immediately as Pierrot comes to terms with his Commedia past, which is symbolized by crystal. Over the course of the third section, Pierrot returns to his home, both as a physical place and as an artistic tradition. This slender narrative is further explicated in the head notes to each poem in Part II.

Susan Youens' interpretation of the narrative has never been seriously challenged. She credits Schoenberg for creating the narrative by pruning and reordering the poems from Giraud's "non-cyclic" order, which she describes as having "little apparent structure or schematic organization."[17] Robert Vilain, while generally accepting Youens' interpretation of the narrative, has objected to Youens' description of Giraud's order, countering that Giraud's work progresses "from easy-going confidence, via disarray, disaster and suicidal despair, back to a renewed but more solidly founded self-possession."[18] Vilain also notes that Hartleben's translation was not informed by the poetological debate—the sense of being caught between artistic movements—that vexed Giraud and resonates in Schoenberg's ordering.[19]

As previously discussed in chapters 2 and 3, before meeting Schoenberg, Albertine Zheme selected twenty-two poems for a 1911 recital. Zehme's selection of poems was also a likely influence on Schoenberg's ordering of the poems. As Reinhold Brinkmann has shown, Schoenberg was revising the order as he composed: he composed in one order, speculating the placement of the melodramas in a second order, only to make a final ordering at a much later date. Thus, he composed "Gebet an Pierrot" first and placed it first in the manuscript, on pages 1–2. However, he composed "Der Dandy" second and placed it on pages 5–7 of the manuscript, leaving pages 3–4 open for "Valse de Chopin," which he anticipated would be the second melodrama.

"Gebet" must have been of considerable importance to Zehme, as it was the first poem in her 1911 recital. As is well known, Zehme insisted on wearing a Pierrot costume for the premiere and first tour of Schoenberg's *Pierrot*.[20] Zehme's 1911 ordering of the poems makes her costume more logical. She began with "Gebet," addressing Pierrot literally as if she were another character (Columbine?), and ends with "Böhmischer Kristall," the last poem in Giraud's collection. In "Böhmischer Kristall," not set by Schoenberg, the second stanza reads, "I've disguised myself as Pierrot / To bring her that I love / A moonbeam, well preserved / In a glass of bohemian crystal."[21]

That Zehme fancied herself a persecuted artist—if not quite an artist of Schoenberg's caliber—can be easily inferred from her writings. For example, she titled the short text found in the program of her 1911 recital "Why I Must Speak These Songs." When she talks of restoring the ear to its appropriate position, which is to say, emphasizing sound as well as meaning, she boldfaces the first person pronoun (*Ich*), which is the only emphasis in the essay. Moreover, she uses the word *zurückerobern*, which is commonly used in military contexts to indicate that a position has been forcefully reconquered. Much later, in her 1920 book, she discusses Sprechmelodie as a talent of heroic liberators (*Freiheitshelden*) who dare to extend music beyond the realm of theory. Such musical pathfinders blaze forth on feeling alone, "igniting an unequal fight: one—against a world of rejections."[22]

Schoenberg's ordering of the poems includes twelve of the twenty-two poems Zehme selected. Most of the overlapping poems were set in the first month of composition, perhaps suggesting that the influence of Zehme's order diminished over time. Furthermore, in a letter of 17 May, Zehme expresses her delight that Schoenberg chose to set "Madonna" and suggests "Mein Bruder" and "Herbst" be added to the collection. Curiously, none of these poems appeared in Zehme's 1911 recital. "Mein Bruder" casts the narrator as a brother of Pierrot jointly suckling at the breast of the moon goddess. Thus, if Zehme imagined a scenario by which she identified with Pierrot, and dressed as Pierrot, "Mein Bruder" would presumably strengthen her relationship to the character and further justify her costume. But by 17 May, Schoenberg was nearly finished and had certainly made his own decisions about the remaining poems to set.

INSTRUMENTATION

Schoenberg chose the instrumentation of *Pierrot lunaire* as he began to compose. The contract expressly called for "piano accompaniment, perhaps with the accompaniment of two additional instruments."[23] However, over the first month of composition, Schoenberg expanded the ensemble to the quintet of two strings, two winds, and piano. This ensemble, which has come to be called the *Pierrot quintet*, has proven a remarkably balanced combination of resources. The instrumentation has been the basis of so many new music ensembles, and so many subsequent compositions, that it is arguably as influential as Sprechmelodie.

However, Schoenberg's choices were not only practical, but also prompted by his reading of the poems. In fact, Schoenberg sketched a number of ideas directly on his copy of the texts. As Christian Martin Schmidt has noted, "in these annotations a formative factor becomes evident which is also important in the final working out of the pieces: the realization in sound. It is as important a characteristic as the pitch organization."[24]

Elsa Bienenfeld was perhaps the first person to suggest that Schoenberg had used the timbral qualities of the instruments to heighten the sense of the poem, when she wrote in her review, "Presumably a particularly characteristic mood is also expressed through the lines of the instruments in each poem."[25] The first instrument he added to the piano and Sprechstimme is the clarinet. The opportunities for facile articulation on the clarinet—the first passage he wrote for clarinet, mm. 2–3 of "Gebet an Pierrot," spans two octaves and a tritone in three beats—suggest the clowning aspect of Pierrot. But the low chalumeau register of the clarinet also has a mournful dimension. Schoenberg used the clarinet again in "Der Dandy," the second melodrama he composed, and added the piccolo. In the immediate context of "Der Dandy," the piccolo suggests the fantastic moonbeam of the first verse. However, over the course of work, and especially in Part I, the flute is often used to personify the moon as a source of poetic inspiration. Aside from the technical achievement of setting a poem for flute and recitation alone, "Der kranke Mond" puts Pierrot in direct contact with the moon-as-flute, brought down to his level by sounding primarily in the same register.

The violin was first played in the introduction of "Mondestrunken," the third melodrama he composed. The cello—Schoenberg's own instrument—was certainly considered at this time as well. Schoenberg set "Mondestrunken" aside on 17 April, presumably to await confirmation from Zehme to add a fifth instrument. In the interim, he composed "Der kranke Mond" for flute and Sprechstimme and "Eine blasse Wäscherin" for flute, clarinet, and violin. By 25 April, Schoenberg must have received confirmation because he composed "Serenade," the first completed melodrama that uses the entire quintet. When he returned to "Mondestrunken" on 29 April, the cello enters rather dramatically on the word *Poet,* thus perhaps representing the more noble aspects of Pierrot's creativity and subtly associating Schoenberg the cellist with the Pierrot character.

The flute and clarinet alternate with standard substitution instruments: the flute alternates with piccolo and the clarinet alternates with bass clarinet. The flute substitution was and remains a typical feature of playing the flute and many large orchestral works of the period require one or two flutes to "take" the piccolo in the course of a work. The clarinet substitution was a little less common, as bass clarinetists tend to specialize in the lower instrument.

Kalman Bloch, who played for Schoenberg's recording of *Pierrot*, had to borrow a bass clarinet and take lessons to play the part. Finally, Schoenberg requires the violinist to play the viola. As Steuermann recalled, the viola substitution "was at that time most unusual—our violinist Maliniak was certainly not used to it."[26] "Rote Messe," the seventh melodrama composed, effectively completes the instrumentation in that it uses all five players and all three substitutions. The piccolo had already been used in "Der Dandy," but the viola and bass clarinet are both used for the first time.

The substitutions are an integral part of another celebrated aspect of *Pierrot*: the instrumentation is varied for each melodrama. No two pieces have the exact same instrumentation. Schoenberg carefully distinguishes between the later inclusion of instruments in the piece (e.g., "flute, violin, piano; *later* cello). Dika Newlin remembered a composition lesson in 1940 when Schoenberg taught by the example of his instrumentation of *Pierrot*:

> Just to give me a bare idea of the possibilities I was neglecting, he named all the possible combinations of the five instruments, and asked me to write them down and count them. I did so, and discovered there were thirty. Add to that the different combinations of melody and accompaniment within those instrumental combinations, and you have over one hundred! He thinks it a good idea to list combinations in this way and thus have a better conception of your variety of resources. That is what he did for the instrumentation of *Pierrot lunaire* and as a result in all of the twenty-one pieces there is only one duplication of combination. [The final melodrama, "O alter Duft" uses all the instruments.][27]

Because of the highly contrapuntal nature of his music, Schoenberg treats the instruments as a group of soloists. The writing is virtuosic, but fairly traditional. It is the combination of instruments that is unusual. However, the combination is not entirely without precedent. Just as Brahms' music influenced Schoenberg's developmental technique, it also provided a model for the mixed chamber ensemble. As Boulez noted, "Chamber music in which the piano played an important part was an increasingly marked feature of the last decades of the nineteenth century. In old piano quartets and quintets the instrumental writing remained clearly defined from beginning to end, emphasis being laid on the cohesion of the ensemble as a whole. In *Pierrot* on the other hand, each piece draws attention to an individual color, a special instrumental combination."[28] Brahms also wrote some of the first significant chamber works for clarinet, including the Clarinet Trio (with piano and cello), op. 114, the Clarinet Quintet, op. 115, and the op. 120 Clarinet Sonatas. As noted, the clarinet was the first instrument added to the *Pierrot* ensemble. Schoenberg was fond of the clarinet and featured it prominently in a number of chamber works. Later in life, Schoenberg was keenly aware of the influence of Brahms on the *Pierrot* instrumentation. Dika Newlin wrote of a composition lesson when Schoenberg "talked a bit about the novel combinations of instruments in *Pierrot*, some of which he does not like any more—says this due to influence of Brahms, who was very much interested in such combinations."[29] Table 4-1 lists the instrumentation and details of composition for each melodrama.

FORM

As explored in chapter 2, Schoenberg's early music is deeply concerned with refitting traditional musical forms with new technical and expressive resources. However, when Schoenberg's music was no longer governed by tonality, he lost the form-building potential of harmonic organization as it relates to a tonic. As Schoenberg often said in retrospect, this resulted in works that were extremely expressive but also fell short for want of a suitable principle for large-scale organization. Schoenberg was able to find a provisional organizational principle as a result of his text setting, because he noticed that "compositions for texts are inclined to allow the poem to determine, at least outwardly, their form."[30] As he explained his lecture "Composition with Twelve Tones":

> I discovered how to construct larger forms by following a text or poem. The differences in size and shape of its parts and the change in character and mood were mirrored in the shape and size of the composition, in its dynamics and tempo, figuration and accentuation, instrumentation and orchestration. Thus the parts were differentiated as clearly as they had formerly been by the tonal and structural functions of harmony.[31]

Pierrot lunaire is a composition in which the musical design is closely allied with the textual design, and specifically, the textual design Schoenberg created by reordering a selection of the poems. As Christian Martin Schmidt remarked about the title page, "Schoenberg places the poems and the poet in the foreground and thus makes clear that the composition does not have an absolute function, but serves the performance of the poems, their symbolic representation by musical means."[32] The internal organization of each melodrama furthers each poem's symbolic representation, and prioritizes that concern over the implementation of traditional formal structures.

While previous commentary has sought to find traditional song forms in the *Pierrot* melodramas, Stephan Weytjens has advanced a more flexible model for analyzing the form based on the form of the poems, which create "pivotal moments."[33] According to Weytjens, there are five pivotal moments. The first

Table 4-1. The Instrumentation and Facts of Composition for Each Melodrama

	Melodrama	Instrumentation	Giraud's order	Working order	Order in ms.	Ms. pages	Date begun/ continued
1	Mondestrunken [Moondrunk]	flute, violin, piano; later cello	16	3	5	10–11	4/17, 4/29
2	Colombine [Columbine]	violin, piano; later flute, clarinet	10	6	4	8–9	4/20
3	Der Dandy [The Dandy]	piccolo, clarinet, piano	3	2	3	5–7	4/1, 4/2
4	Eine blasse Wäscherin [A Pallid Laundrymaid]	flute, clarinet, violin	5	5	9	17	4/18
5	Valse de Chopin [Waltz of Chopin]	flute, clarinet, piano; later bass clarinet	26	13	2	3–4	5/7
6	Madonna [Madonna]	flute, bass clarinet, cello; later violin, piano	28	16	18	34–35	5/9
7	Der kranke Mond [The Sick Moon]	flute	21	4	8	16	4/18
8	Nacht [Night]	bass clarinet, cello, piano	19	14	11	21–22	5/9
9	Gebet an Pierrot [Prayer to Pierrot]	clarinet, piano	31	1	1	1–2	3/12
10	Raub [Theft]	flute, clarinet, violin, cello; later piano	14	17	19	34–35	5/9
11	Rote Messe [Red Mass]	piccolo, bass clarinet, viola, cello, piano	29	7	6	12–13	4/22
12	Galgenlied [Gallows' Song]	viola, cello; later piccolo	17	18	21	37	5/12

13	Enthauptung [Beheading]	bass clarinet, viola, cello, piano; later flute, clarinet	24	19	10	18–19	5/23
14	Die Kreuze [The Crosses]	piano; later flute, clarinet, violin, cello	30	10	15	19–30	4/27, 6/9
15	Heimweh [Nostalgia]	clarinet, violin, piano; later piccolo, cello	34	12	20	36	5/5, 5/23
16	Gemeinheit [Mean Trick]	piccolo, clarinet, violin, cello, piano	45	9	14	27–38	4/26, 6/6
17	Parodie [Parody]	piccolo, clarinet, viola, piano; later flute	42	11	7	14–15	5/4
18	Der Mondfleck [The Moon Fleck]	piccolo, clarinet, violin, cello, piano	38	20	17	32–33	5/28
19	Serenade [Serenade]	flute, clarinet, violin, cello, piano	6	8	12	23	4/25
20	Heimfahrt [Journey Home]	flute, clarinet, viola, cello, piano	36	15	13	24	5/9
21	Oh alter Duft [Oh Ancient Scent]	flute, clarinet, viola, cello, piano; later piccolo, bass clarinet, viola	35	21	16	31	5/30

three pivotal moments are the verses that frame the rondel refrain: the third verse, which is the first line that is not part of the refrain; the fifth verse, which begins the second stanza; and the ninth verse, which begins the third stanza. The other two pivotal moments are the refrains: the seventh and eighth verses and the thirteenth verse.

The pivotal moments, as defined by Weytjens, are indeed the places in the poem where musical sections are formally articulated. Just as Schoenberg varied the instrumentation for each melodrama, each setting takes on a different form. "O alter Duft," for example, is remarkable for reprising a melody for each statement of the refrain while "Der Mondfleck" is a fugue that continues in retrograde after the first text refrain. In general, one of two broad designs can be observed in many of the melodramas. One design is loosely related to a two-reprise "rounded binary" form in which the third stanza contains a much-varied reprise of the first stanza. "Gemeinheit," which is modeled after a minuet, is an example of this design. The location and extent of the reprise vary widely. Another design groups the first two stanzas in a larger, continuous section, which is offset by contrasting music for the third stanza. "Madonna" is an example of this design. In part 2, each melodrama is discussed along the lines of these formal designs. However, our formal designations are merely referential: to fit the melodramas into the Procrustean bed of traditional form is to rob them of their individuality and to diminish the form-building role of the poems.

The subject of form at the largest level is a topic of some debate. Some analysts have suggested that the arrangement of melodramas transcends the arrangement of a poetic narrative and serves a high-level musical function. Reinhold Brinkmann was among the first to suggest the possibility of a greater organization in 1977, when he noted "certain leading musical ideas [*Leitideen*] dominate the score of *Pierrot* though the genesis of the individual numbers is very complex and did not follow an irrevocable, overall conception."[34] Jonathan Dunsby has speculated that there is in fact an undiscovered *Grundgestalt*, or basic idea that underlies the composition. Dunsby predicted that the revelation of that *Grundegestalt* would reveal *Pierrot*, "from the most aphoristic to the more apparently densely constructed structures, as a work that despite all its variegated appearances is nevertheless firmly on the road to serialism, and no less spectacular a composition at the height of 'expressionism' for all its yet-to-be revealed constructionist secrets . . ."[35] Supporting this view is the presence of a seven-note figure that can be found in most of the melodramas. This "Pierrot figure" is prominently featured in "Mondestrunken," the first melodrama in the final order, but the third melodrama Schoenberg composed. Elements of the Pierrot figure can be found in the first entrance of the clarinet in "Gebet an Pierrot" and in "Der Dandy"—the first and second melodramas composed. Example 4-1 shows the Pierrot figure in "Mondestrunken," as well as its precedents in the first two melodramas composed and a significant recurrence in "O alter Duft," the last melodrama composed. Many other examples are referenced in part 2.

The theory of higher ordering is also aided by a famous developed reprise of "Der kranke Mond," the last music composed for *Pierrot*, between "Enthauptung" and "Die Kreuze," Schoenberg originally drafted a transition that would serve not so much as a reprise of an earlier melodrama but rather as a collection of motives from several melodramas (Source Aa). Reinhold Brinkmann has thoroughly analyzed the sketch and his transcription and annotations are reproduced in ex. 4-2.[36]

Example 4-1. Four examples of the Pierrot figure.

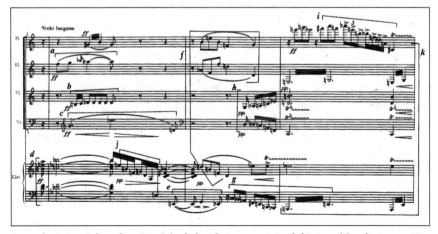

Example 4-2. Schoenberg's original sketch (source Aa) of the transition between "Enthauptung" and "Die Kreuze."

As would be expected, most of the motives anticipate "Die Kreuze," which immediately follows, including the introductory chords in the piano, the final trill of the sketch, and the flute passage at the end (Brinkmann's figures *d*, *k*, and *i* respectively). However, the cello's introductory gesture is from the flute's introduction to "Der kranke Mond" (*c*). The piano left-hand has the principal motive from "Nacht," (*e*) and the flute and clarinet have music from the start of "Eine blasse Wäscherin" (*f*). The sketch also has two variants of the Pierrot figure (*j* and *g*) and the principal motive from "Gemeinheit" (*b*).

Other analysts have generally avoided the issue of larger structuring, accepting that the work is a collection of melodramas cyclically organized by the text. Ethan Haimo recently addressed the issue of cyclic integration and dismissed the importance of the Pierrot figure, asking, "Could one possibly say that isolated motivic similarities are sufficient to create cyclic integration, particularly when the motives in question do not constitute the principal motives of the movements in which they occur and are often buried in obscure locations?[37] Haimo concluded that Schoenberg, still wrestling with the aesthetics he temporarily adopted in 1909, purposefully avoided a higher-level organization beyond what he intuited as he composed.

That Haimo dismissed the cyclic integration of *Pierrot* at the very same conference at which Dunsby speculated a future analysis would reveal a *Grundgestalt*, speaks to the variance of opinion on the issue of large-level form. Given Schoenberg's vast writings and correspondence and his discussions with students and other confidants, it does seem peculiar that there is no document—or even an anecdote—to suggest that Schoenberg was aware of a higher-level organization. Nevertheless, given a music-theoretic culture that delights in increasingly abstruse relationships, it seems likely that stronger connections between the melodramas will emerge over time. David Lewin, whose penetrating insight was matched by a particular sensitivity to text setting, noted in "an enormous leap," that the first eight notes of the Sprechstimme in "Mondestrunken" are united by an invariant trichord—G-sharp, A, and B—that is reproduced, with the same pitches, in the first eight notes of the Sprechstimme in "O alter Duft." Thus the beginning and end are connected by a trichord, which amplifies the meaning of "O alter Duft": the melody is both from "long ago," in that it resembles E major, and from long ago in that it replicates the beginning of *Pierrot*. Lewin concludes, "It seems clear, regardless of disputes over how *Sprechstimme* is to be performed, that the singer will be sensitive to the recollection, if only subliminally."[38] Observations like this can only contribute to a broader understanding of the piece.

THE COMPOSING ORDER AND THE FINAL ORDER

It is generally accepted that Schoenberg's final ordering of the melodramas was directed by his imagined narrative. It is still unclear whether the final order was influenced by musical considerations. However, a consideration of the melodramas in the order he composed them reveals some interesting relationships. Some of these relationships concern superficial details. For example, "Gebet an Pierrot" and "Der Dandy," the first two melodramas composed, are the only melodramas in cut-time. Similarly, "Columbine," "Rote Messe," "Serenade," and "Gemeinheit," all composed 20–26 April are all in three-four meter. This is the longest stretch of the same meter during the composition process. Schoenberg would use three-four meter only once more, for "Der Mondfleck," composed on 28 May.

Other relationships revealed by examining the melodramas in the composing order are more central to Schoenberg's compositional rhetoric. Beginning with "Mondestrunken," there is a group of melodramas with conspicuous repetition—the figuration in "Mondestrunken," the ostinato in the third stanza of "Columbine," the ostinato at the start of "Rote Messe," and the prominently placed ostinato in the middle of "Serenade" (mm. 30–34). All these works were composed between 17 and 28 April. Such repetition is not seen again until the ostinato in "Heimfahrt," and a repetitive ostinato is typical of a barcarolle. There is also more repetition at the phrase level. "Der kranke Mond" and "Eine blasse Wäscherin," composed on the same day of the same week in which he composed the repetitive passages cited above, both end with a thrice-repeated passage. "Der Dandy" begins with a thrice-repeated dyad of A-flat and D-sharp in the clarinet and piccolo. The extended introduction of "Serenade" is filled with a figuration that repeats in the cello and piano.

One other pattern worth noting is an early distribution of melodramas that feature a particular instrument. These concertante works include "Der kranke Mond" (flute), "Columbine" (violin), "Serenade" (cello), "Die Kreuze" (piano), and "Heimweh" (clarinet), which were begun fourth, sixth, eighth, tenth, and twelfth, respectively ("Die Kreuze" was completed later). It seems possible that as part of his elaborate instrumentation design, Schoenberg may have imagined a series of alternating concertante works.

The more superficial relationships among these works amount to little more than continuation of a mode of composing: it is as if Schoenberg began composing "Mondestrunken" before he had washed his hands of "Der Dandy." But the more significant relationships may suggest the observable manifestations of large-scale compositional designs that were either discarded or submerged into the work in a way that can no longer be readily detected.

MOTIVIC ANALYSIS

In his treatise, *Sketch of a New Esthetic of Music*, Busoni wrote of the construc-
tivist potential of new scales and modes. Schoenberg disagreed and expressed
concern that new scales and modes would only create new rules. In his copy
of the 1916 edition, Schoenberg copied the entire flute part of "Der kranke
Mond" and wrote:

> Just let Busoni consider this flute solo from my *Pierrot lunaire* Melodramas.
> Whether this melody is beautiful or good is not under discussion; I don't
> claim that it is, but believe it so. But whether it more resembles the divine
> freedom of a carefree child than that which could arise from the prison of
> his tone rows [*Tonreihen*]! Here there is no procedure other than the inspira-
> tion [*Einfall*] itself (should someone find one, I would swear an oath against
> it); I had no tonic [*Grundton*] or any other tone to work out [*herausarbeiten*];
> I allowed myself to use each of the twelve tones, and was not forced into the
> Procrustean bed of motivic phrasing, or to consider conclusions, sections or
> the beginnings and ends of phrases. As I've said, this melody may *displease
> many*, but everyone must admit that it is *freer* than one composed in one of
> the 113 modes.[39]

The music in *Pierrot* is free with regard to the organization of pitches. However,
Schoenberg used that freedom to further the development of motives. Schoenberg himself provided a model for analyzing his post-tonal music at the phrase
level. In 1932, the conductor Hans Rosbaud programmed Schoenberg's Four
Orchestral Songs, op. 22, to be broadcast in Frankfurt, and he invited Schoenberg to deliver a lecture before the performance. Schoenberg was unable to
deliver the lecture in person, but he did write an analysis to be read before the
performance. The op. 22 songs were composed in 1915, after the completion
of *Die glückliche Hand*, but the analysis addresses the composition in the context
of the seven-year period between 1908 and 1915.

Schoenberg began his analysis by explaining the presentation of the motive. (He does not use the word *motive*; he uses the word *shape* [*Gestalt*]). Using the clarinet melody that begins the first song, "Seraphita," as an example,
Schoenberg demonstrated that the motive is a combination of intervals that
had been prioritized by standard developmental procedures.

> I do not know if it is possible, even after repeated hearings, to perceive
> this passage as melody, in the absence of those repetitions that are usually
> requisite to such perception. However, let the following demonstrate the
> unconscious sway of musical logic. The clarinet melody [ex. 4-3a] consists
> of a series of minor seconds [ex. 4-3b] to which an ascending minor third

is appended [ex. 4-3c]. In the ensuing phrase the minor third and second are combined to yield the following shape [ex. 4-3d].[40, 41]

The analysis continues with an exploration of how the motive is developed in both the orchestra and the voice. Schoenberg's pedagogical writing about tonal music emphasizes developing variation. Jack Boss has noted that many of Schoenberg's statements about the techniques of developing variation in tonal music run parallel to the similar set of procedures he used to create his post-tonal music, albeit with the requisite modifications. One of the most significant differences between tonal and post-tonal development is Schoenberg's conception of the motive. As Boss has shown, in the discussion of the op. 22 Four Songs, when Schoenberg discusses the motive, he speaks largely to the intervals rather than the actual pitches as the motive's melodic feature. Moreover, he limits himself to discussing one motive—one grouping of intervals—and following the development of that motive throughout the work.[42]

As Schoenberg explained in his later pedagogical work, variation is modified repetition.[43] In his post-tonal music, Schoenberg varied motives by changing aspects of its rhythm or its shape. He varied the rhythm of a motive by modifying the duration of notes or changing its metrical placement. He varied the shape of the motive by changing the size of the intervals or reversing the direction of the intervals. Schoenberg also added or subtracted notes from motives, which simultaneously varied the rhythm and the shape. A motive can also be varied by changing its role in the texture, which further varies the harmony and counterpoint. Schoenberg made a point of not discussing the harmonic features of his post-tonal music. As he wrote in the *Harmonielehre*, he felt that the new harmonic resources had not been sufficiently explored and that practice had far outstripped theory. There is a strong implication that preceding the creation of the twelve-tone method, Schoenberg's harmonic choices are primarily intuitive.

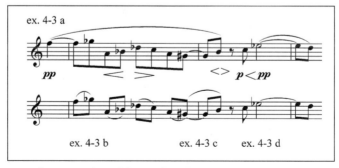

Example 4-3.   Adapted from Schoenberg's analysis of op. 22.

In part 2, each melodrama is analyzed following the precepts of Schoenberg's op. 22 analyses. After a translation of the poem and some remarks on the composition of the melodrama, the short analysis proceeds by identifying the principal motives and their development. The motivic analysis is particularly directed at the Sprechstimme and how it relates to the other voices. By treating the Sprechstimme as one of six *Stimmen*, it will be shown to be a type of pitched speech that actively "participates in a musical form."

NOTES

1. The history of the Pierrot character is masterfully adumbrated in Susan Youens, "The Texts of *Pierrot lunaire*, Op. 21," *Journal of the Arnold Schoenberg Institute* 8/2 (1984): 94–115. A more thorough treatment can be found in Martin Green and John Swan, *The Triumph of Pierrot: The Commedia Dell'arte and the Modern Imagination* (University Park: Pennsylvania State University Press, 1993).

2. Albert Giraud, *Pierrot lunaire: Rondels bergamasques* (Paris: A. Lemerre, 1884).

3. Jean Moréas, "Le Symbolisme," *Figaro*, December 14, 1890; reprinted in André Barre, *Le Symbolisme* (Paris: Jouve, 1911), 110.

4. Robert Vilain, "*Pierrot lunaire*: Cyclic Coherence in Giraud and Schoenberg," in *Pierrot lunaire: Une collection d'études musico-littéraires*, ed. Mark Delaere and Jan Herman (Louvain: Éditions Peeters, 2004), 130.

5. Henri Morier, *Dictionnaire de poétique et rhétorique* (Paris: Presses Universitaires de France, 1975), 931.

6. Max Nordau, *Degeneration*, 2nd ed. (New York: D. Appleton and Company, 1895), 532.

7. *Ferrucio Busoni: Selected Letters*, trans. and ed. Antony Beaumont (New York: Columbia University Press, 1987), 169.

8. R. L.-S., *Münchner neueste Nachrichten*, November 7, 1912; reprinted in Lesure, 25.

9. Charles Rosen, *Arnold Schoenberg* (New York: Viking Press, 1975), 59. Willi Reich, *Schoenberg: A Critical Biography*, trans. Leo Black (New York: Praeger, 1971), 74. Both quoted in Vilain, 128.

10. Youens, 103.

11. The sources of the more recent reevaluation of Giraud are cited and discussed in Vilain's article.

12. Arnold Schoenberg to Erwin Stein, 2 October 1942; reprinted in *Letters*, p. 215.

13. Arnold Schoenberg, *Pierrot lunaire*, The Nash Ensemble, cond. Elgar Howarth, reciter Cleo Laine, RCA Red Label LRL 1-5058, 1974, phonograph. Schoenberg: *Pierrot lunaire*, Da Capo Chamber Players, cond. Oliver Knussen, reciter Lucy Shelton, Bridge Records 9032, 1992.

14. Andrew Porter, "Munching a Beanstalk," in *From Pierrot to Marteau*, ed. Leonard Stein (Los Angeles: Arnold Schoenberg Institute, 1988); Dunsby 1992.

15. Youens, 114.

16. Bienenfeld, 58 and 59.

17. Youens, 107.

18. Vilain, 131.

19. Vilain, 139.

20. Smith, 276; Eduard Steuermann, "*Pierrot lunaire* in Retrospect" in *Juilliard News Bulletin* 1 (Feb. 1963): 8.

21. *Ich hab mich als Pierrot verkleidet—/ Ihr, die ich liebe, bring ich dar / Den Strahl des Mondes, wohl verschlossen / Im Glas of böhmischen Kristall.* Hartleben's translation is gender-specific; the French is better translated, "to offer to the one I love" (*Pour offrir à celle que j'aime*).

22. Zehme 1920, 36.

23. Brinkmann 1995, 227.

24. Christian Martin Schmidt, "Analytical Remarks on Schoenberg's *Pierrot lunaire*," in *From Pierrot to Marteau: An International Conference and Concert Celebrating the Tenth Anniversary of the Arnold Schoenberg Institute*, University of Southern California School of Music, March 14–16, 1987, ed. Leonard Stein (Los Angeles: Arnold Schoenberg Institute, 1987), 41.

25. Bienenfeld, 59.

26. Schuller and Steuermann, 24.

27. Newlin 1980, 186–87.

28. Pierre Boulez, "*Pierrot lunaire* and *Le marteau sans maître*," trans. Martin Cooper, in *From Pierrot to Marteau*, ed. Leonard Stein (Los Angeles: Arnold Schoenberg Institute, 1988), 12.

29. Newlin 1980, 267.

30. Schoenberg, "Analysis," 3.

31. Schoenberg, "Composition with Twelve Tones," *Style and Idea*, 217–18.

32. Christian Martin Schmidt, "Analytical Remarks on Schoenberg's Pierrot Lunaire," trans. John C. Crawford, in *From Pierrot to Marteau*, ed. Leonard Stein, (Los Angeles: Arnold Schoenberg Institute, 1988), 41.

33. Stephan Weytjens, "Text as a Crutch in Schoenberg's *Pierrot lunaire?*" in *Pierrot lunaire: Une collection d'études musico-littéraires*, ed. Mark Delaere and Jan Herman (Louvain: Éditions Peeters, 2004), 109–26.

34. Reinhold Brinkmann, "On Pierrot's Trail," trans. Paul A. Pisk, *Journal of the Arnold Schoenberg Institute* 2/1 (1977): 45.

35. Jonathan Dunsby, "Schoenberg's Pierrot keeping his *Kopfmotiv.*" In *Pierrot lunaire: A Collection of Musicological and Literary Studies*, ed. Mark Delaere and Jan Herman (Louvain: Éditions Peeters, 2004), 75.

36. Reinhold Brinkmann, "What the Sources Tell Us . . . A Chapter of *Pierrot* Philology," *Journal of the Arnold Schoenberg Institute* 10/1 (1987): 22. See also Brinkmann 1977, 46–47 and Brinkmann 1995, 215–16.

37. Ethan Haimo, "Schoenberg's *Pierrot lunaire*: A Cycle?" in *Pierrot lunaire: A Collection of Musicological and Literary Studies*, ed. Mark Delaere and Jan Herman (Louvain: Éditions Peeters, 2004), 150–51.

38. David Lewin, "Some Notes on *Pierrot lunaire*," in *Music Theory in Concept and*

Practice, ed. James M. Baker, David Beach, and Jonathan W. Bernard, Eastman Studies in Music (Rochester, NY: University of Rochester Press, 1997), 435–36. The connection is also observed in Brinkmann 1997. We cannot resist noting that Lewin, a student of Josef Polnauer and Eduard Steuermann [!], refers to the performer who executes the recitation as a *singer*.

39. H. H. Stuckenschmidt, ed., *Ferruccio Busoni: Entwurf einer neuen Ästhetik der Tonkunst. Faksimile einer Ausgabe von 1916 mit den handschriftlichen Anmerkungen von Arnold Schönberg. Im Anhang Transkription der Anmerkungen und Nachwort von H. H. Stuckenschmidt* ([Frankfurt am Main]: Insel Verlag, 1974), 74–75.

40. Schoenberg, "Analysis," 4–5.

41. In Schoenberg's lecture, each of these lettered excerpts is presented as different examples, numbered 5–8.

42. Jack Boss, "Schoenberg's op. 22 Radio Talk and Developing Variation in Atonal Music." *Music Theory Spectrum* 14/2 (1992): 131. Our discussion greatly simplifies Boss' article, which is a detailed exploration of developing variations as chains of ordered intervals.

43. Arnold Schoenberg, *Fundamentals of Musical Composition*, 2nd ed., ed. Gerald Strang and Leonard Stein (London: Faber and Faber Limited, 1970), 10.

Young Albertine Zheme. Photo courtesy of the Leipziger Blätter.

Frank King Clark.

The Zehme family. Photo courtesy of the Leipziger Blätter.

Albertine Zehme in 1912. Photo courtesy of the Arnold Schoenberg Center.

Arnold Schoenberg in 1911. Photo courtesy of the Arnold Schoenberg Center.

Karl Essberger, Jakob Maliniak, Arnold Schoenberg, Albertine Zehme, Eduard Steuermann, Hans Kindler, and Hans W. de Vries, the Choralionsaal, 16 October 1912. Photo courtesy of the Arnold Schoenberg Center.

Josef Polnauer, Eduard Steuermann, Anton Webern, Paul Königer, Gertrude Schoenberg, Marya Freund (?), Mathilde Schoenberg, Heinrich Jalowetz, unknown, Arnold Schoenberg, unknown, Emil Hertzka (?), Edward Clark with Georg Schoenberg, Albertine Zehme, Erwin Stein, unknown, unknown, and Hans Nachod (?). Assembled in Grautzsch on the grounds of Villa Albertine for the Leipzig premiere of Gurrelieder, 1914. Photo courtesy of the Arnold Schoenberg Center.

Part I, Numbers 1–7

NO. 1 MONDESTRUNKEN (MOON DRUNK)

Den Wein, den man mit Augen
    trinkt,
Giesst Nachts der Mond in
    Wogen nieder,
Und eine Springflut
    überschwemmt
Den stillen Horizont.

The wine that one with eyes
    drinks
Poured at night by the moon in
    waves descending
And a spring tide
    overflows
The still horizon.

Gelüste, schauerlich und süss,
Durchschwimmen ohne Zahl
    die Fluten!
Den Wein, den man mit Augen
    trinkt,
Giesst Nachts der Mond in
    Wogen nieder.

Desires, horrible and sweet
Swim through the currents
    without number!
The wine that one with eyes
    drinks
Poured at night by the moon in
    waves descending.

Der Dichter, den die Andacht treibt,
Berauscht sich an dem heilgen
    Tranke,
Gen Himmel wendet er verzückt
Das Haupt und taumelnd saugt
    und schlürft er
Den Wein, den man mit Augen
    trinkt.

The poet, by his prayers driven,
Intoxicated with the sacred
    drink,
Toward the heavens turns in rapture
His head and stumbling sucks
    and slurps
The wine that one with eyes
    drinks.

The Text and Translation

"Mondestrunken" is the sixteenth poem in Giraud's collection. Following the generally accepted models of narrative sketched in chapter 4, the poem introduces the moon as the source of poetic inspiration and Pierrot as a poet. Hartleben's translation makes no material changes to the poem, although in the original, the descending waves are described as green (*A flots verts*). Hartleben's translation is dedicated to Heinrich Hart (1885–1906), a theater critic and, along with Hartleben, a member of the Friedrichshagener Dichterkreis in Berlin.

Details of Composition

Schoenberg began "Mondestrunken" on 17 April 1912, having already completed "Gebet an Pierrot" on 12 March and "Der Dandy" on 1–2 April. After some preliminary work, he set "Mondestrunken" aside and completed five other melodramas before completing "Mondestrunken" on 29 April. The place of "Mondestrunken" in the order of composition is significant, as it was the first melodrama composed that requires the violin and cello. Schoenberg had expanded the original commission from reciter and piano to reciter and five instruments. It is possible Schoenberg set it aside to await confirmation from Albertine Zehme that he could use the additional instruments. There is a pattern of expanding instrumentation in the next group of melodramas he composed: following "Der kranke Mond" for flute and recitiation only, "Eine blasse Wäscherin" and "Columbine" use the violin; "Rote Messe," "Serenade," "Gemeinheit," and "Die Kreuze" use both violin and cello.

Musical Materials

Like most of the melodramas, "Mondestrunken" has three sections that align with the three stanzas. The first two sections are similar and the third section presents a departure in instrumentation, dynamics, and texture. The three sections are united by a compound accompanimental motive that is introduced in the first two measures, consisting of a seven-note motive in the piano and a three-note motive in the violin, pizzicato. As noted in chapter 4, this seven-note figure, with its characteristic rhythm and metric placement, occurs so frequently in other melodramas that it has come to be known as the Pierrot figure.

The initial presentation of this motive text-paints the moon pouring down in waves. The repetition suggests the accompaniment patterns one might encounter in a nineteenth-century lied, comparable to the running sixteenths that represent the spinning wheel in Schubert's "Gretchen am Spinnrade." The first five pitches of the piano are five of the six notes of a whole-tone scale. The missing note, F-sharp, is the first note in the violin. Taken together, these six notes form two symmetrical augmented triads to which a third augmented triad is added from the other transposition of the whole-tone scale, as shown in ex. 5-1.[1]

Schoenberg lightly develops this accompanimental figure throughout the melodrama, subjecting it to extension, sequencing, canonic imitation, and augmentation. In addition to the motive, the easily identifiable sound of the whole-tone scale returns in structurally significant places—in the piano in m. 10 as a chord and suggested in the pattern of thirds that follows, mm. 11–12; in the sequencing of the motive, mm. 25–28 (discussed below); in the Sprechstimme, mm. 35–36; and in the cello, mm. 35–38. Whole-tone sonorities return at the end of each section.

In the first section, the Sprechstimme is the *Hauptstimme*. Marked at a slightly higher dynamic, the Sprechstimme is more chromatic and thus stands in relief against the more symmetrical pitch material in the piano and violin. The first two verses of the poem are set with an unusual emphasis on A-natural, appearing as a weak-syllable anacrusis to the first two phrases. The second phrase ends with A_3 appearing on the last eighth of m. 6.

The Sprechstimme in the first section is integrated into the contrapuntal texture. As shown in ex. 5-2, the descending pattern of the Sprechstimme, particularly on the verse *geißt nachts der Mond*, is imitated in the piano, left hand, m. 5 and violin, in the pickup to m. 6. The pattern is also found in the flute, mm. 4 and 6. Furthermore, the last verses of the first stanza in the Sprechstimme have anchoring notes that are heard in the instrumental texture. The D-sharp/E-flat in mm. 8–9 are heard in the flute and violin, respectively, and the E, G, and B of *den stillen Horizont* are found in places that discreetly reinforce those pitches. See ex. 5-4 for the imitation of *den stillen Horizont* found in the violin, mm. 15–16.

The dynamic indications in the first stanza greatly contribute to a sense of shape. Of the seven hairpins (the crescendo and diminuendo symbols) in the

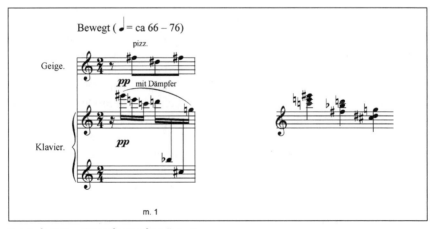

Example 5-1. "Mondestrunken," m. 1.

Example 5-2. "Mondestrunken," first stanza.

first section, the crescendo to D-sharp in m. 8 is the boldest, rapidly increasing intensity to the local climax, marked *forte*. The arrival can be accentuated with a rolled *r* in *Spring*; however, the word must be short to properly observe the rest. The return to enharmonic E-flat in m. 9 is marked with lighter crescendo, which tapers some of the energy of m. 8. The sudden drop to E-natural$_4$ on *stillen* in m. 10 is marked by a contrast of register, dynamic, and tone production. Here, as elsewhere, vibrato on the notes marked *gesungen* provide maximum contrast to Sprechgesang, especially if followed by an immediate return to a straight tone at *gesprochen* for the normal Sprechstimme delivery. At the end of the phrase on the word *Horizont*, most vocalists feel a strong tendency to continue the ascending motion with glissando, which is best if the glissando is not overly emphasized (it is a statement, not a question) and the quarter rest is observed.

The second section features the violin, which, beginning in m. 15, is marked a dynamic above everything else and is further marked *hervortretend* in

m. 19.[2] The violin enters in m. 15 with a paraphrase of the Sprechstimme in m. 10—*stillen Horizont*. This motive, which consists of a third and a second in different octaves, is developed by the violin in the second section. As shown in ex. 5-4, in m. 20, the violin's development of the motive takes on the rhythm and registration of the violin's gesture in m. 7. The octave displacement of adjunct pitches is the most characteristic form of the violin's motive.

In the second section, the Sprechstimme begins with a step progression ascending C-D-E on the accented syllables of the first verse: *Gelü-ste, Schauerlich und süß*. On *süß*, Schoenberg uses a short melisma that emphasizes a minor third (E/C-sharp) and text-paints the word (*sweet*). That same minor third sounds an octave lower in m. 22, preceded by notes in m. 20 that approximately invert the contour of m. 19. The repetition of the minor third, an octave lower, provides a sense of closure to the new verses of the second stanza; the two verses that follow are the text refrain from the first stanza. Moreover, the setting of the new verses of the second stanza also parallels the setting of the second verse of the poem, mm. 4–6: both are bounded by a pitch event an octave apart. In the text refrain, mm. 23–26, the octave is slightly expanded to the augmented octave between A_4 and A-flat$_3$.

The transition between the second and third stanzas, mm. 25–28, is uncharacteristically symmetrical. Beginning in m. 25, the piano plays the motive three times, descending in major thirds. In m. 27, the tail is sequenced in major thirds. Thus, the transposition maps onto the first three notes of the motive—G-sharp, E, and C. Instances of model and sequence are fairly rare in *Pierrot* and tend to be used to text-paint descent. A similar device, contrapuntal imitation, is used to depict the descent of giant black butterflies in the passacaglia melodrama "Nacht," which begins Part II.

The third section begins with the cello playing a melody that is doubled at the unison by the piano. Unison doubling is highly uncharacteristic of Schoenberg and of chamber music in general but is used here to highlight the entrance of the cello on the important word *Dichter*. The new melody and the cello itself

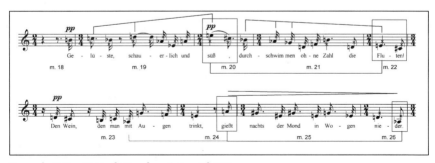

Example 5-3. "Mondestrunken," second stanza.

personify the poetic aspect of *Pierrot*. The melody begins as a bifocal line, which develops from the dramatic leaps in the violin from the second part. As if to further this association, the violin enters with a counter-melody that similarly develops the derived motive from the second section. In m. 33, the violin and cello alternate climactic statements of the most dramatic motive form from the second part on the pitches G, F-sharp, and B-flat, as shown in ex. 5-4.

Significantly, this same three-voice motive was used at the beginning of the third section in the Sprechstimme on the words *Der Dichter*. The rising

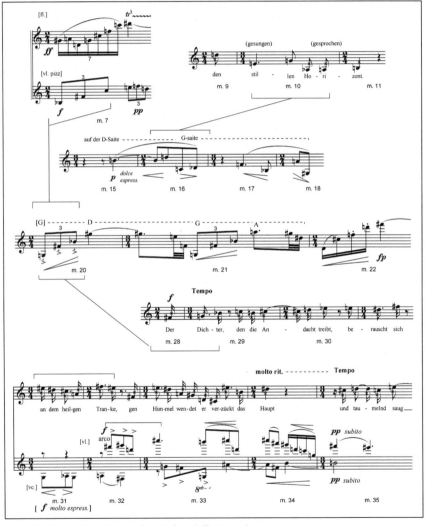

Example 5-4. "Mondestrunken," the violin's motive.

minor third is echoed almost immediately in m. 31 on *berauscht sich*, which makes a subtle connection between the words *poet* and *intoxicated*. The text of this passage is significant, and Schoenberg has taken care to have no syllables enunciated at the same time the piano left hand strikes one of its droning bass chords. At the climactic moment, mm. 32–34, the Sprechstimme is also written with large leaps to heighten the sense of hysteria. Despite the intensity, the text can be communicated by heightening the percussive consonants.

At the end of the last section, the Sprechstimme returns to motivic elements from the beginning. In mm. 35–36, the pitches are largely culled from the same whole-tone scale that creates the accompanying figure at the beginning, while the final words of the text reprise, *den mit Augen trinkt*, begin with the familiar descending seconds and thirds found in each setting of that text. "Mondestrunken" ends as it began with a quiet, mysterious depiction of the moonbeams of inspiration. But before the calm is restored, the intoxicating effect of the ostinato of moonbeams is demonstrated in the third stanza with the brief appearance of the slightly crazed Pierrot.

NO. 2 COLUMBINE

Des Mondlichts bleiche Blüten,	The moonlight's pale blossoms,
Die weißen Wunderrosen,	The white wonder-roses.
Blühn in den Julinächten—	Bloom on July nights—
O brach ich eine nur!	Oh to pluck one only!
Mein banges Leid zu lindern,	My anxious suffering to relieve,
Such ich am dunklen Strome	I seek at the dark stream,
Des Mondlichts bleiche Blüten,	The moonlight's pale blossoms,
Die weissen Wunderrosen.	The white wonder-roses.
Gestillt wär all mein Sehnen,	Stilled would be all my longing,
Dürft ich so märchenheimlich,	Could I with fairy-tale slyness
So selig leis—entblättern	So blessedly soft—scatter
Auf deine braunen Haare	On your brown hair
Des Mondlichts bleiche Blüten!	The moonlight's pale blossoms!

The Text and Translation

"Columbine" is the tenth poem in Giraud's collection. Unlike "Mondestrunken," which is in the third person, "Columbine" is in the first person. It seems to be the narrative voice of Pierrot, longing for Columbine, a fellow servant, sometimes depicted as the daughter of Cassander. In the original French, Giraud's first-person narrator seeks the blossoms along the Lethe—the river of forgetfulness in Greek mythology. Otherwise, Hartleben makes no significant changes to the text.

Details of Composition

Columbine was the sixth melodrama completed, composed entirely on 20 April, two days after Schoenberg composed "Der kranke Mond" and "Eine blasse Wäscherin." Those previous melodramas did not include the piano. Columbine includes the piano, features the violin as a concertante instrument, and adds the flute and clarinet for the last stanza. This is the first melodrama with four instruments that Schoenberg completed. ("Mondestrunken" was begun, but not completed until 29 April.)

Musical Materials

"Columbine" is a flowing waltz in three sections that align with the three stanzas. The first two sections are homogeneous, and the final section presents changes in character, instrumentation, and texture. The traditional waltz rhythms are continually varied throughout "Columbine." The solo violin sits comfortably in the meter. Most of its arrivals are on downbeats, and hairpins are arranged to peak on the downbeats. The principal material found in the violin part is a bifocal melody that first appears in mm. 1–5, shown in ex. 5-5. The higher portion of the bifocal melody descends in a step progression from the initial G-sharp$_5$ to the G-sharp$_4$ at the end of m. 4 (doubled an octave higher by the Sprechstimme). The G-sharp is registrally displaced an octave lower in m. 5.

The piano part supports the violin during lyrically sustained statements with legato counterpoint. However, between these statements, it also punctuates with staccato chords, which tend to vary the traditional waltz rhythms. In the first measure, the piano fills the measure with even eighth notes, marked *cantabile* and slurred. The eighth notes are arranged such that the first two are in a low register while the second and third beats are higher—a subtle variant of an *ohm-pah-pah* pattern. Throughout the first and second sections, the piano develops a rhythmic motive that suggests the second and third beat—the *pah-pah*—of the traditional waltz rhythm.

As ex. 5-5 shows, the Sprechstimme begins with a Brahms-like superimposition of duple meter. Beginning with the note on the second beat of the first measure, the Sprechstimme proceeds as if in two-four for the first two verses of the poem (with a three-four bar suggested between mm. 4 and 5). The wide range of the opening line and the beautiful vowels in *Wunderrosen* (also empha-

Example 5-5. "Columbine," mm. 1–5.

sized in mm. 25–26) create a sense of calm and bring this initial pattern to a close. For the next two verses of the first stanza, rhythmic roles are more varied. The Sprechstimme and violin continue in increasingly halting gestures, which culminate in the prurient statement, *O bräch ich eine nur!*, mm. 9–12. Melismas are uncommon in the text setting, but for this passage, Schoenberg uses melismas on three syllables for a tentative delivery. The melismas on *bräch* and *eine* use the same pitches, which also appear in the violin between these two words.

The second section continues the musical materials of the first. The violin resumes and develops the bifocal line of m. 1. In m. 17, the Sprechstimme resumes with the same hesitant delivery used for the end of the first stanza. The second stanza begins with four chromatic notes, but a distinct articulation of each note would better serve the text than a continuous glissando. The *b* in *banges*, in particular, can be delayed to give the impression of a throbbing pain. The text refrain, mm. 21–26 shown in ex. 5-6, begins with the same metric scheme as mm. 1–5. However, for the second verse of the refrain, the Sprechstimme aligns with the given meter and the violin superimposes two-four meter (with a final suggested six-eight).

The third section is a sudden departure in texture and tempo. It begins with a cadenza-like transition for the Sprechstimme and violin. The violin is legato and lyrical. The Sprechstimme returns to the halting delivery of the end of the first stanza and beginning of the second stanza, here communicated by ritardando and dynamics. For *Gestillt wär all mein Sehnen*, mm. 29–30, the hairpins over the last three notes communicate the hesitancy. On first glance, the

Example 5-6. "Columbine," mm. 21–26.

hairpins may seem reversed: the taper is in the middle, not at the ends. In fact, Schoenberg originally composed the passage with the hairpins emphasizing the E-flat in m. 29, but then lined-through the hairpins in the manuscript and added the revised hairpins as they appear in the published score.[3] As published, the sudden diminuendo on *Sehnen* (senses) heightens the sense of hesitancy and yearning, as does making the text, *So selig leis*, quite short, as written.

For the final verse, the violin has a flowing cantilena while the Sprechstimme remains aligned with the meter, its attacks only slightly longer than the staccato attacks in the accompanying ostinato. The B-flat on *Mondlichts* is an important pitch: it is one of three pitches missing from the ostinato. (The other pitches, B-natural and C, are introduced in the Sprechstimme and the violin, but the violin does not play the B-flat until m. 39, giving it first as a low trill then as a high note.) After the sung note, the Sprechstimme completes the final verse, in a rhythm that matches the previous two statements of the refrain. The sudden appearance of the Pierrot figure in the violin, m. 38, breaks the spell of the ostinato. The close imitation of the flute, piano, and clarinet suggests a disarrayed Pierrot, suddenly stirred from his prurient daydream at the abrupt conclusion of the melodrama.

NO. 3 DER DANDY

Mit einem phantastischen Lichtstrahl	With a fantastic light beam
Erleuchtet der Mond die	The moon illuminates the
krystallnen Flakons	crystalline vials

Auf dem schwarzen, hochheiligen
  Waschtisch
Des schweigenden Dandys
  von Bergamo.

On the black, holiest
  washstand
Of the quiet dandy from
  Bergamo.

In tönender, bronzener Schale
Lacht hell die Fontäne,
  metallisehen Klangs.
Mit einem phantastischen
  Lichtstrahl
Erleuchtet der Mond die
  krystallnen Flakons.

In the resounding, bronze basin
Laughs brightly the fountain, a
  metallic din.
With a fantastic light beam

The moon illuminates the
  crystalline vials.

Pierrot mit wächsernem Antlitz
Steht sinnend und denkt: wie er
  heute sich schminkt?
Fort schiebt er das Rot und des
  Orients Grün
Und bemalt sein Gesicht in
  erhabenem Stil
Mit einem phantastischen
  [Mondstrahl].

Pierrot with waxen face
Stands pensive and thinks: how
  should he wear make-up today?
Away he shoves the Red and
  Orient's green
And paints his features in a
  grand style
With a fantastic [moonbeam].

The Text and Translation

"Der Dandy" is the third poem in Giraud's collection—the only example of Giraud's order matching Schoenberg's final order. The text presents us with Pierrot, here identified as the quiet dandy of Bergamo—the traditional home of the Pierrot character—preparing to put on his performing face. It is notable that Pierrot keeps his make-up in crystalline vials. In "Heimweh," which Schoenberg placed at the beginning of Part III, a *crystalline sigh* represents the nostalgia Pierrot feels for Bergamo. In both melodramas, Schoenberg text-paints *crystalline* with the high register of the piano.

Giraud's first verse reads, "*D'un rayon de Lune fantastique.*" Harteben translated the first verse, "*Mit einem phantastischen Lichtstrahl,*" moving the moon to the second verse of the poem for smoother German syntax. Schoenberg is faithful to Hartleben's translation at the beginning of the poem and at the first text refrain. However, he changes the last word of the poem from Hartleben's *Lichtstrahl* to his own *Mondstrahl,* which puts the word *moon* in the last two measures, where it is musically depicted.

Details of Composition

"Der Dandy" is the second melodrama that Schoenberg composed. Having composed "Gebet an Pierrot" on 12 March, he waited more than two weeks before composing "Der Dandy" on 1–2 April. Schoenberg's *Textvorlage* has an undated sketch of the clarinet part in m. 13 next to the fifth verse of the poem.[4] "Der Dandy" also shows the accretion of instruments. "Gebet" contains only piano, clarinet, and reciter; "Der Dandy" adds the flautist, here playing piccolo. The addition is significant, as the flute or piccolo is often invoked to represent the moon. In "Gebet" the moon is mentioned only in an ironic aside; in "Der Dandy" the moon is integral to the poem, and the piccolo suggests a *fantastic moonbeam.*

Musical Materials

"Der Dandy" makes a strong immediate impression because of the quick *alla breve* tempo and high register. Of the three sections that parallel the three stanzas, the first two sections are in a broad duple meter, and the Sprechstimme emphasizes the meter through quarter-note triplets. The third section, *Langsammer,* is more easily heard in four. The Sprechstimme is often the meter-defining element of the musical texture, and the rhythms should be strictly observed in performance.

Regarding the tessitura, the vast majority of notes are above middle C. While the instrumentation accounts for some of this, the piano is also written in a higher range: in fourteen of the thirty-one measures, the bottom staff of the piano's grand staff is written in treble clef. The high tessitura gives the monodrama an ethereal quality, more a reflection of the moonbeam than Pierrot.

Whereas most of the melodramas of the first section use familiar texture devices (the ostinato of "Mondestrunken," the homophonic song-form textures of "Columbine," and "Valse de Chopin," etc.), the constantly changing texture of "Der Dandy" is more like "Gebet an Pierrot," the first melodrama composed. However, while "Gebet" makes conspicuous use of the Sprechstimme for motivic development, "Der Dandy" relies more on the resources of the ensemble. As a result, Schoenberg uses the *Hauptstimme* brackets for the first time (both in order of composition and in the final order) in "Der Dandy" to indicate the principal line. Here and elsewhere, Schoenberg never marks the Sprechstimme as the *Hauptstimme.*

Schoenberg begins "Der Dandy" by establishing the fantastic moonbeam in the high clarinet and piccolo, shown in ex. 5-7. On the downbeat of the first complete measure, they form a perfect fourth (a doubly diminished fifth, actually: D-sharp and A-flat), which is sustained with some embellishment through the first three measures. The ascent to the sustained enharmonic fourth and the embellishments recall the seven-note motive of "Mondestrunken." The winds arrive at the enharmonic fourth three times, which is paralleled by the three arrivals in the Sprechstimme on F-natural, F-sharp, and F-natural (spelled with enharmonic E-sharp).

Schoenberg uses dynamics to great effect in the first section to give us this first portrait of Pierrot. The dynamics are unified throughout the ensemble in the first two measures. In mm. 3–5, the dynamics are varied in each part. The piano plays the *Hauptstimme*, marked pianissimo, in a high register. In contrast, the Sprechstimme has a bifocal line; the lower notes frame a D$_4$, often two octaves lower than the piano. The higher notes are marked louder than the lower notes, presenting a challenge for balancing the ensemble.

The frenzy of the first five measures is met with a dramatic change in m. 6. The five measures that follow give us a musical depiction of the uninspired Pierrot. For text describing the black washstand of the silent dandy, the piccolo—suggesting the moon—rests, and the clarinet—typically suggesting the clowning qualities of Pierrot—plays a mournful tune. The Sprechstimme here contrasts the leaps of the first five measures with a more narrowly ranging line that emphasizes the notes D and C. This passage is filled with undulating seconds. The minor seventh B-flat$_4$ to C$_4$, marked *gesungen* in the Sprechstimme, is inverted to B-flat$_4$ to C$_5$ in the piano and marked as the *Hauptstimme* in mm. 6–7.

In sum, the first section presents the listener with extremes. Schoenberg uses sudden changes of dynamics in each part and between the parts. There are

Example 5-7. "Der Dandy," mm. 1–4.

also extremes of register, rapid changes from singing to speaking to whispering, and a graduated tempo change from *rasch* to *langsam*. These extremes, combined with the staccato *Hauptstimme* in the piano, mm. 3–5, present a musical picture of *Pierrot* as a nervous and fickle dandy, given to bouts of melancholy, suggested by narrow ranges and repetition.

The second section develops many of the materials of the first five measures, including: the thrice-stated perfect fourth, here in the piano, m. 11; the repeated F-naturals of the Sprechstimme, here moved to the piccolo's enharmonic E-sharp in m. 12; the emphasis on quarter-note triplets in the Sprechstimme; and the piano's chords, leaping between hands. However, the third section presents a sudden change, shown in ex. 5-8. Pierrot is called by name for the first time in m. 21. This event is marked by a parody of an operetta-style melody in the piano. The melody, in the left hand, begins in E major, but the tonality is obscured by enharmonic spelling and the use of an ostinato in the right hand of the piano, which consists of three notes that are not in E-major. The melody is quickly fragmented into a short segment that sounds like a bass-chord piano accompaniment and sequenced down—like a music box unwinding—to comically mime the action: Pierrot stops to consider his stage paint.

The poem ends with Pierrot's decision to use the moonbeam for his makeup. Schoenberg depicts this with two events, shown in ex. 5-9. In m. 29 the piano has a motive marked as the *Haupstimme*. The figure is played with the left hand under a chord that is held with the right hand, but never attacked. The held notes will produce resonance because of their relationship to the notes played by the left hand. As shown in ex. 5-9, each note in the held chord is a common tone with either the second or third partial in the overtone series

Example 5-8. "Der Dandy," mm. 21–23.

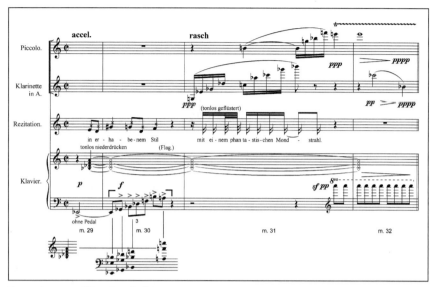

Example 5-9. "Der Dandy," mm. 28–30.

of the notes struck by the left hand. The common tones in the overtone series cause the chord to sound through sympathetic vibration.[5] The special effect, often called *piano harmonics*, recalls the opening measures in an oblique way. The high resonance in the piano recalls the high piccolo and clarinet, while the triplets in the left hand recall the Sprechstimme in mm. 2–3, as well as the clarinet's opening figure.

The final gesture is a depiction of the moonbeam make-up. The last verse of the poem is whispered quickly, which essentially removes all sense of pitch and emphasizes the consonants. The clarinet and piccolo, imitating the motive in the piano, m. 29, each play variants of their motive-forms from the opening measure, rising precipitously to an E_6 and E_7, respectively. The high E creates a final perfect fourth between the piccolo and piano's repeating A. This final fourth is a half-step above the fourth that is repeated at the beginning of the melodrama. Similarly, the clarinet's last notes are F—the same F_5 repeated in the Sprechstimme, mm. 2 and 4 (enharmonically)—"resolving" down a ninth to an E. The final E in the clarinet matches the half-step transposition of the perfect fourth, but while the fourth is further transposed an octave higher, the E is inverted an octave lower. Thus, Schoenberg accomplishes a subtle but sophisticated piece of text-painting: the music depicting the moon, illuminating the make-up in the crystal vials in the first few measures, is subjected to distorted inversion—as if seen through a funhouse mirror—to depict Pierrot's face reflecting the same moonlight.

NO. 4 EINE BLASSE WÄSCHERIN (A PALE LAUNDRESS)

Eine blasse Wäscherin
Wäscht zur Nachtzeit bleiche
 Tücher;
Nackte, silberweisse Arme
Streckt sie nieder in die Flut.

A pale laundress
Washes the nighttime's bleached
 fabrics;
Naked, silver-white arms
She stretches down in the current.

Durch die Lichtung schleichen
 Winde,
Leis bewegen sie den Strom.
Eine blasse Wäscherin
Wäscht zur Nachtzeit bleiche
 Tücher

Through the clearing creeps
 wind,
Lightly it stirs the stream.
A pale laundress
Washes the nighttime's bleached
 fabrics.

Und die sanfte Magd des Himmels,
Von den Zweigen zart
 umschmeichelt,
Breitet auf die dunklen Wiesen
Ihre lichtgewobnen Linnen
Eine blasse Wäscherin.

And the placid maid of the heavens,
By the branches tenderly
 beloved,
Spreads on the dark meadows
Her light-woven linens
A pale laundress.

The Text and Translation

"Eine blasse Wäscherin" is the fifth poem in Giraud's collection. Hartleben's translation does not include a specific reference to the moon, but Giraud's identifies the moon as the pale laundress with his title, "Lune au Lavoir" (Moon as Laundress). Schoenberg ultimately placed "Eine blasse Wäscherin" fourth, right in the center of the first cycle, which creates a symmetrical design: the first, fourth, and seventh melodramas are characterizations of the moon. Here the moon is depicted as a young maiden with white arms—a feature that suggests both the moon and youth.[6] There is also a progression from the moon as muse in "Mondestrunken," to the more prosaic laundress in "Eine blasse Wäscherin," and finally to the moon as a patient fatally ill with tuberculosis in "Der kranke Mond."

Details of Composition

"Eine blasse Wäscherin" was fifth in order of composition, composed completely on 18 April, the same day as "Der kranke Mond." It uses the violin, which had only been added to the ensemble the previous day for the first draft of "Mondestrunken."

Musical Materials

"Eine blasse Wäscherin" consists of a short introduction followed by three sections that align with the stanzas. An extraordinary feature of this melodrama is the use of texture to contrast the sections. Throughout the first and third sections, the instruments play chords with constantly shifting voicings: from eighth note to eighth note, the soprano, tenor, and inner voice switch between instruments. This technique has come to be known as *Klangfarbenmelodie*, after Schoenberg's coining of the term in the last pages of his *Harmonielehre*.[7] Schoenberg makes his intentions clear through two score notes and the use of a piano reduction. The score notes explain that the instruments should all play at the same volume, without expression, and that the Sprechstimme accompanies the instruments.[8] Finally, he provides a piano reduction below the score, a technique that resembles the notation of *a capella* choral music.[9]

The *Klangfarbenmelodie* technique complicates the traditional voice leading roles of soprano and bass. The ear tends to follow the tone color that has been playing the most salient line, even as it moves to the middle of the texture. Moreover, the varying strengths of the instruments in different registers—the clarinet and violin are louder than the flute in lower registers—pose a challenge to the instrumentalists who seek to achieve the balance that Schoenberg demands. Schoenberg challenges the instrumentalists further by using pizzicato in the violin for a single note (m. 4), *col legno gestrichen* (m. 12), and the lowest string of the violin for higher notes.[10] Similarly, the full range of the clarinet is exploited.

Unlike most of the introductions in *Pierrot*, the introduction to "Eine blasse Wäscherin" does not merely introduce an accompanying pattern: it is a self-contained musical unit. The constantly shifting voices distort the musical lines, as the reflection of the moon would be distorted in the stream the laundress uses to wash clothes.[11] As shown in ex. 5-10, the introduction presents a melody in the soprano in the first three bars that is immediately varied. The melody's most recognizable feature is the neighbor-tone group in m. 2. However, the use of minor thirds in outer voices is also prominent. These two features form the initial motive in the Sprechstimme, which is varied with each text refrain.

In the first section, the Sprechstimme stays in a low register: it is largely notated below A_4. Unlike "Der Dandy," in which the Sprechstimme often defined the meter, here the Sprechstimme is cast in durations that subdivide the beat. Schoenberg marks the Sprechstimme with a slightly higher dynamic, but the low tessitura and abundance of consonants makes this passage challenging for the reciter. Against the Sprechstimme, the instruments gradually achieve independence from the homorhythmic texture of the introduction. After the first group of seven chords, each successive gesture is smaller, and the gestures in m. 8 each have some rhythmic independence.

Example 5-10.   **"Eine blasse Wäscherin," introduction.**

In the middle section, which begins on the third beat of m. 9, the description of wind creeping through the clearing is depicted with increased rhythmic independence in the instrumental parts. The instrumental parts largely vary the music presented in the introduction and first section. For example, the first chord of the middle section, on the third beat of m. 9, can be found in the same register with a different voicing in m. 6, on the fourth beat. Of the seven chords in m. 6, this common chord is the only accented chord and, in both places, it features the highest note heard to that point in the melodrama. Thereafter, the flute alternates F and D like the lower voice in the first two measures, while the clarinet emerges from the texture to play a lyrical third, much like it did at the end of m. 8.

The Sprechstimme plays a more definitive role in the texture of the second section, since it is one of four essentially equal voices. At the end of the second section, the Sprechstimme and instruments combine for the text refrain. Example 5-11 shows all three statements of the first verse.

Unlike the first three melodramas, in which the third stanza is met with an adjustment of musical style, the third section of "Eine blasse Wäscherin" returns to the texture of the first section. However, it also drives to a climax in m. 14. The climax itself reflects these two tendencies: it is varied and dramatic but it also reflects a number of elements that have been varied throughout the work.

In m. 13, the measure before the climax, the flute leaps to E_6, which is the highest note thus far (previously heard in mm. 6, 8, and 9). In m. 14, shown in ex. 5-12, the violin leaps to an A_6 as a harmonic, which is the highest note in

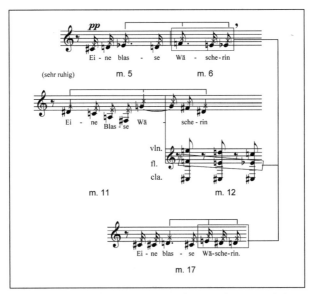

Example 5-11.   "Eine blasse Wäscherin," the text refrains.

the melodrama. The chord with the highest note alternates with a second chord that has a C-sharp$_3$ bass, the lowest note available for this ensemble. The composite soprano line of m. 14, shown in the piano reduction, consists of a minor third between the violin and the flute, displaced registrally by two octaves. The composite minor third resembles a number of salient minor thirds heard in the first two sections, including the composite soprano line from the introduction, the flute's repeating F$_5$–D$_5$ in mm. 9–10, and the clarinet's high minor third in mm. 8 and 10. The composite minor third is also mirrored by the voice leading: the clarinet and the flute both play registrally displaced major sixths—the inversion of the minor third. The clarinet's major sixth is also the bass of the ensemble. The Sprechstimme also has a minor third from a C$_5$—the highest note in the Sprechstimme thus far—to the A$_4$ below, a minor third above the F-sharp in the flute. The role of the Sprechstimme is further enhanced by the direction to sing those notes (*gesungen*). Finally, for the first and only time, the Sprechstimme and the instruments are rhythmically aligned for a gesture. As a result, the dramatic leap in the composite soprano line is only a minor third if only the instruments are considered; in view of the whole ensemble, the leap is actually two octaves from A$_6$ in the violin to A$_4$ in the Sprechstimme. The climactic gesture in m. 14 is thus marked by dramatic events—the homorhythm between Sprechstimme and ensemble, the large leaps, the sung notes, and the extreme range—but ultimately comprises familiar elements, especially the minor thirds and the *Klangfarbenmelodie* texture.

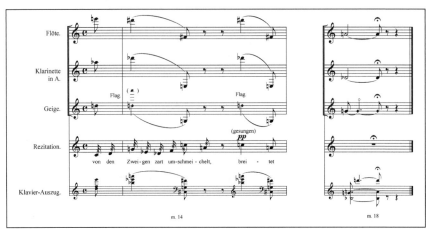

Example 5-12. "Eine blasse Wäscherin," mm. 14 and 18.

Measure 14 depicts the spread of moonlight across the meadow. The remaining four measures have a marked sense of denouement. The Sprechstimme returns to the tessitura from the opening bars, and eventually reprises the motive for the repeated text (ex. 5-11). Against the final text refrain, the instruments repeat a final chord three times. The final chord resembles the climactic chord in m. 14 due to the common tones B-flat and A-natural voiced as a major seventh and the harmonic in the violin. The repeated chord in the instruments, coupled with the narrow profile of the Sprechstimme, provides a word-painting of the laundress slowly wringing the laundry.

NO. 5 VALSE DE CHOPIN (WALTZ OF CHOPIN)

Wie ein blasser Tropfen Bluts	As a pale drop of blood
Färbt die Lippen einer Kranken,	Brightens the lips of an invalid,
Also ruht auf diesen Tönen	So lurks in these tones
Ein vernichtungssüchtger Reiz.	An invitation to annihilation.
Wilder Lust Akkorde stören	Wild lusty chords disturb
Der Verzweiflung eisgen Traum—	Despair, the icy dream—
Wie ein blasser Tropfen Bluts	As a pale drop of blood
Färbt die Lippen einer Kranken.	Brightens the lips of an invalid.
Heiß und jauchzend, süß und schmachtend,	Hot and ecstatic, sweet and languishing,
Melancholisch düstrer Walzer,	Melancholy, dark waltz,

Kommst mir nimmer aus den Sinnen!	Never leave my senses!
Haftest mir an den Gedanken,	Stick to me in my thoughts,
Wie ein blasser Tropfen Bluts!	Like a pale drop of blood!

The Text and Translation

"Valse de Chopin" is the twenty-sixth poem in Giraud's collection. Both "Valse" and "Madonna" (which immediately follows), represent a slight departure from the first four melodramas in Schoenberg's ordering. There is no mention of the moon or any other specific character. We must infer the first-person narrator is Pierrot transitioning from "drunk with the moon" in the first melodrama to despairing of the moon in the seventh melodrama. "Valse" and "Madonna," taken as a unit, parallel "Columbine" and "Der Dandy," and create a symmetrical ordering of the first seven melodramas. The first, fourth, and seventh melodramas are primarily about the moon; the second and third melodramas present other characters (Pierrot and Columbine); and the fifth and sixth melodramas are symbolic vignettes.

Hartleben takes some liberties with the second and third stanzas. Giraud's second stanza continues the contrast of colors—a pale (sick bed) tunic, a red sound, and a white daydream (*Un son rouge—du rêve blanc / Avive la pale tunique*). Similarly, Giraud's third stanza describes a physical savor but a poor aftertaste (*Me laisse une saveur physique / Un fade arrière-goût troublant*). Hartleben's translation is dedicated to Curt Hezel, who was possibly Dr. Kurt Hezel, an attorney in Leipzig.

Details of Composition

Schoenberg composed "Valse de Chopin" completely on 7 May. Like "Madonna," which was composed two days later, "Valse" was composed well after most of the melodramas that make up the first part, which were completed by the third week of April. In Schoenberg's *Textvorlage*, there is a sketch of the bass clarinet part in m. 32 next to the tenth verse of the poem. Unlike all the other annotations in the *Textvorlage*, this annotation was made in blue, which suggests he made the annotation at a different time. "Valse" was the thirteenth melodrama begun. Given Schoenberg's well-documented regard for numerology, it seems hardly coincidental that the thirteenth melodrama was composed on the seventh of May.[12]

Musical Materials

"Valse de Chopin," like "Columbine," is a waltz with three parts aligned with the three sections. However, unlike "Columbine," the developmental techniques used in "Valse de Chopin" create a busy and variable texture. The *Hauptstimme* is more consistently marked here than in any other melodrama. In mm. 3–6, Schoenberg required four different *Hauptstimme* brackets. Moreover, the brackets overlap in mm. 14, 22–27, and 32–33, thus creating a *Hauptstimme* and *Nebenstimme* (although the *Nebenstimmen* are not distinguished with their own marking). Perhaps reflecting this variability, Schoenberg provides his clearest statement of the *Hauptstimme* principle as a footnote: "The passages with the ⌐ symbol are to be emphasized, played espressivo, until the sign ¬ because they are the *Hauptstimme* or first *Nebenstimme*. The other parts given simultaneously should step back; they are accompaniment."

The principal motive, presented in the clarinet mm. 2–3, consists of three notes with a step down and a leap further down. As shown in ex. 5-13, it is joined by the flute playing the motive in diminution in m. 3 before the clarinet can complete the first statement. It returns to the clarinet for two diminished statements in m. 5 with a simultaneous statement in the flute even further diminished. This basic form of the motive is easily found in all the parts; see especially the piano in m. 8 and the flute and the clarinet in mm. 24–26. Inversions, retrogrades, and reorderings—such as the piano right hand in m. 4—are also easily found, most importantly in the bass clarinet in mm. 32–35; mm. 34–35 (shown on p. 127, in ex. 5-16), present an inverted and prime form of the motive in each measure.

Example 5-13 also shows accompanimental motives that are related to the waltz topic, the most important of which are found in the first measure of the piano. Here the right hand provides the chordal pattern typical of dance forms, while the left hand provides a broad gesture that spans two and a half

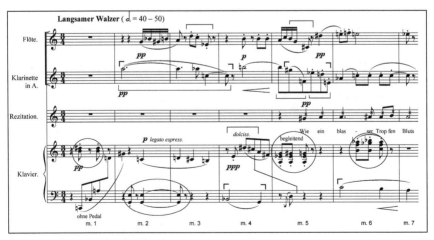

Example 5-13. "Valse de Chopin," mm. 1–5.

octaves in five notes. This gesture is doubly inverted in mm. 2–3; the voices switch hands and register, and the higher voice in the right hand inverts the lower voice from m. 1, moving mostly down by seconds instead of up by sevenths. These two accompanimental motives occur frequently in the piano to continue the conceit of a waltz by Chopin. The chords are frequently filled in with a neighboring chord as in m. 5. The broad gesture is frequently seen in the varied inversion, as in the left hand, mm. 6–8. Finally, the accompanimental motive and the main motive intersect in mm. 3–4, where the descending lines in the piano right hand and the clarinet drop to the left hand to form the half-step and minor third of the main motive (B, B-flat, G in piano; A, B-flat, G in clarinet and piano). These connections occasion the peculiar one-bar *Hauptstimme* brackets in m. 4.

The Sprechstimme enters in m. 5 and provides a third important element—the highlighting of a note through repetition or *noodling*. In the first entrance of the Sprechstimme, it emphasizes an A_5, approaching it from below, repeating it, and providing an upper neighbor before returning to the A in m. 7 (creating parallel octaves with the piano!). At the same time the clarinet also noodles around A_5. The busy texture makes it somewhat difficult for the reciter to be heard at pianissimo. A slight increase of volume is advisable as long as the delirium of the verse is preserved. The Sprechstimme proceeds, alternating between noodling in a narrow range and explosive bursts, especially in mm. 8–9, where the word *Kranken* is emphasized by a sudden drop into the lower range of the voice.

The second section, mm. 14–26, can be further partitioned into new material, mm. 14–19, and a developed reprise of the music from the beginning to accompany the text refrain, mm. 20–26. The new material text-paints the wild chords with a three-measure unit in the piano, mm. 14–16. The three-measure unit, shown in ex. 5-14, is immediately varied for three more measures. Combined, both units form a whole in that they superimpose two-four meter established in the first three measures and continuing in the next three measures.

The Sprechstimme joins the pattern on the last bar of the three-bar grouping with a very distinctive motive form, which is varied in m. 19—the last bar of the second three-bar grouping. As ex. 5-14 also shows, with the entrance of the Sprechstimme, the winds add to a sense of delirium by playing passages in close imitation. The text refrain that ends the second section, shown in ex. 5-15, reprises many of the elements from mm. 1–9 in a disjointed way. For example, in m. 21, the piano left hand plays the same motive it played in m. 1, but the right hand continues with chords. The music in the right hand in m. 1 is first reprised by the winds. When the right hand reclaims that figure in m. 23, the winds begin to play the clarinet's motive from mm. 2–3 in close imitation. The Sprechstimme returns to its earlier delivery, noodling around

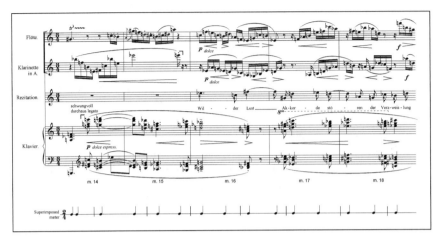

Example 5-14. "Valse de Chopin," mm. 14–18.

Example 5-15. "Valse de Chopin," mm. 20–25.

the note A_5 and reprising D, E-flat, and F for *einer Kranken* (compare mm. 8–9 to mm. 22–23).

The final stanza begins with four adjectives. The delivery superimposes two-four meter to emphasize these words while the rest of the ensemble sits comfortably in the three-four meter. While there are many leaps in this line, the general direction is down to the low sensual part of the voice on the word *Walzer*. The word *Walzer* on the low A is the thing that sticks to the narrator's thoughts. To make the move down to the A more unified, the reciter could connect *schmachtend* with a slightly exaggerated slide to convey the *languishing*. Immediately thereafter, the music changes dramatically. The superimposition of two-four comes to an abrupt halt and the piano *vamps* two measures with yet another variant on waltz rhythms. All the instrumental parts are marked pianissimo, and while not marked, the Sprechstimme should also decrease in volume to increase the sense of drama for *melancholisch düstrer Walzer*. A slightly exaggerated slide would also be appropriate for *Walzer*, followed by a closely observed rest on the downbeat of m. 32 before returning to the delirium and noodling delivery on A₅ leading to the last text refrain.

The last text refrain returns to the piano chords in the second section. In m. 34, the bass clarinet introduces a new motive form that joins the leaps in the piano from m. 1 to the descending motive found in the clarinet and flute, mm. 2–3. The Sprechstimme also returns to the descending motive from mm. 2–3 and frames it with two significant minor thirds—D-natural and F-natural, which has been an important dyad in each text refrain and which is found almost simultaneously in the bass clarinet, and D-sharp and F-sharp, which, along with the leap in the bass clarinet (E-flat and B-natural), are members of the last chord in the piano (which is ultimately a development of the dyads in the piano right hand in m. 1).

"Valse de Chopin" ends by reprising some of the musical materials from earlier in the melodrama. However, the end does not feel like a reprise, but rather an incomplete resolution. The repetition of a figure in the piano, mm. 40–47, resembles the use of repeated figures at the end of "Eine blasse Wäscherin" and "Der kranke Mond." On the other hand, unlike those conclusions, the repeated figure at the end of "Valse" is not the very last thing. Instead, the figure is repeated on a note a half-step lower, comprising another set of three—three half-notes, of which the first, beginning on the second beat of m. 40, is subdivided into three eighth notes and an eighth rest. The somewhat mechanical figure in the piano has a feeling of winding down, which, coupled with the long diminuendo in the winds and the text, can easily be construed as the final breaths of a consumptive.[13] The lone notes that follow are eerily still

Example 5-16. "Valse de Chopin," mm. 32–35, 40.

and isolated. In the loose narrative of the first part, "Valse de Chopin" marks a change in Pierrot's fortunes. Some part of his creativity dies in the final bars, and he fails to regain his prior good humor in the funereal "Madonna" or the desperate "Der kranke Mond."

NO. 6 MADONNA

Steig, O Mutter aller Schmerzen,	Rise, O Mother of all sorrow,
Auf den Altar meiner Verse!	To the altar of my verses!
Blut aus deinen magern Brüsten	Blood from your withered breasts
Hat des Schwertes Wut vergossen.	Has by the raging sword been shed.
Deine ewig frischen Wunden	Your eternally fresh wounds
Gleichen Augen, rot und offen.	Like eyes, red and open.
Steig, O Mutter aller Schmerzen,	Rise, O Mother of all sorrow,
Auf den Altar meiner Verse!	To the altar of my verses!
In den abgezehrten Händen	In your worn-out hands
Hältst du deines Sohnes Leiche,	Hold you your son's corpse,
Ihn zu zeigen aller Menschheit—	To show to all humanity—
Doch der Blick der Menschen meidet	But the gaze of humanity avoids
Dich, o Mutter aller Schmerzen!	You, O Mother of all sorrow!

The Text and Translation

"Madonna" is the twenty-eighth poem in Giraud's collection. As noted above, "Madonna" can be paired with "Valse de Chopin" for their similar role in the structure of the first section. Moreover, like *Valse*, Madonna is in the first person, names no established characters, and presents a view of poetry as an affliction visited upon the first-person poet. The central image proved controversial. In a letter from 1922, Marya Freund wrote that while her Paris performances, sung in French, were enthusiastically received, Madonna met with some resistance.[14] Schoenberg replied that he had noticed a similar reaction in Geneva and Amsterdam with not only "Madonna," but also "Rote Messe" and "Die Kreuze." He protested that he could not understand how anyone would take these poems as a critique of religion, and that he had never been antireligious or even unreligious.[15]

Hartleben, whose translation is dedicated to the poet Caesar [Cäsar] Flaischlen (1864–1920), takes some liberties in his translation. Giraud's title for the poem was "Evocation." Hartleben's title emphasizes the Madonna—a conceit for poetry itself—instead of the poet. Similarly, Giraud evokes the "Madonna of hysteria" (*O Madone des Hystéries!*) but Hartleben addresses the "mother of all sorrows," and the word *Madonna* is never pronounced. Finally, Giraud's third stanza is more graphic. Hartleben describes the son as a corpse, but Giraud describes the son with green limbs and wilting, putrid flesh (… *members déjà verts, / Aux chairs tombantes et pourries*).

All editions of the score before the 1996 *Gesamtausgabe* contain a text error. The word *magern* (withered) is misspelled as *magren*, in both the melodrama and the preliminary list of poems. Schoenberg has it spelled correctly in his manuscript, but it was misspelled in the program for the first performance.[16]

Details of Composition

Schoenberg composed "Madonna" on 9 May along with "Nacht," "Heimfahrt," and "Raub." All four melodramas allude to an established composition type. However, while Schoenberg labels "Nacht" a passacaglia and "Heimfahrt" a barcarolle, the listener must infer the relationship of "Raub" to an operatic *scena* and the similarity of "Madonna" to a Baroque aria. All four melodramas also contain repeating figures or processes. In particular, the repetitive figuration at the beginning of "Madonna" resembles the figuration at the beginning of "Heimfahrt."

Musical Materials

Unlike the more typical tripartite musical structure that follows the stanzas, "Madonna" is in two sections: the first section groups the first two stanzas together and the last section is a dramatic departure. In Schoenberg's 1922 letter to Marya Freund, he seems to suggest that the relationship of "Madonna" to conventional religion can only be inferred by the text of the poem.[17] However, the first section of "Madonna" suggests a religious topic with a number of style features of the Baroque era. The instrumentation recalls Baroque music: the bass clarinet seems a substitute for a more exotic instrument (such as the oboe d'amore). The "walking bass" resembles a basso-continuo and plays in a register far below the flute and bass clarinet, in the manner of the Baroque trio sonata.[18] Finally, the Sprechstimme proceeds in regular three-bar phrases—(pickup) mm. 2–4, mm. 5–7, mm. 8–10, and mm. 10 to 12. Here, m. 10 is counted twice because the entrance of the phrase, along with the main motive, is metrically displaced.

The principal motive is presented immediately by the flute in the first measure, which Schoenberg identifies with his slur and short caesura mark. The motive consists of a long note followed by five shorter notes. The motive is particularly multivalent and the three distinct rhythmic groupings can be varied for the number of contours that are developed in the first section. Example 5-17 shows how some of the motivic contours map onto the Sprechstimme in the first four measures.

Schoenberg's direction of "very inwardly" can be established immediately with a breathy attack on the word *Steig*. While the Sprechstimme proceeds in precise rhythmic unison with the cello, the motivic material of the Sprechstimme is derived from the flute and bass clarinet. A short breath after *Steig* will heighten the connection to the flute part and set apart the motive as it appears for *o Mutter*. Schoenberg has drawn special attention to that form of the motive with hairpins. Special care should be taken for all three note groupings in the first twelve measures where the second syllable is accented and placed in a metrically strong position—*den Altar, vergossen, und offen.* To accommodate the text *meiner Verse* in mm. 3–4, Schoenberg adds a note to what would otherwise be one of these groups (where the second syllable of *meiner* is metrically weak, if displaced registrally).

The first two phrases of the Sprechstimme are similar in rhythm and contour, although displaced metrically. Thus, m. 3 is similar to m. 6. However, the meaning and mood of *hat des Schwertes Wut vergossen* is quite different and suggests a more forceful presentation. The Sprechstimme in mm. 8–9 is a departure, but the final phrase is the poetic refrain and returns to the motivic material of the first two phrases. This *ppp* "high and sweet" entrance of the Sprechstimme is particularly accentuated by the first two beats of m. 10 when all the instruments play the same rhythm—a variant of the three-note motive—in a crescendo. For the refrain, Schoenberg reworks the text-setting to favor a three-note grouping for *meiner Verse* by beginning on a strong beat.

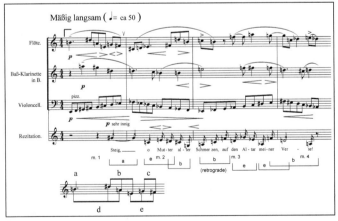

Example 5-17. "Madonna," mm. 1–4.

Thus, each of the four initial phrases ends with a cadential motive form in the Sprechstimme.

In the second part, the mostly conjunct motion of the cello in the first section is contrasted in mm. 15–16 by a version of the motive form *d* with octave displacement, marked as the *Hauptstimme*. The wind instruments play variations of motive form *c*. The reciter is directed to begin calmly with a full sound and gradually increase intensity until m. 21. The increase in intensity in the Sprechstimme is greatly aided by the ascending lines, which reflect and develop motive forms from the first part. The Sprechstimme begins in m. 16 with a development of the music in m. 6 (and thus also m. 2). The Sprechstimme in m. 20 is strongly related to the Sprechstimme in mm. 8–9, and as in those measures leads to the climactic measure of the section, m. 21.

The Sprechstimme soars to a climax in m. 21 on the word *Mutter*, the longest held and loudest note in the melodrama. Measure 21 is the climactic moment not only for "Madonna," but for the entire first part of *Pierrot*. The F-sharp in the Sprechstimme is approached by the largest leap in Part I, which is further shaped by the ascending scalar passage in the cello and clarinet. With the entrance of the piano and violin, m. 21 is the first time (in the final ordering) that all five instrumentalists appear in the same melodrama, even if they don't all play at the same time. Measure 21 is the first use of *fortissimo* since the beginning of "Der Dandy" (discounting a brief emphasis of a piano trill in m. 28 of "Valse de Chopin"). But beyond these objective measures, m. 21 just feels like a dramatic arrival. Following the excitement of "Valse," the beginning of "Madonna" is a dramatic reduction in an intensity that is only regained and exceeded in the run-up to m. 21.

Taken as a whole, "Madonna" feels like the true conclusion of Part I. It is the dramatic apogee of the first part, and the conclusion recalls elements from previous melodramas. "Madonna" and "Mondestrunken" are the only melodramas in Part I to use the cello, and the cello figures prominently in the conclusion of both melodramas. In "Madonna," the final B-natural in the cello recalls the initial B in the flute part, which seemed to "resolve" the hanging A-sharp from "Valse de Chopin." The initial B in the flute part went immediately to a D-sharp, which is recalled by the occurrences of B-natural and D-sharp in the violin. D-sharp also figures prominently in the final chord in the piano, which, combined with the cello's final B, vaguely recall the final chords in the cello at the end of "Mondestrunken" and the B major triad at the end of "Valse." Like the end of "Valse" and other conclusions, including the end of "Der kranke Mond," the repetition of the chord and the cello's figure adds a sense of finality. If the end of "Valse" suggests the symbolic death of Pierrot's creativity, the end of "Madonna" is a public eulogy, as well as a bitter indictment of Pierrot's fickle muse.

NO. 7 DER KRANKE MOND (THE SICK MOON)

Du nächtig todeskranker Mond
Dort auf des Himmels schwarzem
Pfühl,
Dein Blick, so fiebernd übergross,
Bannt mich, wie fremde Melodie.

You nocturnal gravely ill moon
There on the sky's black cushion,

Your countenance, so feverishly enlarged,
Enchants me, like a strange melody.

An unstillbarem Liebesleid
Stirbst du, an Sehnsucht, teif
erstickt,
Du nichtig todeskranker Mond
Dort auf des Himmels schwarzem
Pflühl.

An unhealing love wound
Kills you, with longing, deeply
smothered,
You nocturnal gravely ill moon
There on the sky's black cushion.

Den Liebsten, der im Sinnenrausch
Gedankenlos zur Liebsten [geht,]
Belustigt deiner Strahlen Spiel—
Dein bleiches, qualgebornes Blut,
Du nächtig todeskranker Mond!

The lover, who in sensual delirium
Indifferently to his lover [goes,]
Delights in your beams' play—
Your bleached, agony-wrenched blood,
You nocturnal gravely ill moon!

The Text and Translation

"Der kranke Mond" is the twenty-first poem in Giraud's collection. The first-person text marks the nadir in the relationship between the narrator and the moon. The moon is first depicted as the fount of poetic inspiration in "Mondestrunken," and indifferent and ineffectual in "Eine blasse Wäscherin." In "Der kranke Mond," the moon is depicted as terminally ill and unhealthy to poets and lovers.

In Hartleben's translation, which is dedicated to Wilhelm von Hohenhausen, the first verse is less specific than Giraud's original. The French *O Lune, nocturne phtisique* actually provides the moon's ailment: a phthisic has tuberculosis. If the moon has tuberculosis, also called *the white plague*, then the moon can be identified as the sick woman (*Kranken*) whose lip is colored with a "pale drop of blood" at the start of "Valse de Chopin."

Schoenberg made one change to the poem. Hartleben translated the tenth verse, "Gedanklos zur Liebesten schleicht." Schoenberg changed the verb *schleicht* (slinks) to *geht* (goes). In doing so, Schoenberg unwittingly came closer to the spirit of the original French (*L'amant qui passe insoucieux*), which casts no aspersions on how the lover passes.

Details of Composition

"Der kranke Mond" was the fourth monodrama composed. He completed it along with "Eine blasse Wäscherin" on 18 April 1912. Even though it uses only a flute with the Sprechstimme, "Der kranke Mond" is one of the first melodramas to be composed with the final ensemble in mind; he had added the violin and cello to begin working on Mondestrunken on 17 April. All editions of the score published before the *Gesamtausgabe* number the measures incorrectly.

Musical Materials

"Der kranke Mond" is in three clear sections that align with the stanzas. Each section ends with a cadential leap in the voice. The first and second sections are followed by a transition in the flute. As previously seen in "Eine blasse Wäscherin," "Valse de Chopin," and "Madonna," the end of "Der kranke Mond" is signaled by the repetition of a figure.

The most striking feature of "Der kranke Mond" is the instrumentation of only flute and Sprechstimme. In this sparse texture, the pitches of the Sprechstimme assume considerable importance. Moreover, as detailed in chapters 4 and 6, the principal musical materials from the first and third sections of "Der kranke Mond" are repeated near the end of Part II as a transition between "Enthauptung" and "Die Kreuze."

The first section begins with an ascending sixth in the flute. Perhaps because it is exposed and slow, Ferrucio Busoni described it as "descended from the '*traurige Weise*' in *Tristan*" in a letter to his former student Egon Petri.[19] It is unclear if Busoni discussed this with Schoenberg. When Schoenberg read Busoni's 1916 edition of *Sketch of a New Esthetic of Music*, he was moved to annotate the section on exotic scales by copying out the entire flute part of "Der kranke Mond" and calling it a "flute solo." (Schoenberg's annotation is quoted in chapter 4.) The connection may be purely coincidental, or it may be that Schoenberg was reproving Busoni with an excerpt of Schoenberg's music that he knew Busoni admired.

The Sprechstimme enters with a series of notes in chromatic pairs in the first phrase. In three of the four pairs, the first note is accented to give the sense of an appoggiatura. The sense of appoggiatura is conveyed only through rhythm—there is no tonal basis for nonharmonic tones—and can be heightened by some light dynamic shading. The chromatic pair for -*kranker* is reversed: the accent is on G-natural, the first syllable. However, that is only the first two of a four-note group that resolves to the G as a melisma. As previously noted, most of the text-setting in *Pierrot* is syllabic. The use of melismas in the first section contributes to the depiction of a sickly mood. In addition, the words that have melismas, *Mond, Himmels schwarzem Pfühl*, and later, *Liebesleid*, essentially summarize the first two stanzas.

For most of the first section, the Sprechstimme is above the flute. The second section of "Der kranke Mond" is a significant contrast. In this section, shown in ex. 5-18, the Sprechstimme is clearly the *Hauptstimme*, as the flute is marked at a lower dynamic and its pitch content is greatly reduced. The voice remains below the flute, and often below the range of the flute. As the text describes the suffering of the moon, the Sprechstimme begins the second section with a new motive form, derived from the first section, consisting of a group of four notes—a second and a third separated by a leap.

The development of this motive eventually takes the Sprechstimme down to E_3—the lowest pitch in the first part of *Pierrot*, and well below the range of the flute—which begins the text refrain. A small breath after *du* and again

Example 5-18. **"Der kranke Mond," the second section motive.**

before *todeskranker* would emphasize the motivic design. Like many of the text refrains in *Pierrot*, the motive used for the second verse of the poem is the motive that returns.

After a varied reprise of the flute's motive from m. 1, the third section begins with new music for a new idea in the poem. To represent the lover passing by, the Sprechstimme, which moves at a quarter note impulse for the first two sections, is dominated by eighth notes. Measures 22–23 are primarily homorhythmic as the flute begins a motivic sequence that represents the play of the moonbeams. A quasi-staccato delivery in the Sprechstimme would emphasize the new rhythmic design and stand in stark contrast to the music that follows.

Like the second section, the third section flows into the text reprise without a formal articulation. The elements that compose the final text reprise are found in mm. 22–23. However, as ex. 5-19 shows, its elements are already found in the previous text refrains using the same pitches. Moreover, a comparison of examples 5-18 and 5-19 reveals the similarity between the motive form for the text refrain and the motive form for the second section.

Example 5-19.   Text refrains in "Der kranke Mond."

Like "Eine blasse Wäscherin," composed on the same day, the final phrase is repeated three times. This figure is arguably the most memorable and melodic passage for the Sprechstimme in the first part of *Pierrot*. In the reprise of "Der kranke Mond," near the end of the second part, this passage is the only passage from the Sprechstimme marked as the *Hauptstimme*. The sudden abundance of articulations and written directions attests to the importance of these measures.[20]

At the start of the third stanza, the flute and Sprechstimme have a similar rhythmic design. However, in mm. 24–26, the flute slows to emphasize a network of thirds that have been important earlier in the work; in m. 24 especially, the sudden half-notes in the flute seem like the presentation of a *cantus firmus* in a superimposed three-two meter. (A variable three-two meter in the flute can be back-formulated to the start of the third section.) However, in the last three measures, the Sprechstimme and flute occupy the same narrow pitch range. While ranging both higher and lower than the flute, presentation of the Sprechstimme can emphasize the connection to the flute with the wide vibrato marked in m. 25. The wide vibrato will imitate the breathy beating of the flute in its lower register and, coupled with the repetition, contribute to a sense of exhaustion. At the end of the first part, Pierrot is neither melancholy nor desperate; he is drained.

NOTES

1. The whole-tone scale is a mode of limited transposition. There are only two discrete collections—the whole-tone scale beginning on C-natural and the whole-tone scale beginning on C-sharp. While music theorists have developed more elegant nomenclatures, we will generally restrict ourselves to referring to the C transposition (C, D, E, F-sharp, G-sharp, and A-sharp) and the C-sharp transposition (C-sharp, D-sharp, F, G, A, B).

2. In Schoenberg's second copy, he pencils in *pp* for the Sprechstimme's pickup to m. 19. Source D2, 6.

3. Source B, 10.

4. Source Ab, 710 verso. The sketch is written for A clarinet in the correct transposition and is quite close to the way it appears in the score. Schoenberg changed the eighth and two sixteenths to a dotted-eighth and two thirty-second notes. Moreover, he changed the octave E-flat/E-flat to a diminished octave, E-flat/ E-natural.

5. Schoenberg first used this device in the opening measures of the first of his Three Piano Pieces, op. 11 (1909), a seminal post-tonal work. The listing of harmonics follows numbering the fundamental as the first harmonic. Thus, the third harmonic is 3/f.

6. In Schoenberg's *Erwartung*, "the woman" describes her rival as "*die Frau mit den wießen Armen . . .*" (the woman with the white arms). In Marie Pappenheim's text, the

world of *Erwartung* is lit by a sickly moon, not unlike the world of Giraud/Hartleben's *Pierrot lunaire*.

7. *Klangfarbenmelodie* is typically understood to mean a melody of tone colors, especially where the pitches are of secondary importance. See our discussion of *Klang-farbenmelodie*, including Schoenberg's famous quote from *Harmonielehre*, in chapter 3.

8. Above the first system, Schoenberg notes, "The three instruments in the exact same volume [*Klangstärke*], all without expression." Above the Sprechstimme, he notes, "The Sprechstimme here is wholly an accompaniment to the instruments; it is the accompanying line [*Nebenstimme*], the principal line [*Hauptstimme*] is the instruments."

9. The piano reduction does not appear in the manuscript, but he leaves a blank staff, marked *Clavierauszug* [*sic*] for later notation (Source B, 17).

10. *Col Legno* is an indication to use the wooden shaft of the bow. Typically, string players tap the string with the wood for *col legno battuto*—the execution that is typically suggested by *"col legno."* However, *col legno gestrichen* presents a challenge because the wooden shaft does not "catch" the string. Violinists typically compensate by applying the bow at an angle to use a small amount of the bow hair.

11. Schoenberg may have associated the *Klangfarbenmelodie* technique with water. In *Eine blasse Wäscherin*, the laundress dips the clothes in a stream, which is stirred by the wind. In *Heimfahrt*, Pierrot travels on a small stream, depicted with *Klangfarbenmelodie* voice-exchange in mm. 14, 16, and 19. Finally, Schoenberg first made extensive use of the technique in the third movement of his op. 16 *Fünf Orchesterstücke*. When asked for a descriptive title for that movement, Schoenberg suggested *Sommermorgen an einem See (Farben)* [*Summer Morning by a Lake (Colors)*]. In "Enthauptung," Schoenberg used the technique to present the moon as if in a state of delirium in mm. 11–16, which is not literally related to water, but nonetheless similar in the sense of the wavelike alteration of perception associated with changes in neurochemistry.

12. Regarding Schoenberg's involvement with numerology, see Colin C. Sterne, *Arnold Schoenberg: The Composer as Numerologist* (Lewiston, NY: E. Mellen Press, 1993).

13. It is interesting that the final chord in "Valse de Chopin" emphasizes B as a soprano. As is well known, Alban Berg used B for his "invention on a note," the second scene of the third act of *Wozzeck* (1914–1922). There, the repeating B is a menacing harbinger of death that precedes and accompanies Wozzeck's murder of Marie.

14. Letter from Marya Freund, December 12, 1922 (LC/ASC).

15. Letter to Marya Freund, December 30, 1922 (LC/ASC).

16. Program for "Dreimal sieben Gedichte aus Albert Giraud's 'Lieder des Pierrot lunaire,'" premiere performances at the Choralion-Sall, Berlin, 1912; The Library of Congress, Washington, DC, 5.

17. Letter to Marya Freund, December 30, 1922 (LC/ASC).

18. Schoenberg was probably not familiar with the "walking bass" in early forms of jazz. One possible precursor is the slow movement of Brahms' second Cello Sonata, op. 99. The pizzicato cello at the start of that movement similarly strikes modern listeners as *jazzy*.

19. Busoni to Egon Petri, 19 June 1913; Busoni/Beaumont, 169.

20. Schoenberg's direction, "different but not tragic!" has led to some confusion about the insurance anecdote quoted in our discussion of "Die Kreuze." See chapter 6, note 11.

6

Part II, Numbers 8–14

NO. 8 NACHT (NIGHT)

Finstre, schwarze, Riesenfalter
Töteten der Sonne Glanz.
Ein geschlossnes Zauberbuch,
Ruht der Horizont—verschwiegen.

Aus dem Qualm verlorner Tiefen
Steigt ein Duft, Erinnerung mordend!
Finstre, schwarze Riesenfalter
Töteten der Sonne Glanz.

Und vom Himmel erdenwärts
Senken sich mit schweren Schwingen
Unsichtbar die Ungetüme
Auf die Menschenherzen nieder . . .
Finstre, sehwarze Riesenfalter.

Murky, black, giant butterflies
Killed the sun's brilliance.
A closed spell-book,
Sprawls on the Horizon—furtively.

From the smoldering of lost depths
Arises a scent, killing memory!
Murky, black, giant butterflies
Kill the sun's brilliance.

And from heaven earthward
Descending on heavy wings
Unseen the monsters
To human hearts below . . .
Murky, black, giant butterflies.

The Text and Translation

"Nacht" is the nineteenth poem in Giraud's collection. Hartleben's translation intensifies the sense of the butterflies as a collective cloud. On the other hand, the third stanza is actually less graphic in translation. Giraud's third stanza describes the butterflies as monsters with sticky suckers seeking blood (*Des monstres aux gluants suçoirs / Recherchent du sang pour le boire*) and feeding on our despair.

Hartleben's translation is dedicated to Otto Julius Bierbaum (1865–1910). Bierbaum's 1897 novel *Stilpe* was an inspiration for Ernst von Wolzogen to open the Überbrettl cabaret where Beirbaum was an occasional contributor and where Schoenberg conducted for the 1901–1902 season. Moreover, Bierbaum edited the anthology of light poems *Deutsche Chansons*, from which Schoenberg selected texts for his *Brettl-Lieder* of 1901, including Bierbaum's own poem *Gigerlette*.

Details of Composition

"Nacht" was the eleventh melodrama composed and was one of four completed on 9 May, along with "Heimfahrt," "Madonna," and "Raub." In the first ten measures, the imitation of the passacaglia "spine" in the lower part of the texture is similar to the low repetitive figuration in "Heimfahrt" and "Madonna." Like most of the melodramas in Part II, "Nacht," composed for bass clarinet, cello, and piano with the Sprechstimme, is primarily set in a low register.

Musical Materials

The visceral imagery of the poem is met with mimetic features in the music. "Nacht" is a passacaglia organized in three lightly articulated sections that align with the three stanzas. Schoenberg understood passacaglia to mean a slow, serious movement in three with continuous variations over a ground bass, such as J. S. Bach's *Passacaglia in C-Moll für Orgel* (BWV 582).[1] The use of a passacaglia is an inspired choice for this poem. Like most passacaglias, "Nacht" increases in textural density as it proceeds, and most contrapuntal strands are a variation of the ground bass. The effect is similar to a cloud of flying insects. "Nacht" also reflects the poem in the consistent use of low register, which suggests the sinister.

The passacaglia "spine" is a three-note head followed by a chromatic tail. As is typical of Baroque imitative works, the head is more characteristic than the tail. Unlike so many of the *Pierrot* melodramas that vary the intervals of a motive, in "Nacht," the intervals of a minor third and a major third are strictly observed. The three-note head is presented with a three-bar introduction that ends with a fermata, shown in ex. 6-1. The introduction presents overlapping statements of the head, each beginning a minor third apart, until they complete the octave (E, G, B-flat, D-flat, E). One additional set begins on A. Most of the overlapping sets are in the piano. The last, which completes the series, is in the cello and bass clarinet.

For the first section, the instruments enter in four points of imitation in successive measures, shown in ex. 6-2. Each point of imitation consists of the

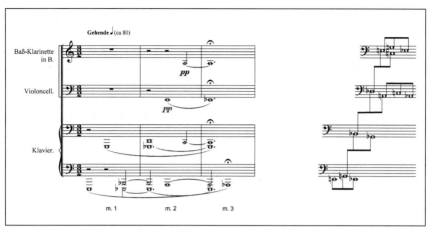

Example 6-1. "Nacht," mm. 1–3.

Example 6-2. "Nacht," mm. 4–10.

head and a seven-note tail, descending chromatically and ending with a rising of a diminished seventh. (The cello's leap in m. 6 is to correct for register, but it does accentuate the leap in the bass clarinet.) The diminished seventh actually creates another version of the head motive because it is the enharmonic inversion of the minor third. With a chromatic step before and after this leap, the characteristic major/minor third of the head is sounded. After the tail, each voice has free development of elements of the tail, the most important of which is a presentation of the head in smaller diminutions. The close imitation and the low chromatic lines are descriptive and suggest the slow rotation and descent of the moths.

In the first ten measures, the Sprechstimme varies two ideas—the tail, refitted with a new rhythm, and the head. The initial descending line is based on the tail; it even has the ascending diminished seventh, which is used for *Riesenfalter*, the giant butterflies. The head is first suggested for *Zauberbuch* (mm. 7–8). The head is then presented dramatically in m. 10, sung (*gesungen*) as the lowest notes in all of *Pierrot*. The approach to those notes is significant. In m. 9, the Sprechstimme begins as it began in m. 4, transposed up a third. Where the Sprechstimme leaped *up* a diminished seventh in m. 5, it leaps *down* a diminished seventh for the low notes on *verschwiegen*. The low notes are much preferred to the *ossia*. If the low notes are not always reliable, the singer should try raising the chin, not lowering it. If the notes come out somewhat breathy, they can be heard against the sparse texture and the mood is all the more enhanced and spooky.

For the second and third sections, the ideas of the passacaglia are developed and accelerated through progressively smaller diminutions, from the half-notes of the introduction to the sextuplets that begin in m. 18. The texture grows busier, and effects such as tremolo and *sul pointicello* add to the sense of a proliferation of creeping insects.

The second stanza has three points of imitation, shown in ex. 6-3: the cello in m. 11 is imitated by the bass clarinet in m. 12 at varying intervals (a third, an octave, a sixth) and by the piano in m. 13 (sometimes imitating the cello's pitches, sometimes the bass clarinet's pitches). A significant development of this section is the expansion of the leap at the end of the tail into a motive of two leaping major sevenths.

Once again, the Sprechstimme simultaneously varies and develops what the instruments present. At the end of m. 12—thus between the bass clarinet and cello entrances—it loosely begins a point of imitation. The words *Erinnerung* and *mordend* are marked with continuous diminuendo as though being choked off. The sudden forte on text refrain, m. 14, uses the tail from the first section—same pitches, different rhythm. This passage is challenging for the reciter. A presentation of the vowels as far forward and "snarly" as possible will give the Sprechstimme some definition against the busy instrumental texture.

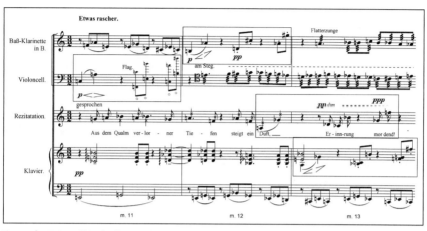

Example 6-3. "Nacht," mm. 11–13.

For the last stanza, the two staves of the piano part have forms of the motive playing in close imitation separated only by an eighth-note. As a result, it appears as if one hand plays mirror retrograde of the other. The strong chromatic descent found in the piano's working of the motive and the more obvious descending half-steps of the cello resemble the tail. The last text reprise gives the motive—pitch-specific E, G, and E-flat—on the text *finstre, schwarze* and adds a G-flat before returning to a variant of the tail for *Riesenfalter*. The final three measures, shown in ex. 6-4, combine the prevailing chromatic descent with a compression of the introduction in the piano in m. 24. The last four notes in the bass clarinet and cello echo the Sprechstimme's *finstre, schwarze* in m. 23, transposed down a third.

Example 6-4. "Nacht," mm. 23–26.

In addition to the pitch materials, the final measures also recall the beginning with the sudden reduction in rhythmic activity. For nineteen measures, the texture is made increasingly busy with the use of increasingly smaller durations. In m. 24, the accumulated motion abruptly gives way to half notes, recalling the rhythmic motion of the introduction. It is as if the engine has suddenly stalled, leaving us to float momentarily before the final coup de grâce in the bass clarinet and cello. Like "Mondestrunken," "Nacht" begins one of the three parts with a repeating figure that builds momentum. Unlike "Mondestrunken," the repeating figure is more pervasive and more determinant, as the poem's narration completes a small character arc from concern, to terror, to abject resignation.

NO. 9 GEBET AN PIERROT (PRAYER TO PIERROT)

Pierrot! Mein Lachen	Pierrot! My laughter
Hab ich verlernt!	I have unlearned!
Das Bild des Glanzes	The picture of brilliance
Zerfloß—zerfloß!	Dissolved—dissolved!
Schwarz weht die Flagge	Black waves the flag
Mir nun vom Mast.	Now from my mast.
Pierrot! Mein Lachen	Pierrot! My laughter
Hab ich verlernt!	I have unlearned!
O gib mir wieder,	O give me again,
Roßarzt der Seele	Horse doctor of the soul
Schneemann der Lyric,	Snowman of the lyric,
Durchlaucht vom Monde,	Lord of the moon,
Pierrot—mein Lachen!	Pierrot! My laughter!

The Text and Translation

"Gebet" is the thirty-first poem in Giraud's collection and the only poem that addresses Pierrot in the first person. The first-person poems in the first part, "Columbine," "Madonna," and "Der kranke Mond," seem to feature the voice of Pierrot himself. In "Gebet" a second character berates Pierrot for his inability to please. It is plausible that the narrator is Columbine, and in Schoenberg's arrangement of poems, this second poem of the second part may reflect her dissatisfaction with the tryst he so anxiously desired in "Columbine," the second poem of the first part.

Hartleben's translation is dedicated to Otto von Grotte (1620–1687), a Baroque literary figure and member of the Fruchtbringenden Gesellschaft. Hartleben's translation shortens the verses considerably and, as a result, condenses the imagery. In the refrain, Giraud's original complains of a coil of laughter that has snapped between the teeth (*O Pierrot! Le resort du rire, / Entre mes dents je l'ai cassé*). The dissolved picture of brilliance is a shortening of Giraud's more theatrical "clear décor disappearing in a Shakespearean mirage" (*Le clair décor s'est effacé / Dans un mirage à la Shakespeare*).

As noted in chapter 4, "Gebet" must have been of considerable importance to Albertine Zehme, as it was the first poem in her 1911 recital and the first poem Schoenberg selected.

Details of Composition

Schoenberg composed "Gebet" first on 12 March 1912, the day after he signed the contract and weeks before the final instrumentation was negotiated. As detailed in chapter 4, the contract specified a piano accompaniment with possibly two other instruments. "Gebet" is composed for piano and clarinet with the Sprechstimme. The use of clarinet is particularly appropriate, as it suggests the clownlike nature of Pierrot, perhaps even taking the role of Pierrot in dialogue with the reciter. But the clarinet is also capable of a more sensuous expression, and the mournful low notes of the clarinet's chalumeau register resonate with the text: the narrator finds Pierrot a despairing and disappointing clown.

Musical Materials

Like O alter Duft, the last melodrama composed, "Gebet" resembles a lied. The melodrama is in three short sections that align with the stanzas.[2] The overall tessitura continues the exploration of the low register begun in "Nacht," which is appropriate to the narrative. The Sprechstimme is present in every measure, and the piano is found in almost every measure. Textural relief is achieved through varying the density of texture and especially through alternating the clarinet and the piano. There is a particular emphasis on the Sprechstimme, which is the *Hauptstimme* throughout, which features more articulations and shadings than is common in the other melodramas.[3] The reciter is asked to sing (m. 13), hiss (m. 5), recite pitiably (m. 9), and execute a trill (m. 9) and a tremolo (mm. 11–12) in the Sprechstimme delivery.

In contrast to the steady pulse of the previous melodrama, the passacaglia "Nacht," the tempo of "Gebet" is flexible and the rhythms often play against the meter. Between "Nacht" and "Gebet," Schoenberg asks for a "long pause, quasi in tempo." The new tempo, a moderato cut time (*Mäßige*) in which the half note is just a shade slower than the quarter in "Nacht," must be established immediately. However, once established, only eight of twenty measures play at the marked tempo. The second and the third sections end with dramatic ritardandi, and the third begins with an accelerando. Even in the measures that proceed in tempo, there is a tendency to superimpose triple meters. For example, beginning with the pickup measure, the first five bars superimpose three-two meter, as can be seen in ex. 6-5. Note the three-two meter downbeats on the downbeat of m. 2, the second beat of m. 3, and the downbeat of m. 5, where on the second beat, a superimposition of three-four occurs.[4] Such fluidity of tempo is more typical in the liedlike melodramas.

The principal motive of "Gebet" is sounded in the Sprechstimme in m. 1 on the word *Pierrot*. The motive has a short-short-long rhythm and a distinctive contour comprising two linear intervals—a descending minor third and an ascending augmented fourth. The interval between the first and third note is an augmented second. In the next measure, the motive is developed with interval expansion for the words *mein lachen*. The interval expansion—the minor third becomes a perfect fifth, the augmented fourth becomes an augmented octave, and the augmented second becomes an augmented fourth—places an unexpected accent on the second syllable of *Lachen* (laughter), which makes the word an ironic, painful cry. Schoenberg emphasizes *Lachen* with the hairpin crescendo and with his choice of notes; D and D-sharp are the last two notes of the total chromatic aggregate to be introduced. It is also accented metrically because it occurs after the first structural downbeat; the downbeat of m. 2 is the first downbeat common to cut time and the superimposed three-two meter.

As ex. 6-5 shows, the Sprechstimme for the rest of the first section stays close to the motive and ends in m. 5 with a near retrograde of m. 1. There, the word *zerfloss* (dissolved) is text-painted by Schoenberg's indication *gezischt* (hissed). Hissing emphasizes the consonants in the word, especially when said quickly, and the sound of the voice literally dissolves.

In the second part, the piano and the clarinet play a more significant role in the texture. The Sprechstimme explores the lowest register with lyrical lines. Schoenberg returns to the motive in the Sprechstimme for the text refrain, mm. 9–12, shown in ex. 6-6. Indeed, the collection of pitches in the Sprechstimme, mm. 9–12, is nearly identical to mm. 1–3. In m. 10 of the text refrain, the second syllable of *Lachen* is accented by a wide leap using the same notes—D-sharp and D-natural. In addition to pitch, other elements such as contour and durations reveal that the text reprise in mm. 9–12 is a modified retrograde. Strict observance of the vocal directives will suggest choked sobs. The staccato and the shake on the first two syllables of *Pierrot* deemphasize the first two pitches and emphasize the D-sharp, which the piano sounds prominently at the beginning of m. 9. The hairpins on *Lachen* and *hab ich* emphasize

Example 6-5. "Gebet an Pierrot," mm. 1–5.

those pitches—which strongly recall mm. 1–2—and contribute to a musical depiction of suppressed weeping. Finally, the rolled *r* (long) on both syllables of *verlernt* (*verrrr—lerrrnt*) emphasizes the last appearance of this word and may be considered a final, abortive effort to laugh.

The third section of "Gebet" is a remarkable development of the ideas presented in the first two sections, as the character veers between angry contempt and quiet desperation. The motive from m. 1 is largely relegated to the piano and clarinet. The Sprechstimme develops the initial minor third with particular attention to the notes around E_4—the initial note in the Sprechstimme. By the end of the third section, the minor third between E_4 and G_4

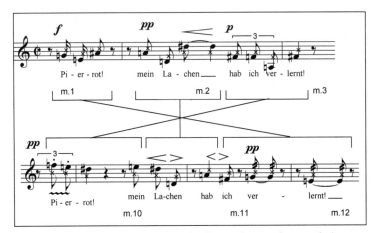

Example 6-6. "Gebet an Pierrot," the first and second text refrains.

from m. 1—which is heard again at the end of the first text reprise—is reworked as the E-flat$_4$ to C$_4$ that ends the melodrama.

After the piano begins the third section with a varied reprise of the chords from m. 1, the reciter is asked to sing E$_4$ before returning to the Sprechstimme delivery to begin a bifocal line. As can be seen in ex. 6-7, the upper half of the bifocal line, mm. 15–19, descends in a precipitous step progression from the G-sharp$_5$ in m. 15 to the G-sharp$_4$ in m. 19. The bottom half of the bifocal line runs a more modest course from the E$_4$ sung in m. 13 and reactivated in m. 15, to the C$_4$, first heard in m. 18 and heard again as the final note in the Sprechstimme. The gestures that form the bottom half of the bifocal line are parallel and progressive: mm. 15 and 17 end with falling gestures to D$_4$, and mm. 18 and 20 end with falling gestures to C$_4$. These gestures have the rhythmic feeling, if not the tonal disposition, of cadential appoggiaturas.

The bifocal line beginning in m. 15 can be emphasized with slight differences in timbre and presentation between the higher and lower parts. The higher line is more accusative, and effects such as a glottal stop in *Roßarzt*, m. 15 (even though it is one word), would be appropriate. The lower line is more circumspect and suggests a lighter presentation. Schoenberg carefully places the louder attacks in the piano between the syllables of the line for better clarity. The last two measures present an opportunity to set the higher and lower parts of the bifocal line—and the angry and despairing qualities—into relief. The rhythm for the word *Pierrot* in m. 19, while marked pianissimo, recalls the accusatory tone of the first measure. However, the last measure recalls the anguish of the first refrain, mm. 9–12. A novel effect can be achieved here by slightly and softly "frying" the vocal chords on the final word, *Lachen*. However, the pitches should be observed as they complete a process of development that ends with the final C$_4$.

Example 6-7. "Gebet an Pierrot," mm. 13–20.

NO. 10 RAUB

Rote, fürstliche Rubine,	Red, baronial rubies,
Blutge Tropfen alten Ruhmes,	Bloody drops of ancient glory,
Schlummern in den Totenschreinen,	Slumber in the coffins,
Drunten in den Grabgewölben.	Down in the burial vaults.
Nachts, mit seinen Zechkumpanen,	By night, with his drinking buddies,
Steigt Pierrot hinab—zu rauben	Climbs Pierrot down—to rob
Rote, fürstliche Rubine,	Red, baronial rubies,
Blutge Tropfen alten Ruhmes.	Bloody drops of ancient glory.

Doch da—sträuben sich die Haare,	But there—stands up his hair,
Bleiche Furcht bannt sie am Platze:	Pallid fear fixes them in place:
Durch die Finsternis—wie Augen!—	Through the darkness—as eyes!—
Stieren aus den Totenschreinen	Glaring from the coffins
Rote, fürstliche Rubine.	Red, baronial rubies.

The Text and Translation

"Raub" is the fourteenth poem in Giraud's collection. Hartleben makes no significant changes, although Giraud is a little less direct about identifying the scene as a burial vault, noting only the horror of an underground chamber (*Dans l'horreur des longs souterrains*). In the context of Schoenberg's order, "Raub" provides a sense of comic relief in Part II before returning to the more dramatic themes introduced in "Nacht" and continued in "Rote Messe."

Details of Composition

"Raub" was the seventeenth melodrama completed, composed entirely on May 9. However, on the *Textvorlage* there is a sketch of the cello part in mm. 7–8 after the first stanza (where it appears in the melodrama). "Raub" was composed on the same day as "Nacht," "Heimfahrt," and "Madonna," and shares with those others a notable use of repetitive elements. However, the mood of comic relief is quite different from the macabre elements of "Nacht" and "Madonna" and the optimism of "Heimfahrt."

Musical Materials

Schoenberg's setting of "Raub" takes the form of a miniature *scena* as from an opera buffa—a music-rhetorical device that is similar to the classical form of *melodrama*. While it is never marked, the Sprechstimme is the *Hauptstimme* throughout. The details of the text direct the events of through-composed melodrama, using elements of recitative and more traditional text-setting. While the three stanzas are distinct, "Raub" is not as sectional as most of the melodramas. Rather, like "Nacht," composed on the same day, "Raub" is shaped like an expanding wedge of increasing intensity. Unlike "Nacht," the instrumentation of "Raub" keeps the pitch materials in a fairly high register, which is markedly different from most of the melodramas in Part II.

The accompaniment is created almost entirely of chromatic segments, arranged in patterns of three and four notes. The resulting group of seven notes resembles the Pierrot figure—a resemblance that continues in the next melodrama, "Rote Messe." Linearly and harmonically, the chromatic segments form clusters, as can be seen in ex. 6-8. To introduce the clusters, Schoenberg is deliberate with the pitches in the beginning. For example, after the leaps in the flute in mm. 1–2, the same three pitches, D, E-flat, and E-natural, are used for the violin part in m. 3. The E-natural and E-flat (written as D-sharp) are ultimately the outer voices of the chord sustained for the entrance of the Sprechstimme. As noted below, these pitches conspicuously recur at structural moments in "Raub." Also in m. 3, the clarinet and cello fill in all the notes between G-sharp and B. Added to the notes in the violin, they form an incomplete cluster, as there is no F-natural. However, in the next measure, the sustained chord plus the cello provide all the chromatic notes between C-sharp and F-sharp, thus overlapping and completing the previous cluster.

Example 6-8. "Raub," mm. 1–5.

The Sprechstimme enters as *recitativo accompagnato* over a sustained chord. That chord, mm. 4–5, is comprised of the same notes that form the head of the "Nacht" passacaglia, composed on the same day. The entrance of the voice over pianissimo chord is one of the most exposed moments for the Sprechstimme in all of *Pierrot*. The florid line of the Sprechstimme contrasts the noodling of the instruments. Schoenberg indicates it is to be delivered in tempo, and it presents the most significant motive in the melodrama. Part of the strength of this line may come from the fact that the first eight notes are essentially in A-flat harmonic minor (spelled enharmonically); the accented syllables fall on members of an A-flat minor triad. The rhythm of the Sprechstimme is also distinctive in that it contrasts the instrumental parts by adding a dotted-eighth and sixteenth rhythm. The dotted rhythm is used for all three text refrains, albeit punctuated for dramatic effect for the second text refrain (mm. 10–13). However, dotted rhythms are conspicuously underrepresented in the instrumental parts. One notable exception is the exaggeration of a dotted rhythm—a double-dotted rhythm—in the cello part, mm. 7–8, a passage that Schoenberg sketched on his copy of the text.

Three of four verses in the first stanza are set in recitative declamation. The last verse, in m. 7, elides the resumption of the texture established in the introduction. The flute and violin resume the sixteenth-note impulse arranged once again around E-natural and E-flat and further accentuated by the clarinet's dramatic D-natural/E-flat gesture at the end of m. 8. The second stanza begins at the end of m. 8 with a stage whisper, adding "tone" for the notes around the E-flat and E-natural. The renewed texture activity is interrupted almost as soon as it begins for the text refrain. Rather than a full stop, the ensemble keeps the momentum going by punctuating the phrases with chords.

The final stanza is climactic but also revisits elements from the beginning of the melodrama. The strings take a more prominent and descriptive role in the accompaniment, using *sul ponticello* to suggest Pierrot's hair standing on end and string harmonics to suggest the glow of the eyes. These two devices are stock effects of Romantic descriptive music—both figure prominently in Berlioz's "Dream of the Witches Sabbath" in *Symphonie fantastique*—and had become clichés long before the turn of the century. Their use here contributes to an ironic sense of horror, or what Pierre Boulez called "playing with fear."[5] The harmonics, mm. 16–17 hold G-sharp and A—notes that figured prominently in the first sixteenth-note texture in m. 3—while the sixteenth-note figure in the flute and clarinet returns to D, E, and E-flat. After one final dramatic run in the clarinet, the final text refrain returns to the rhythm from m. 5 set against chromatic, descending staccato sixteenth-notes in the ensemble—a gesture of frightened surrender or even fainting.

NO. 11 ROTE MESSE (RED MASS)

Zu grausem Abendmahle,
Beim Blendeglanz des Goldes,
Beim Flackerschein der Kerzen,
Naht dem Altar—Pierrot!

Die Hand, die gottgeweihte,
Zerreisst die Priesterkleider
Zu grausem Abenedmahle,
Beim Blendglanz des Goldes.

Mit segnender Geberde
Zeigt er den bangen Seelen
Die triefend rote Hostie:
Sein Herz—in blutgen Fingern—
Zu grausem Abenelmahle!

To a horrible communion,
With the dazzling brilliance of gold,
With the flickering light of candles,
Nearing the altar—Pierrot!

The hand, consecrated by God,
Rips the priestly attire
For a horrible communion,
With the dazzling brilliance of gold.

With a blessing gesture
He shows the worried souls
The gushing red host:
His heart—in bloody fingers—
For a horrible communion!

The Text and Translation

"Rote Messe" is the twenty-ninth poem in Giraud's collection. Hartleben makes no significant changes. Hartleben's translation is dedicated to Felix Hausdorff (1868–1942), a mathematician known for his contributions to topology and set theory.[6]

Details of Composition

"Rote Messe" was the seventh melodrama composed and was completed on 22 April. "Rote Messe" uses all the substitution instruments together (piccolo, viola, and bass clarinet) for the first time, and, with the cello and piano, it is the first melodrama Schoenberg composed using all five instruments. The ostinato bears a strong relationship to the Pierrot figure from "Mondestrunken," begun five days earlier and completed seven days later. This relationship is strengthened with the appearance of the Pierrot figure in the piano, mm. 20–21.

Musical Materials

Following the character pieces "Gebet an Pierrot" and "Raub," which largely emphasized the Sprechstimme, "Rote Messe" returns to some of the musical concerns introduced in "Nacht." Like "Nacht," the music dramatizes the sinister and grotesque aspects of the poem. The tessitura is predominantly low, but set in relief by high, registrally distinct figures and gestures played by the piano and piccolo. While not a contrapuntal form, "Rote Messe" is a return to contrapuntal textures and a more balanced distribution of activity between the ensemble and reciter. Unlike "Nacht," "Rote Messe" is in three clear sections that align with the stanzas and rises to peak intensity in the middle before an extended denouement.

The first section of "Rote Messe" actually begins in the last measure of "Raub." The final cluster in m. 20 is re-voiced, transposed, and transferred to the piano.[7] In the brief transition, Schoenberg exploits a feature of his voicing in which adjacent voices are a major seventh apart, which inverts to a minor second, and alternating voices are a major ninth apart, which is a major second, displaced one octave. In the ostinato that begins "Rote Messe," the first four descending notes have a similar relationship; the adjacent notes are a perfect fourth and a diminished fourth and the alternating notes are a major seventh and a minor seventh. This technique is like a miniature bifocal line, but is also related to the interlocked voicing of the strings. The first four notes of the piano ostinato form a motive that is developed throughout the melodrama. The ensuing trills and figuration also occur frequently in varied form. See ex. 6-9 and ex. 6-11, farther below.

As ex. 6-9 shows, the ostinato is accompanied by low chords in the bass clarinet, viola, and cello. The register of the chords makes for a dark and murky sound, which is enhanced by the primarily adjacent voice leading. The chords superimpose two-four meter.

The Sprechstimme is the *Hauptstimme* in the first section and occupies a tessitura between the piano and the instruments playing chords. While the tessitura is low, the reciter can project with the aid of the short durations, bright vowels, and hard consonants. The reciter enters with a seven-note figure—three pick-up notes and a new motive for *Abendmahle* in a metrically strong position. The new motive is derived from the first four notes of the piano's ostinato, and like that ostinato, it cultivates relationships between alternating notes, as shown in ex. 6-9. However, the relationships between adjacent notes are also significant. In particular, the first statement of the text refrain establishes the tritone A-flat and D. These notes appear as an adjacent pair on *Abendmahle*, *Goldes*, and *Pierrot*, and as an alternating pair on *Naht dem Altar*. As noted below, the A-flat and D tritone returns in focal moments of the second and third sections.

The pace of the Sprechstimme is slackened in mm. 4–5 by means of slightly longer durations. Here, the vowels should be held for their full duration. There is a simultaneous decrease in intensity in the ensemble as the instruments playing the chords settle on a single chord at the end of m. 4. A short interlude, mm. 7–9, dispels the forward motion of the first section as the piano and piccolo alternate and the tone of the strings is weakened by *sul ponticello* and *col legno*.

Example 6-9.   Transition to "Rote Messe."

The second stanza commences with a sudden and dramatic change of mood to match the narrative of the poem. The Sprechstimme is no longer the most salient element, but must compete with the ensemble playing as a homorhythmic unit, one of the most forceful gestures in *Pierrot*. In a musical depiction of Pierrot theatrically ripping his clerical robes, the ensemble commences in m. 10 with the elements presented at the beginning. The strings play a chord more forcefully than the beginning as the piano plays a more aggressively articulated version of the second half of its ostinato from m. 1. In m. 11, the piano continues the ideas in m. 10, adding the descending four notes from the beginning of the ostinato. Here, at the exact moment Pierrot rips the robe, the Sprechstimme has the descending four-note motive in a form that most resembles the piano ostinato from m. 1 (as shown on p. 157 in ex. 6-11). It is followed immediately by a dramatic glissando for *zerreißt* that expands the last two notes, G-sharp and D. The word *zerreißt* signals the dramatic highpoint of "Rote Messe," which is sustained through m. 15. The glissando is dramatic, but the pitches are significant in that they amplify the G-sharp and D-natural at the end of *geweihte*. A strongly rolled *r* will emphasize the D-natural as the note of arrival.

Another sign of the dramatic significance of mm. 11–12 is the use of the piccolo. Throughout the first two sections, the piccolo is used to text-paint the flickering of candles and their illumination of gold, appearing on the words *Kerzen* in m. 4, *Blendeglanz* in m. 16, and *Goldes* in m. 17. The ascending arpeggio of the piccolo in m. 7 suggests the gentle flicker of the candles as Pierrot approaches the altar. However, in m. 12, the rapid ascending arpeggio balances the descending glissando of the Sprechstimme and signifies the action: the sudden movement of Pierrot's hand causes the candle's flame to sputter.

The climactic plateau of the second section comes to an end in m. 15. As shown in ex. 6-10, the four-note motive can be seen in different metrical positions in the piano (both staves), cello, and viola, and is augmented in the Sprechstimme. The busy texture makes it difficult for the Sprechstimme to be heard, but a careful observance of the rhythm will keep the higher piano chords between the notes of the Sprechstimme—a hocket effect that reflects the relationship between alternating notes as explored in the first section. The Sprechstimme pitches not only feature the recurrent G-sharp and D-natural pairing, but reprise the four-note motive from the start of the ostinato with a precise diminution of the intervals; each interval from the piano ostinato is two half-steps larger than the comparable interval in the Sprechstimme, as shown in ex. 6-11.

The intensity of the second section dissipates in mm. 16–17. Like the end of the first section, the strings play *sul ponticello* to decrease the force

Example 6-10.   "Rote Messe," beginning and end of the second section.

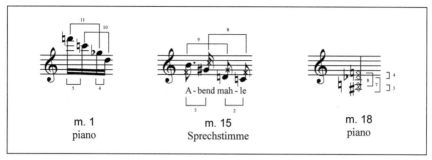

Example 6-11. "Rote Messe," the manifestations of the ostinato.

of tone, if not the volume. Against the ensemble passagework, based on the four-note motive, the Sprechstimme has a *subito* pianissimo in m. 16, which is mirrored in the ensemble at the end of m. 17. The gesture suggests a Pierrot frightened by the intensity of his own actions and given pause by the flickering of gold.

After a brief caesura, the third section begins on the second eighth-note of m. 18 and presents the same motivic material with a different character. Like the first and second sections, the third section begins with chords in the bass clarinet, viola, and cello, as shown in ex. 6-12. However, these instruments, which thus far had been either chordal supporting elements or rhythmically aligned with the piano, emerge as contrapuntal voices at the forefront of the texture, marked by the first use of *Hauptstimme* brackets. They present a half-step sigh in close imitation, derived largely from the voice leading of the chords beginning in m. 1. The piano ostinato is reworked as a chord sustained as piano harmonics. The voicing of the chord is similar to the first four notes of the ostinato, also shown in ex. 6-11. Like the piano harmonics in "Der Dandy," the pitches held by the piano are activated by other sounding pitches with common tones in their overtone series. The rhythmic activity of the ostinato is supplied by the figuration in the left hand of the piano, derived largely from the seven-note Pierrot figure. In m. 23, the piano harmonic stops and the piano and other ensemble instruments exchange roles; the bass clarinet and viola play fragments of both the ostinato and Pierrot figure, while the piano adopts the sigh motive, reworked with chords that resemble the chords at the beginning.

The Sprechstimme in the third section begins with motive forms closely related to the motive forms cultivated in the first two sections, as also shown in ex. 6-12. The motive derived from the ostinato, first used in the Sprechstimme for the word *Abendmahle* in m. 15, is reprised with the same pitches for the words *treifend rote* in m. 23, and in a modified form for the words *Mit segnender Geberde*, thus making a subtle connection for the words *communion, with blessing*

Example 6-12. "Rote Messe," mm. 18–23.

gesture, and *gushing red* (*host*). Most of the Sprechstimme in the third section develops the minor second and minor third intervals in this motive. In mm. 20 to 23, there is a developmental process, shown in ex. 6-12, that establishes the minor third F-sharp and D-sharp in m. 20 and slowly elaborates that third, with neighboring half-steps, until it arrives at the minor third E and C-sharp in m. 23. The pitches used in this process are carefully chosen; they correspond to the pitches held in the piano chord. Having already sounded the low A and the F-sharp in m. 20, Schoenberg begins the developmental process with an F-natural in m. 20, the soprano of the chord. At the arrival in m. 23, the C-sharp is the only note in the chord yet to be sounded in the Sprechstimme. Finally, note that the center of this developmental process contains the repetition of the word *bangen* (worried). This is the only instance of Schoenberg repeating a word in his text-setting in all of *Pierrot*. Here, the repetition serves several functions. It keeps the F-natural active as a tone in the piano. It defines the second step of the process, establishing the minor third a half-step above the arrival. Perhaps most importantly, it continues the image of an agitated Pierrot, still anxious about the dramatic tearing of his clerical garments in the second section and uncomfortable about revealing his bloody heart.

The developmental process in the Sprechstimme, mm. 20–23, is bounded by F_4 and C-sharp$_4$ (not counting the B_4 for the pitch-specific reprise of the motive in m. 23). These two pitches, and their enharmonic equivalents and octave transpositions, dominate the last five measures in the Sprechstimme in a passage of notes largely drawn from the C-sharp transposition of the whole-tone scale, shown in ex. 6-13. As the cello's mournfully slow line rises to a G-sharp$_5$ in m. 24, the Sprechstimme has three notes to sing (*gesungen*). While marked *ppp*, a slightly higher dynamic will be required to set those notes in relief. The combination of voice and cello in m. 24 forms the D- to A-flat dyad that has returned at key moments in this melodrama and returns again, in the cello, in the final measures. Similarly, the motive drawn from the ostinato (ex. 6-11) is reprised in the low register of the piano, mm. 25–27, where it slowly winds down in longer values that sustain. Like mm. 18–22, where the Sprechstimme's development was bound to the piano harmonic tones, the Sprechstimme in mm. 26–29 is closely allied with the sustaining tones in the piano.

"Madonna" used religious imagery in Part I to anticipate the despair in "Der kranke Mond" and the terror of "Nacht." "Rote Messe" uses similar imagery and furthers both the despair and the anticipation of a horrible event, which comes to fruition in "Enthauptung" and "Die Kreuze," which returns to religious imagery for the final time.

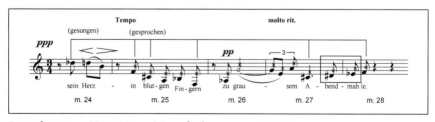

Example 6-13. "Rote Messe," Sprechstimme, mm. 24–28.

NO. 12 GALGENLIED

Die dürre Dirne	The bony whore
Mit langem Halse	With a long neck
Wird seine letzte	Will his last
Geliebte sein.	Lover be.
In seinem Hirne	In his brain
Steckt wie ein Nagel	Stuck like a nail
Die dürre Dirne	The skinny whore
Mit langem Halse.	With a long neck.
Schlank wie die Pinie,	Skinny like a pine,
Am Hals ein zöpfchen—	On the neck a ribbon—
Wollüstig wird sie	Lustfully will she
Den Schelm umhalsen,	The rogue embrace,
Die dürre Dirne!	The bony whore!

The Text and Translation

"Galgenlied" is the seventeenth poem in Giraud's collection. Hartleben changes it considerably. As he did in "Gebet an Pierrot," Hartleben shortens the verses from Giraud's *octosyllabe* meter to a quick five-syllable meter.[8] Also, it is primarily iambic, as opposed to the more common trochaic meter of the other translations. As a consequence of the shorter verses, Hartleben drastically pares the imagery. In Giraud, we learn that the protagonist (presumably Pierrot) is penniless but dreams of gold (*De ce songe d'or sans le sou*) and that he has his reverie while drinking (*Qu'en sa tête enfonce l'ivresse*).

In the imagery of "Galgenlied," the prostitute is a metaphor for the gallows. Therefore, while Schoenberg gives it a somewhat buoyant setting, the poem continues the general decline of the Pierrot character from the despair in "Rote Messe" to the terror of the last two melodramas.

Details of Composition

"Galgenlied" was the eighteenth melodrama composed, all on May 12, three days after writing the similarly comic "Raub."

Musical Materials

"Galgenlied," like "Gebet an Pierrot" and "Raub," resembles an established type of vocal music. For all of the thirteen measures of "Galgenlied," the

Sprechstimme is the *Hauptstimme* and the instruments accompany. The prominence of the Sprechstimme and the fast tempo gives the impression of a patter song, a song type common in operetta and cabaret. As shown in ex. 6-14, the repetition of B-natural as a final note in mm. 2, 4, and m. 8, and the multiple occurrences of those notes in the strings, contribute to a sense of 8-bar double-period structure with two-bar phrases. The B is also repeated and emphasized in the interior of the phrases: it is five of the first nineteen pitches in the Sprechstimme. Despite the patter song elements, one must remember Schoenberg's instructions and resist a "singsong" manner of speaking.

Like "Raub," "Galgenlied" does not divide into sections. Rather, it is one continuous expanding wedge of accelerating tempo, increasing dynamics, and ever-higher register. The first eight bars neatly covers two stanzas using the short-long durations Hartleben used in his translation.

The final five bars present another period structure with parallelism between mm. 9–10 and 11–12. This shorter unit develops the same material presented in mm. 1–8. There is a slight reversal on the last two notes; the longer unit closes in m. 8 with an A to B, whereas the shorter unit closes in the same register with the notes reversed. Unfortunately, this detail is lost in performance against the ascent of the piccolo to its highest note.

Example 6-14. "Galgenlied," mm. 1–8.

NO. 13 ENTHAUPTUNG (BEHEADING)

Der Mond, ein blankes Türkenschwert	The moon, a shining scimitar
Auf einem schwarzen Seidenkissen,	On a black silk cushion,
Gespenstisch gross—dräut er hinab	Ghostly large—menaces down
Durch schmerzensdunkle Nacht.	Through sorrowfully dark night.
Pierrot irrt ohne Rast umher	Pierrot stumbles without rest around
Und starrt empor in Todesängsten	And stares up in mortal terror
Zum Mond, dem blanken Türkenschwert	At the moon, a shining scimitar
Auf einem schwarzen Seidenkissen.	On a black silk cushion.
Es schlottern unter ihm die Knie,	Rattling under him his knees,
Ohnmächtig bricht er jäh zusammen.	Swooning he collapses completely.
Er wähnt: es sause strafend schon	He imagines: it whisks vengefully already
Auf seinen Sündenhals hernieder	Towards his sinning neck rushing
Der Mond, das blanke Türkenschwert.	The moon, a shining scimitar.

The Text and Translation

"Enthauptung" is the twenty-fourth poem in Giraud's collection. Hartleben makes no substantial changes, but his word choices in the second and third stanzas intensify Pierrot's horror. The comma after the first two words is also found in the original (*La lune, comme un saber blanc*), and is reflected in Schoenberg's prosody. Hartleben's translation is dedicated to Alfred Oehlke (1862–1932), a teacher, editor, and later the publisher of the *Breslauer Zeitung*.

Details of Composition

"Enthauptung" was composed on May 23. However, the transitional reprise of "Der kranke Mond" was composed later and is believed to be the last music Schoenberg composed for *Pierrot*. "Enthauptung" was the nineteenth melodrama composed and the first composed after "Galgenlied." This is the only instance of two adjacent melodramas composed in the same order in which they would ultimately appear in the final order. Schoenberg took a break of 11 days between "Galgenlied" and "Enthauptung," which is the longest break he took after beginning in earnest on 1 April.

Musical Materials

"Enthauptung" is unique in a number of ways. At tempo, more than half of the melodrama is the transition, which reprises significant portions of "Der kranke Mond." The first half—the actual setting of the text—is quite short, and should run under a minute at tempo. Despite the brevity, "Enthauptung" consists of an introduction and three sections that align with the three stanzas. Moreover, the sections are arranged in a familiar pattern in which the second section is a significant contrast and the last section resembles the first section in many details. "Enthauptung" is similar to "Nacht" and "Rote Messe" in that it features the same core ensemble of piano, viola, bass clarinet, and cello that contribute to the dark sound and low tessitura.

The introduction, shown in ex. 6-15, presents the significant musical materials. The motive in the cello in m. 1 and the counterpoint motive in the piano, mm. 1–2, are essentially the same; the arrival notes in the cello form the same profile—and even the same intervals—as the motive in the left hand of the piano. The introduction ends with the descending scale pattern—the deadly stroke of the scimitar—that informs the second part of the melodrama.

Like "Raub," the Sprechstimme begins in a manner that resembles *recitativo accompagnato*. The Sprechstimme is the *Hauptstimme* throughout (the *Hauptstimme* brackets for the cello cease in m. 5 and do not return until the transition, the pickup to m. 23). Unlike "Raub," the sustained chords in the bass clarinet and strings create tension with dynamics and chordal gestures in the piano. The initial words, *Der Mond*, are slightly offset and recall the pickup to the downbeat of m. 1. The Sprechstimme is formed of close reiterations of

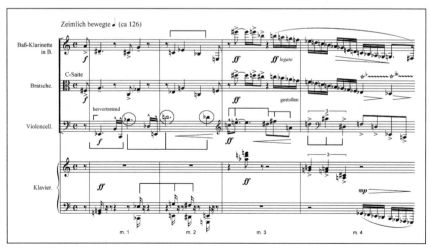

Example 6-15. "Enthauptung," mm. 1–4.

the motive from the introduction. The motive appears in its purest form on *Türkenschwert*—the key image of the melodrama. It is surrounded by variants in retrograde and inversion with slight interval expansions and octave displacements. Following the close patterning of motive forms in mm. 5–8, the instruments emerge from their accompanying to reprise the motive as first heard in m. 1 against the last verse of the first stanza.

The first stanza of the poem establishes the metaphor of the moon as an executioner's sword. Pierrot is not mentioned. The second stanza text-paints Pierrot stumbling in terror through the use of a cross-voice *Klangfarbenmelodie* technique in the ensemble. Unlike "Eine blasse Wäscherin," in which Schoenberg used the technique to depict the moon reflected in a nearby stream, here *Klangfarbenmelodie* represents Pierrot's perception of the moon in his state of delirium. The relative equality of voices is offset by a series of accents, the accented notes of which form gestures that largely relate to figures from the introduction—the thirds in the piano part, the major seventh leap in the cello, and the intervals between the homorhythmic bass clarinet and viola. The Sprechstimme for the second stanza is also largely composed of motive forms, but here they are mostly inverted, as if the depiction of Pierrot in the second section is a mirror image of the depiction of the moon in the first section.

The second section builds intensity by increasing the frequency of the accented notes. Example 6-17 shows the increased occurrence of the accented notes until m. 16, where every other note is accented. The text refrain is slightly altered in the poem to make the syntax continuous. The continuity between the second and third verse of the second stanza is incorporated into Schoenberg's setting as well, where the music for the refrain actually begins on the word *Todesängsten*. In contrast to the narrow range and close motive forms of the first setting of that text (mm. 5–7 in ex. 6-16), ex. 6-17 shows how the second text refrain sprawls over two octaves. In mm. 13 and 15, the initial half-step for *Der Mond* in m. 5 is expanded to a major seventh. The leaps in the Sprechstimme recall the leaps in the cello, mm. 1 and 8–9, which return in dramatic fashion for the third section. Also, the leaps create a bifocal line where the top half ultimately descends two octaves to the F-sharp$_3$ in m. 16. The characteristic motive is fragmented into combinations of seconds and thirds.

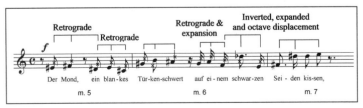

Example 6-16.   "Enthauptung," Sprechstimme, mm. 5–7.

Example 6-17. **"Enthauptung," mm. 13–16.**

Just as the instruments emerged from accompanimental chords with a statement of the motive in m. 9, the instruments emerge from their accompanimental role in the second stanza with a similar emphasis on the motive in mm. 17–19. These last five measures of the melodrama parallel the first five measures, beginning with a statement of the motive in the piano (the top notes of each chord) that is a pitch-specific reprise of the cello in m. 1. After a two-bar development, the descending scale pattern from mm. 3–4 is reprised in the piano, beginning with the same pitches. The return of this descending run, paired with the glissandi in the ensemble, and the return of the two-octave text refrain in the Sprechstimme join several elements of this short melodrama in a dramatic text-painting of the descending saber.

Like most of the transition passages in *Pierrot*, the transition at the end of "Enthauptung" has no special heading (e.g., *Zwischenspiel*) and continues the measure numbering of the prior melodrama.[9] Similarly, no indication on the score or in the carefully prepared front matter alludes to the fact that the fourteen-measure transition reprises and develops material from the twenty-six measures of "Der kranke Mond." The flute reprises its part from "Der kranke Mond" and is, for most measures, a literal repeat, marked *Hauptstimme*. The voice part of "Der kranke Mond" is literally reprised in only the second measure (m. 24). All other instances of the voice part are either subtly changed (the second and third note in m. 23 are reversed; the third note in m. 26 is shortened) or more thoroughly reworked (the reprise of the last motive, mm. 33–36, is augmented and begins in a different metrical position, relative to the flute).

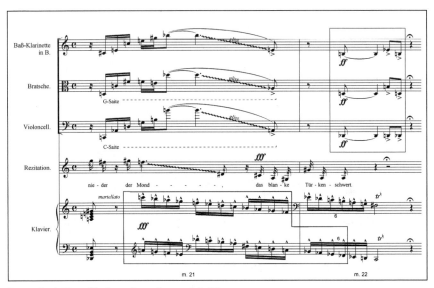

Example 6-18. "Enthauptung," mm. 21–22.

Example 6-19. "Enthauptung" transition, mm. 22–26 paired with "Der kranke Mond," mm. 1–4.

The transition compresses the three sections of "Der kranke Mond" into two parts, largely by omitting the material from the second section. The first six measures correspond to the first six measures of "Der kranke Mond." Against the literal reprise in the flute part, the voice part sounds first in the bass clarinet, then in the cello. The other instruments imitate details from the voice part. After a few bars of less literal development (mm. 29–31), the last five bars reprise and condense the last six bars of "Der kranke Mond."

One should resist the temptation to draw conclusions about the performance of "Der kranke Mond" based on this reprise. The flute is marked *Hauptstimme* throughout. While it is true the voice part in the bass clarinet is initially marked *begleitend* (accompanying), it is also marked *espressivo* and serves as the basis for points of imitation in the first three bars. Similarly, at the end of the work, mm. 33–36, the voice part is also marked *Haupstimme* and *poco espressivo* at a slightly higher dynamic. Thus, there is a certain degree of parity between the voice and flute parts, as presented in this transition.

Similarly, one should be wary of overestimating the structural significance of this reprise. In the context of Part II, it provides a certain sense of contrasting relief between the dark tension of "Enthauptung" and high drama of "Die Kreuze." "Raub" provides comedic relief between "Gebet an Pierrot" and "Rote Messe," and "Galgenlied" provides comparable relief between "Rote Messe" and "Enthauptung." Thus, the extended transition completes a pattern of alternating tension and release between "Gebet" and "Die Kreuze." Moreover, it brightens the instrumental palette. The transition features the flute, which is underrepresented in Part II. It also begins with bass clarinet and ends with clarinet in A—the opposite of the switch from clarinet to bass clarinet in "Valse de Chopin" in Part I and "O alter Duft" in Part III. Finally, the quartet that plays the transition returns in m. 10 of "Die Kreuze." There, the quartet, further brightened by the change from viola to violin, follows a dramatic piano fantasia with an ensemble texture beginning with the subdued affect of the transition. (See ex. 6-23, below.)

The role of the transition between "Enthauptung" and "Die Kreuze" in the larger context of *Pierrot lunaire* is less obvious. While Schoenberg had the final order in mind when he composed this transition, it is altogether more likely that the placement of this reprise is more extra-musical than structural. Perhaps the reason for the reprise is esoteric. As Ethan Haimo has observed, given Schoenberg's mysterious involvement with numerology, the reprise of material from the seventh melodrama at the end of the thirteenth melodrama "may have been intended to counteract the negative influence of thirteen (in Schoenberg's eyes, a terrible number)."[10]

The transition is ultimately programmatic. There is a rough symmetry to the fact that the first poem with religious imagery, "Madonna," is followed by "Der kranke Mond," and the last poem to use religious imagery, "Die Kreuze," is preceded by the reprise of "Der kranke Mond." "Rote Messe," the only other poem with religious imagery, falls roughly between these two melodramas, creating an overlapping pattern that begins near the end of Part I and continues through the end of Part II. Pierrot's creativity, as nourished by the moon, dies at the end of "Valse de Chopin." "Madonna" signals the beginning of Pierrot's darkest period, which continues until "Die Kreuze." The melodramas of Part II are more episodic than the character studies of Part I. Before "Die Kreuze" begins, Schoenberg uses the reprise of "Der kranke Mond" to wordlessly revisit the misery of Pierrot one last time before bringing the section to a close.

NO. 14 DIE KREUZE (THE CROSSES)

Heilge Kreuze sind die Verse,	Holy crosses are the verses,
Dran die Dichter stumm verbluten,	To which poets silently hemorrhage,
Blindgeschlagen von der Geier	Struck blind by the vultures
Flatterndem Gespensterschwarme!	Fluttering in a spectral swarm!
In den Leibern schwelgten Schwerter,	Their bodies are fodder for swords,
Prunkend in des Blutes Scharlach!	Profligate with blood's scarlet fever!
Heilge Kreuze sind die Verse,	Holy crosses are the verses,
Dran die Dichter stumm verbluten.	To which poets silently hemorrhage.
Tot das Haupt—erstartt die Locken—	Dead the head—congealed the tresses—
Fern, verweht der Lärm des Pöbels.	Far-off, wafts the roar of the mob.
Langsam sinkt die Sonne nieder,	Slowly sinks the sun low,
Eine rote Königskrone.—	A red kingly crown.—
Heilge Kreuze sind die Verse!	Holy crosses are the verses!

The Text and Translation

"Die Kreuze" is the thirtieth poem in Giraud's collection. Hartleben makes a few changes. In the last stanza, the decapitation imagery—a head with tresses mottled with dry blood—is not found in Giraud. In Giraud's original, the head is only invoked as a place for the sun as crown. Hartleben dedicated his translation to Maria Janitschek (1859–1927), a poet and novella writer who was strongly identified with the late-nineteenth-century women's movement in Europe.

Details of Composition

"Die Kreuze," written for the entire ensemble on their principal instruments, was begun on 27 April, the day after "Gemeinheit." Like "Gemeinheit," it was left incomplete until June. It was finished on 9 June, three days after he finished "Gemeinheit."

Musical Materials

Unlike "Der kranke Mond," which ends Part I with a quiet and reflective mood, "Die Kreuze" ends Part II in a grand style. Like "Madonna" and "Valse de Chopin" from Part I, "Die Kreuze" groups the first two stanzas into a continuous section with Sprechstimme and the most virtuosic piano writing in *Pierrot*. The third stanza stands as a second section, differentiated by a varied texture and the introduction of new instruments, followed by a bravura coda.

The imagery and mise-en-scène of "Die Kreuze" are similar to that of "Rote Messe" and "Madonna," but the affect and expression are quite different. "Rote Messe" is a narrative, and like most of the melodramas in Part II, it plays like a dramatic scene. The text of "Madonna" is more conceptual; it is an extended metaphor, and the Sprechstimme is marked *sehr innig* (inwardly). "Die Kreuze" is also conceptual but spoken with a public voice. Schoenberg marked the Sprechstimme *ernst* (seriously) at the beginning and again at m. 11. This direction gave rise to a famous anecdote. During the rehearsals before the premiere, Schoenberg worked with Zehme to capture the right tone for the Sprechstimme. In the unpublished essay "Pathos," dated April 1928, Schoenberg describes the scene thus:

> As I've told Steuermann, once during a *Pierrot* rehearsal, I said to Frau Zehme regarding "Kreuze": "If you want to speak [*sprechen*] this piece with the correct expression then you must think of a life-insurance policy!!" And I always stressed that these pieces must not be tragically but rather lightly recited [*leicht vorgetragen*].[11]

While this anecdote speaks to Zehme's flair for sentimental theatricality, it also suggests a more detached and objective delivery. The textures and rhythms suggest an almost formal presentation of the materials in the first two measures.

In the opening two measures, the piano and Sprechstimme present several related motives. The two chords that begin the melodrama disturb the serene recollection of "Der kranke Mond" with an urgent sense of in media res. These two chords, marked M_0 in ex. 6-20, constitute a motive that generates the many chordal passages in the piano part. The first eight notes in the Sprechstimme can be parsed into two related motives. The defining characteristics of the first of those motives, marked M₁ in ex. 6-20, are the dotted rhythm and the final ascending leap following descending steps. The characteristic feature of the second motive, marked M_2, is alternating notes that are the same or similar, not unlike the motivic development in "Rote Messe." The piano left hand in m. 1 presents a three-note motive, marked M_3, which inverts and rearranges the last three notes of M_1 in the Sprechstimme.

The relationships between these motives are revealed through their combination. A combination of the two motive forms in the Sprechstimme can be found at the end of m. 2, where the alternating similarity of M_2 is concluded with the major third leap from the end of M_1. In the piano, beginning with the pickup to m. 2, a figure is created with the chords from M_0, the contour of M_1 (with octave displacement), and the intervallic profile of M_3 (inverted and with a half-step expansion of the intervals).

The dynamic indication and the busy texture of the piano make the first nine measures particularly difficult for the reciter. The dramatic effect of the first two chords in the piano can be heightened if the first beat is slightly elongated, continuing in tempo with the Sprechstimme on the second beat. To make the Sprechstimme project against the percussiveness of the piano, the reciter should take breaths liberally (except on the second beat of m. 2, where Schoenberg uses a slur to the D-sharp, prefiguring the pitches for *verbluten* at the end of the verse). More contrast can be achieved if the reciter takes a little time before *blindgeschlagen* in m. 3 and the pianist takes a little time before the third beat of m. 3. These slight breaths will help offset the first two verses, because after the third beat of m. 3, there is an attack on almost every sixteenth through m. 9. Similarly, the cadential feeling of *Gespensterschwarme* in the Sprechstimme in m. 4 should accentuate the close of the first stanza. There, the Sprechstimme presents two further variations of the first motive found in the

Example 6-20. "Die Kreuze," mm. 1–3.

Sprechstimme; the final leap of a third becomes a descending leap on *flattern-dem* to a B$_4$, then a descending leap of a fifth to an A$_4$ on *Gespensterschwarme*. As shown in ex. 6-21, the motive form on *Gespensterschwarme* closes the first stanza and generates the piano interlude in m. 5, which also prominently features the B-natural and the A-natural at the ends of each motive form in m. 4.

The short caesura at the end of m. 5 divides the stanzas, but the music that follows is not sufficiently different to call it a new section. The Sprechstimme stays close to the motive forms presented in mm. 1–4, as shown in ex. 6-22. The first motive is inverted in m. 6, and its relationship to the third motive is more obvious, especially during the text refrain, mm. 7–10.

The lyrical expansion at the end of this section may also be heightened with extra time, which will aid the listener in the recognition of reprised motives. In mm. 7–8, the first three notes of the text reprise should be clear, as the last chord in m. 7 and the first chord of m. 8 recall the chords from the beginning.

After a dramatic sequencing of the motive in the piano, m. 9, the second section begins with a timbral modulation. The flute, clarinet, violin, and cello enter imperceptibly, their attacks masked by a cluster of tones sustained by the piano. As the ring of the piano decays, the sustained ensemble becomes increas-

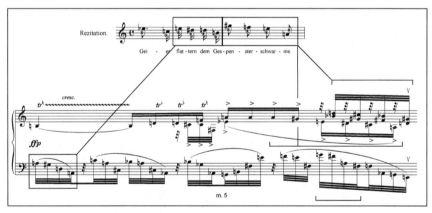

Example 6-21. "Die Kreuze," mm. 4–5.

Example 6-22. "Die Kreuze," Sprechstimme, mm. 6–7.

ingly present. Every note of the entering instruments is a significant tone in the spectrum created by the piano's cluster: the flute's A-flat is third harmonic above the piano's D-flat; the clarinet's D is the fourth harmonic above the piano's D; the violin's G is the twelfth harmonic above the piano's low C and the fifth harmonic above the E-flat (held over from the trill, and rearticulated in the cello), and the cello provides a new fundamental, one octave below the E-flat held over from the trill in m. 9. The cello's E-flat is the only attack that should be heard. Schoenberg's conducting copy of the score indicates he subdivided the third and fourth beat of m. 10, but the downbeat of 11 should not come until all the elements of the harmonics are in place.[12]

The beginning of the second section, shown in ex. 6-23, is a dramatic change. The volume and rhythmic energy of the first section is supplanted by a thin and quiet texture, and the piano is replaced by an ensemble that recalls the reprise of "Der kranke Mond." Schoenberg marks the Sprechstimme *ernst* again, but the rhythmic grouping suggests a halting delivery for the gruesome images that begin the third stanza. The quality of Sprechstimme in the last section can be connected with the beginning by performing each segmented motive legato.

Example 6-23. "Die Kreuze," mm. 9–13.

The second section is a continuous crescendo of volume and activity. With the invocation of the roar of the crowd, m. 13, the ensemble emerges from static chords with long lines in three-part counterpoint. Simultaneously, the piano adopts a more regular rhythm, which in m. 15 becomes a descending sequence as the narrative describes the sun sinking low. The goal of the third stanza is the sudden arrival of the chord in m. 17. The chord is held for the pronouncement of the text reprise, which is surprisingly close to the original statement in m. 1, inexactly transposed a fifth, as shown in ex. 6-24.

The coda that concludes "Die Krueze" is derived from the motivic material used in the Sprechstimme. As ex. 6-24 shows, the final melody in the clarinet, marked *Schalltrichter hoch* ([hold the] bell high) like a climactic melody in a Mahler symphony, is derived from motive 2, especially as it appears in the Sprechstimme in m. 9 and in the clarinet and flute in m. 15. Moreover, the clarinet's alternation around D-sharp and the climactic note A recalls the repetition of the D-sharp and A tritone in mm. 2–3 approaching the word *verbluten* (see ex. 6-20).

"Die Kreuze" ends with the two chords that began the movement, bolstered by the other instruments in the ensemble. In m. 1, these chords create the impression of raising the curtain on a scene already in progress. At the end, they close the melodrama and Part II with a sense of finality. The swarm of giant butterflies that menaced Pierrot at the start of Part II caused debilitating fear. But the swarm of vultures in "Die Kreuze," feeding on bodies where "swords have feasted," are not related as personal turmoil, but rather with a

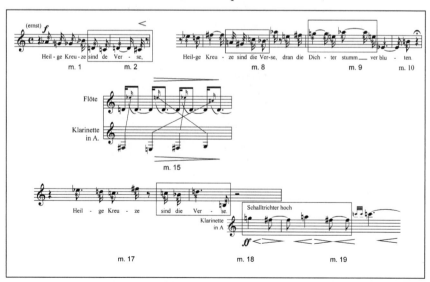

Example 6-24. "Die Kreuze," development of motive 2.

larger sense of resigned martyrdom. Whereas Part I leaves us with a Pierrot consumed with his own worries, Part II ends with a rejuvenated Pierrot, infused with a larger sense of self as poet and mystic.

NOTES

1. This definition, including the example, is abstracted from "Passecaille" (*sic*) in *Meyers Konversationslexikon*, 4th ed. While Schoenberg had read and written much about music by the time he wrote *Pierrot*, his early self-instruction included studying the articles of this encyclopedia. See Willi Reich, *Schoenberg: A Critical Biography*, trans. Leo Black (New York: Praeger, 1971), 2.

2. It is worth noting that the distribution of measures in the sections—mm. 1–6, 7–12, and 13–20 (6+6+7)—resembles the distribution of lines in the rondel (4+4+5). This relationship is more significant here as "Gebet" has exactly twenty measures and was the first of what was originally planned to be twenty melodramas.

3. The score note at the bottom of the first page of *Gebet*—*Die Rezitation hat die Tonhöhe andeutungsweise zu bringen*—was mistakenly printed in the first published score and every subsequent edition prior to the *Gesamtausgaben* edition of 1996. As detailed in chapter 3, this annotation was a first attempt at articulating the definition of Sprechstimme and is subsumed—if not improved—by the preface. Schoenberg circles it in red and adds the delete sign in his second conducting copy (Source D2, 29). See Brinkmann 1995, 150.

4. In Schoenberg's second conducting copy, there is a bold diagonal stroke through the eighth rest on the second beat of m. 1—a clear indication of a strongly conducted beat to cue the reciter and keep the hemiola in time (Source D2, 29).

5. Pierre Boulez, "*Pierrot lunaire* and *Le marteau sans maître*," trans. Martin Cooper, in *From Pierrot to Marteau*, ed. Leonard Stein (Los Angeles: Arnold Schoenberg Institute, 1988), 15.

6. In the spring of 2006, the authors learned of a privately owned copy of the book *Sant' Ilario: Gedanken aus der Landschaft Zarathustras* (Leipzig: Verlag C. G. Naumann 1897), written by Felix Hausdorff under the pen name Paul Mongré, that was signed by Hausdorff and inscribed to Albertine Zehme. The inscription read, "*Der Freundin Italiens, Frau Albertine Zehme, widmet dies Buch südlichen Himmels verehrungsvoll der Verfasser.*"

7. The last cluster, on the downbeat of m. 20, spells Bach's name—B–A–C–H; in traditional German notation, *B* is B-flat and *H* is B natural. Bach used this motive, most notably in *Der Kunst der Fuge*. Schoenberg later made reference to the motive in his String Quartet No. 3, op. 27 (1927) and the Variations for Orchestra, op. 31 (1926–1928).

8. Hartleben shortened the verses for only two poems, "Gebet an Pierrot" and "Galgenlied" (17 and 45 in the original order). Schoenberg chose both shortened poems, as had Zehme in her 1911 recital. Otto Vrieslander set a shortened version of "Rot und Weiß," no. 25, which can be found in the second edition of Hartleben's translation. Hartleben, Otto Erich, Albert Giraud, and Otto Vrieslander, *Albert Giraud, Pierrot*

lunaire (München: G. Müller, 1911), xi. Gregory Richter identifies this shorter version of "Rot und Weiß" as an alternate version by Hartleben (Richter, xxiiii). There is some evidence that Schoenberg had access to the 1911 edition of the poems (Brinkmann 1987, 12), but in his presumably cursory examination of Vrieslander's settings, he may not have noticed that the version of no. 25 set by Vrieslander was different from the version in the cycle of poems. In any event, Schoenberg's working copy of the poems contained the longer form of the *Rot und Weiß* (Source Ab, 719 recto).

9. Schoenberg does use the word *Zwischenspeil* (interlude) to describe this transition in his list of instrumentation appended to his copy (Source D2).

10. Haimo 2004, 153.

11. "Pathos" (1928) (ASC). Steuermann has written that this exchange occurred after the last three measures of "Der kranke Mond." According to Steuermann, Schoenberg "would step behind her when "Der kranke Mond" became too tearful, saying in the rhythm of her speech, "Don't despair, Mrs. Zehme, don't despair; there is such a thing as life insurance!" Steuermann 1963, 7; reprinted in Brinkmann 1995, 244.

12. Source D2, 45.

7

Part III, Numbers 15–21

NO. 15 HEIMWEH (HOMESICK)

Lieblich klagend—ein krystallnes
  Seufzen
Aus Italiens alter Pantomime,
Klingts herüber: wie Pierrot so
  hölzern,
So modern sentimental geworden.

Und es tönt durch seines
  Herzens Wüste,
Tönt gedämpft durch alle Sinne
  wieder,
Lieblich klagend—ein krystallnes
  Seufzen
Aus Italiens alter Pantomime.

Da vergisst Pierrot die Trauermienen!
Durch den bleichen Feuerschein
  des Mondes,
Durch des Lichtmeers Fluten
  —schweift die Sehnsucht
Kühn hinauf, empor zum
  Heimathimmel,
Lieblich klagend—ein krystallnes
  Seufzen.

Gently objecting—a crystalline
  sigh
From Italy's ancient pantomime,
Echoes down: that Pierrot so
  wooden,
So fashionably sentimental has become.

And it sounds through his
  heart's wasteland,
Sounding muted through all senses
  again,
Gently objecting—a crystalline
  sigh
From Italy's ancient pantomime.

Then forgets Pierrot the tragic facade!
Through the pale-fire glow of
  the moon,
Through the surge of light's ocean
  —disperses the longing
Intrepidly flying, rising to the
  homeland sky,
Gently objecting—a crystalline
  sigh.

The Text

"Heimweh" is the thirty-fourth poem in Giraud's collection. Hartleben makes no significant changes but does dedicate his translation to Fritz Mauthner (1849–1923), a philosopher of language. Hartleben and Mauthner were among the writers that founded *Gesellschaft der Zwanglosen.*

"Heimweh" is an important poem in the construction of the narrative. Giraud entitled this poem "Nostalgie." Hartleben's "Heimweh" means *nostalgia* but also *homesickness.* The German title changes Pierrot's anxiety from a more general longing for the past to a more specific longing for Bergamo, the traditional home for Commedia.

In Giraud's collection, "Heimweh" is followed by "O alter Duft" (number 35) and "Heimfahrt" (36). These three poems, along with "Das Alphabet" (39), a poem that Schoenberg did not include, constitute a brief episode of nostalgia and longing in Giraud's collection. Eventually, the nostalgia subsides, and Pierrot returns to his old tricks of tormenting Cassander and interacting with the moon. Schoenberg took three of the nostalgia poems and put them at the beginning and end of Part III, which gives the entire section a context and a narrative goal: Pierrot is going home.

Composition

"Heimweh" was the fifteenth melodrama composed and was dated 5 May, the day after the composition of "Serenade." The short but significant transition was composed on 23 May. At an earlier date, Schoenberg sketched the introduction in the margin of his copy of the text.

The materials and techniques of "Heimweh" are closely related to "Die Kreuze," which was composed one week earlier. The piano writing resembles "Die Kreuze" (compare especially m. 5 of "Die Kreuze" with mm. 16–17 of "Heimweh"). Even the entrance of the Sprechstimme is similar: *Heilge Kreuze sind die Verse* is rhythmically similar to *Lieblich klagend ein krystallnes Seufzen* in Schoenberg's prosody. Finally, both "Die Kreuze" and "Heimweh" make dramatic use of harmonics to emphasize a change of texture between sections.

Musical Materials

As a first melodrama in a section, "Heimweh" is comparatively tranquil. "Mondestrunken," the first melodrama in Part I, and "Nacht," the first in Part II, both make use of repeating figures to build intensity. "Heimweh" does contain some repetitive elements, especially the repeating chords in the piano, but with the exception of m. 18, these repeating figures do not have the effect of building intensity. Rather, they fill passages with a sense of contented repose, not unlike the music of contemporary impressionist composers. Similarly, the chords and melodic figures, while still post-tonal, tend toward symmetrical groups of notes—whole-tone segments, chords in fourths, and extended triads. "Heimweh" groups the first two stanzas into a continuous first section. The third stanza begins a second section with sharp contrast, but quickly returns to the affect and materials of the opening.

The principal motive of "Heimweh" came to Schoenberg early, and he sketched it on his copy of the poem.[1] It consists of two adjacent notes and an intervening note that is approached and left by leaps. As stated by the violin in m. 1, shown in ex. 7-1, the motive consists of three notes from the whole-tone scale that can be arranged as the root, third, and seventh of a dominant seventh chord. The materials that frame the violin's statement are similarly composed of variants of that motive—the piano's figuration in the pick-up measures, the piano chords in mm. 2–5 (a modified inversion of the pickup), and the scalar passage in the clarinet.

As the work proceeds, the motive retains most of its features and is often found with one additional note at the end, which is typically lower than the intervening note; this pattern is established by the clarinet in mm. 1–2.

The rhythmic character of the motive suggests a lilting "Viennese rhythm," which some composers have used to suggest yearning. Here, it suggests Pierrot's yearning for his home. Similarly, Schoenberg's indication of many variations in the tempo (*abwechslungreicher Bewegung*), coupled with the many slight modifications (free, accelerando, lingering), suggests a flexible rhythmic movement of this melodrama. For example, the initial gesture, with high piano and the pizzicato violin, is static, frozen. It is the crystalline sigh of

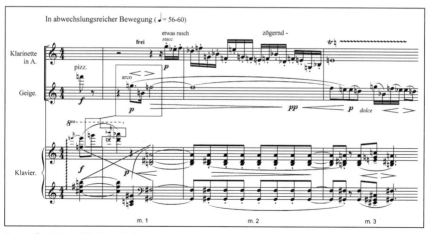

Example 7-1. "Heimweh," mm. 1–3.

the poem. That gesture immediately expands with the crescendo in the piano, and is contrasted by the yearning presentation in the violin. The clarinet combines elements of these two gestures. Each clarinet note is staccato, but the entire gesture changes from *somewhat fast* at the start to *lingering* at the end of m. 2. The accompanying piano also combines elements of the crystalline and the sigh with both a slur and staccato dots.

The opening suggests the opposition of two ideas—a rhythmic language that eagerly presses ahead, and one that reluctantly lingers. Even the details of the piano writing suggest opposition. In mm. 4–5, Schoenberg alternates between the "motive chord" and a contrasting chord. Furthermore, the voicing of these chords suggests an opposition; the alternate chord is a combination of two triads, a half-step apart, and in m. 5 the contrast of sharps and naturals informs the voicing of the two chords that conclude the piano's phrase.

The Sprechstimme enters in m. 4 with a compressed version of the motive against more literal statements in clarinet and violin. In mm. 6–7, the seven-note Pierrot figure, first suggested by the clarinet in m. 1 and the repetition of the piano chord in m. 2, dominates the texture. This figure is a temporary departure from the materials presented in the introduction. Measures 8–10, the final words of the first stanza, return to the materials from the beginning. As shown in ex. 7-2, the piano arpeggiates its chord from the pickup to m. 1. Elements of that chord are also found in the Sprechstimme— the prominent grace note in m. 7 using the same intervals as the piano grace note in m. 1, in the

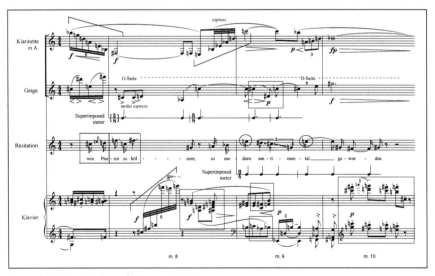

Example 7-2. "Heimweh," mm. 8–10.

clarinet's arpeggiation at the end of m. 8, and the piano chords in m. 10 with another minor-third skip to the grace note. Also in m. 8, the Sprechstimme sounds its most literal statement of the motive thus far, completing a process of expanding intervals from m. 4 to m. 6 to m. 8.

At the end of the first stanza, the intricacies of tempo fluctuation are composed into the cadence. As shown in ex. 7-2, the Sprechstimme has a brief, superimposed three-four meter and the violin has an offset superimposed three-eight meter. The return to the E-natural in the Sprechstimme marks the metrical accent of the superimposed meter, and most of the other pitches are overlapped in the violin (the G-natural is overlapped in the clarinet).

Measures 9–10 have a tapering shape that acts as a cadence. The second section also begins in m. 10, eliding the sense of closure. Despite the cadential articulation, the second section continues with the materials established in the introduction. Indeed, m. 10 sounds like the start of a modified repeat. After the high, icy chords in the piano, the violin sounds the longing motive with the same pitches heard in m. 1, one octave lower. As the piano continues to the motive chord in m. 11, the Sprechstimme and clarinet begin to develop the seven-note Pierrot figure, first introduced in mm. 6–7. The opposition of ideas that inform the introduction is found here as well. The seven-note figure, as it appears in "Heimweh," is largely chromatic. The principal motive, as discussed above, is a subset of the whole-tone scale. The Sprechstimme mediates these extremes. It begins with three notes, E-flat, G, and A, that complete the whole-tone scale begun in the violin. However, as the measure progresses, the Sprechstimme grows more chromatic. The highly chromatic chords of alternation in the piano part, mm. 3–4, are replaced in the modified reprise with chords that belong to opposing whole-tone sets in m. 11.

In short, the second section begins as a condensation of the introduction and the start of the first section. Similarly, the second verse of the second stanza causes the same kind of sudden change as the second verse of the first stanza. In the first section, m. 6, the second verse caused a dramatic tutti seven-note grouping. In the second section, m. 12, there is a dramatic *ritardando* where the piano, marked *espressivo*, returns to the seven-note grouping in a manner that resembles the beginning of "Mondestrunken." This *ritardando* is best subdivided for precision, and the composite gesture should have the Sprechstimme emerge from the complicated texture on the words *Sinne wieder*. Schoenberg text-paints these words by having the Sprechstimme suddenly rise to the highest notes since the entrance of the Sprechstimme in m. 4 just as the *a tempo* leads to the text refrain.

After a brief, impassioned transition, the third stanza begins as a new section. In m. 18, the clarinet arpeggiates the piano chord from m. 2.[2] As shown in ex. 7-3, the piano left hand provides a superimposed triple meter, which,

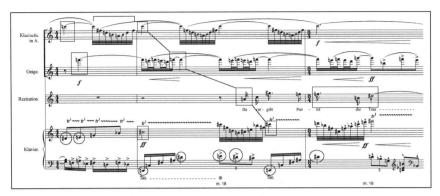

Example 7-3. "Heimweh," mm. 18–19.

like m. 9 in the Sprechstimme, uses the note E to define the important accents. Finally, the sustained notes in clarinet, violin, and piano—A, F, and C-sharp—sound an augmented triad, or whole-tone subset, that has been an important part of the motivic structure.

The last stanza presents a special challenge for the reciter in that it forms a part in a high and loud texture. Schoenberg prioritizes the line for the reciter by using the rhythm of the motive in a high register for the important accented syllables in mm. 19, 21, 22, and 24. The second verses of the first two stanzas occasioned a sudden change to a more vigorous treatment of the seven-note figure. In the third section, the situation is reversed: the third section begins with a vigorous treatment of the seven-note figure and the second verse of the poem occasions a change to the materials presented in the introduction. The clarinet reprises its descending treatment of the motive from m. 2, and in m. 21 the piano returns to the alternating chords from mm. 3–5.

The final text reprise, mm. 25–26, returns to the materials presented by the piano in the pickup to and downbeat of m. 1, shown in ex. 7-4. The piano emerges from the texture with a fragment of the chord it played at the beginning of the third section, m. 18, ringing as a harmonic chord, not unlike the harmonics used to begin the third sections of "Rote Messe" and "Der Kreuze."[3] That chord then reverts to the chord from the beginning of the melodrama, also found in the clarinet, while the violin plays the piano's melody from the beginning.

Without the warmth of the violin on the motive, it falls to the Sprechstimme to balance the iciness of the piano chords with the Viennese rhythm. For the plaintive final verse of the poem, the reciter may take a little extra time on the first syllables of *lieblich* and *klagen*; a bit of lingering on the consonants will particularly recall the beginning, and will nicely contrast the bright vowel on the *krystallnes*.

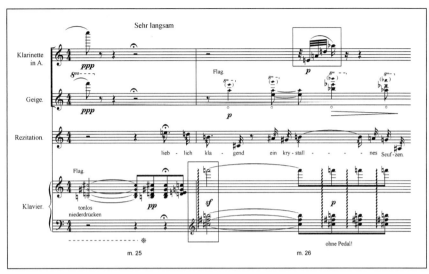

Example 7-4. "Heimweh," mm. 25–26.

NO. 16 GEMEINHEIT (MISCHIEVOUSNESS)

In den blanken Kopf Cassanders,	In the shining head of Cassander,
Dessen Schrein die Luft durchzetert,	Whose screams inundate the air,
Bohrt Pierrot mit Heuchlermienen,	Bores Pierrot with a hypocrite's airs,
Zärtlich—einen Schädelbohrer!	Tenderly—a skull-drill!
Darauf stopft er mit dem Daumen	Thereafter he plugs with his thumbs
Seinen echten turkschen Tabak	His genuine Turkish tobacco
In den blanken Kopf Cassanders,	In the shining head of Cassander,
Dessen Schrein die Luft durchzetert!	Whose screams inundate the air!
Dann dreht er ein Rohr von Weichsel	Then he screws a tube of cherry-wood
Hinten in die glatte Glatze	Behind the smooth bald head
Und behaglich schmaucht und pafft er	And contentedly smokes and puffs
Seinen echten turkschen Tabak	His genuine Turkish tobacco
Aus dem blanken Kopf Cassanders!	In the shining head of Cassander!

The Text

"Gemeinheit" is the forty-fifth poem in Giraud's collection. In addition to the minor change from *Maryland* tobacco to *Turkish* tobacco, Hartleben makes no mention of Pierrot's red lips puffing the tobacco (*A très rouges lèvres*), as found in Giraud's original.

Composition

"Gemeinheit" was the ninth melodrama begun. Most of "Gemeinheit" was composed 26 April, but it was left incomplete until 6 June. Like "Serenade," composed immediately before, "Gemeinheit" features the cello. (Moreover, both melodramas make inappropriate use of poor Cassander's head.) Finally, "Gemeinheit" follows "Columbine," "Rote Messe," and "Serenade" as the last of a series of melodramas in three-four meter written between 20 April and 26 April.

Musical Materials

"Gemeinheit" is a minuet. As a young man, Schoenberg would have read in *Meyers Konversationslexikon* that the minuet "moves in a moderately fast triple meter and has two reprises."[4] Many years after the composition of *Pierrot*, Schoenberg would write that the "only specific rhythmic feature of a minuet is the meter, 3/4 (or, rarely, 3/8). Striking rhythms, like those in scherzos or more modern dances, are seldom found."[5]

"Gemeinheit" is organized as a two-reprise minuet without repeats, which Schoenberg might have graphically represented as || A || B A′ ||.[6] The first section, mm. 1–7, aligns with the first stanza. It presents a five-bar minuet theme in the cello accompanied by the violin and piano emphasizing beats two and three—the *pahs* of an *ohm-pah-pah* accompaniment. The metrical regularity of the accompaniment is contrasted by the Sprechstimme, which enters in a superimposed four-four meter, shown in ex. 7-5. If the Sprechstimme is heard in four, and followed through to the end of the section, the morbid humor of *Schädelbohrer* is increased because it begins on a downbeat of the superimposed common time. As ex. 7-5 also shows, the cello has a hemiola at the end of its phrase that aligns three measures of two-four with the superimposed meter of the Sprechstimme.

The first section ends with a cadential extension that further comments on the darkly comedic effect of the *Schädelbohrer*. The second, contrasting section begins in m. 9 marked *Etwas langsamer*. As is typical of the minuet, the second reprise begins with a short developmental section followed by a reprise—the B and A′ of Schoenberg's schematic. A development of the cello's motive begins in the winds. The piano adds further elaboration of the motive and continues the accompaniment.

The reprise, marked *Tempo I*, is one of the most literal reprises in *Pierrot*. At the start of an eighteenth-century minuet, the theme begins in the tonic

Example 7-5. "Gemeinheit," mm. 1–5.

and typically cadences in the dominant (or relative major). In the reprise of an eighteenth-century minuet, the last third is reworked so that the modulation is thwarted and the minuet can cadence in the tonic (thus, a fourth higher than the first cadence). In "Gemeinheit," Schoenberg playfully alludes to the practice of reworking the theme in the reprise. In m. 16, the violin begins the reprise with the same notes the cello had in m. 1. However, as shown in ex. 7-6, at the end of m. 17, the theme suddenly shifts a tritone higher as if to avoid modulation. Schoenberg continues his feint of tonal relationships in mm. 20 and 21 with C major and G major triads in the piano, voiced like a nineteenth-century piano reduction of an orchestral work.

Like the presentation of the melody at the beginning, the reprise is also counterpointed with a line that superimposes common time, shown in ex. 7-7. Beginning in m. 16, the cello has a descending line marked *Hauptstimme* that can be heard as beginning on beat two of a four-four meter. Hearing it thus

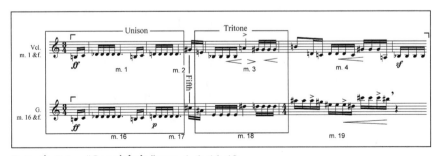

Example 7-6. "Gemeinheit," mm. 1–4; 16–19.

Example 7-7. "Gemeinheit," mm. 16–19.

would put the dramatic pizzicato in m. 19—where Pierrot inserts the tube into Cassander's head—on a downbeat.

Many common features of the eighteenth-century minuet are incorporated into "Gemeinheit." These features ultimately serve a dual role: they text-paint the poem and they comment on the form. The text-painting is easily observed, but the commentary on the form is especially noteworthy. As noted in chapter 4, Giraud cast the poems in a poetic form that was old and out of fashion. In this third part of *Pierrot lunaire*, where the poems speak of a return to Pierrot's homeland and his native ways, Schoenberg matches the rondel form and indeed Pierrot's mischievousness—also a throwback to his native ways, the Commedia—with a Haydnesque minuet.

NO. 17 PARODIE

Stricknadeln, blank und blinkend,   Knitting needles, bright and brilliant,
In ihrem grauen Haar,   In her graying hair,
Sitzt die Duenna murmelnd,   Sits the duenna muttering,
Im roten Röckchen da.   In a red frock.

Sie wartet in der Laube,   She waits in a bower,
Sie liebt Pierrot mit Schmerzen,   She loves Pierrot with heartache,

| Stricknadeln, blank und blinkend, | Knitting needles, bright and brilliant, |
| In ihrem grauen Haar. | In her graying hair. |

Da plötzlich—horch!—ein Wispern!	Then suddenly—listen!—a whisper!
Ein Windhauch kichert leise:	A breeze snickers lightly:
Der mond, der böse Spötter,	The moon, the evil mimic,
Äfft nach mit seinen Strahlen—	Imitates with its beams—
Stricknadeln, blink und blank.	Knitting needles, brilliant and bright.

The Text

"Parodie" is the forty-second poem in Giraud's collection. Hartleben reverses the two words at the end of the last stanza, which allows for a more definite cadence at the end of the poem. Also, in Hartleben's translation, the moon is a more active participant. In Giraud's original poem, the duenna mistakes the wind for a whisper and the moon's beams *seem to resemble* (*ses rais semblent imiter*) knitting needles. In the translation, the anthropomorphic moon laughs and deliberately imitates the duenna.

"Parodie" is an interesting complement to "Eine blasse Wäscherin." Both are placed near the center of their sections and consist of character studies of the moon. However, in "Eine blasse Wäscherin," the moon was an old washer woman, whereas here the moon is a youthful spirit that antagonizes an unidentified character. "Parodie" also complements "Der Mondfleck," the melodrama that follows, in that both present the moon as an antagonist in the center of Part III. The other poems included in Part III suggest a more neutral and less anthropomorphic moon.

Composition

"Parodie" was the eleventh melodrama composed and was dated 4 May, eight days after beginning "Die Kreuze." Schoenberg's copy of the text contains a pencil annotation at the start of the third stanza that reads "viola low, clarinet high," although ultimately he used the flute in the upper register while the clarinet imitates the voice.

Musical Materials

"Parodie" is one of the two contrapuntal works that dominate the middle of Part III; the other, "Der Mondfleck," immediately follows. "Parodie" proceeds as a set of accompanied canons. The first two stanzas are grouped as a section, mm. 1–21, that end with a reprise of the opening for the text reprise.

The second section begins with contrasting material that matches the sudden change in the poem, but ultimately ends with the material from the beginning. Jonathan Dunsby has rightly noted a relationship between the act of knitting fabric and the contrapuntal weaving of musical texture.[7] Moreover, the use of canon-by-inversion would also suggest the texture of knitted fabric, in which one side is more conventionally presentational and the other side, while inversely proportional, is rarely seen.

The first canonic entrances begin with the viola presenting a two-bar incipit (with a pickup), shown in ex. 7-8. The incipit has several characteristic features. Rhythmically, it has the smallest durations in the center, which creates the sense of accelerando and *ritardando*. The rhythmic scheme is also accentuated by the disposition of the intervals. In general, the incipit begins with the smallest intervals and progresses to the major third (A-flat to F-flat) before suddenly widening to a minor ninth, which frames the span of the incipit. It begins with a half-step and ends with a half-step (the minor ninth as an octave-displaced minor second). Between these half-steps, the other notes in m. 1, which affect the rhythmic acceleration, compose five of the six notes of the whole-tone scale. The articulations contribute to a sense that the whole-tone scale notes, which participate in the accelerating rhythm, are distinct from the chromatic notes. The slur and double-sharp at the beginning suggest a slide to the next note. The whole-tone notes that follow are slurred, but suddenly interrupted by the short, accented leap between the final two notes, in m. 3.

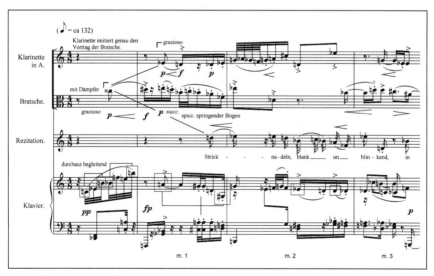

Example 7-8. "Parodie," mm. 1–3.

The incipit is imitated with entrances that follow at two beats and four beats. At two beats, the clarinet enters in inversion. The Sprechstimme enters at four beats in canon at the unison with some slight variations in rhythm. Schoenberg's direction to the pianist, *durchaus begleitend*, makes clear that the piano accompanies. However, it also varies material from the canon. In particular, the minor ninth leap on *blinkend* is imitated in the piano's pickup and first two measures. Moreover, the piano's seven-note figure in m. 1 is reprised with each text reprise (mm. 16 and 27).

The canon-by-inversion begins by matching the viola's D with the clarinet's C. This particular inversion will map two notes onto themselves: G maps onto G and C-sharp maps onto C-sharp, as shown in ex. 7-9. As Stephan Weytjens and Mark Delaere have noted, Schoenberg capitalizes on this relationship by ending the first canon on the note G in the viola (m. 9), which is then answered by the G in the clarinet in m. 10.[8] In m. 10, the Sprechstimme cadences on G, the same note on which the piccolo entered earlier in the bar. Similarly, the second set of entrances ends with the Sprechstimme on C-sharp in m. 14, which is then followed by the C-sharp in the clarinet. The C-sharp is also in the piano. A final cadence of agreement occurs in m. 26, where the viola and flute end on a G before the final rush of notes.

In m. 11, a second set of contrapuntal entrances begins with the Sprechstimme imitated at the unison by the viola and in inversion by the clarinet. The first note is missing in the Sprechstimme but is found in the viola and clarinet. The temporal intervals are the same. This short canon emphasizes the head of the incipit. The melismas on *liebt, Pierrot,* and *Schmerzen* in mm. 12–13 are uncharacteristic and gently mock the duenna's love in much the same way Mozart makes light of Fiordiligi and Dorabella in *Ah guarda sorella* from *Così fan tutte.* The first section ends with the text reprise, which returns to the incipit from the beginning, pairing the Sprechstimme with the piccolo, imitating at the octave. Like the beginning, the clarinet imitates the viola in inversion.

A second, contrasting section begins in m. 22 with the third stanza of the poem. As a depiction of the moon mocking the duenna as a gust of wind, Schoenberg emphasizes the seven-note Pierrot figure, especially in the form heard in the piano as a pickup to m. 1. The viola and flute enter in inverted canon with a new incipit, based on the seven-note figure. The Sprechstimme

Example 7-9. The C-D axial symmetry.

and clarinet proceed as a canon at the octave. As seen in ex. 7-10, the accompaniment in the piano is largely constructed from the materials presented in the first two measures.

As Dunsby has noted, Hartleben's reversal of *blank* and *blinkend* in the final verse of the poem, whereby *blinkend* is shortened to *blink*, loses something in translation.[9] It is also worth noting that Hartleben's sound poetry is intensified in Schoenberg's setting. As ex. 7-11 shows, the abbreviated text reprise is a reduction of the first (and second) setting of the refrain. By omitting the last D-natural, Schoenberg parallels not only the shortness of the final verse of the poem, but also the sense of a sudden stop; which is further paralleled by the melodrama ending abruptly on the last thirty-second note of m. 30. Moreover, he reverses the final leap in the Sprechstimme from a descending ninth to an ascending and interrogatory seventh. The final ascending leap is further intensified because the last three measures constitute one final set of imitative entries, and the piccolo has preceded the entrance of the Sprechstimme by two

Example 7-10. "Parodie," mm. 22–24 and mm. 1–2.

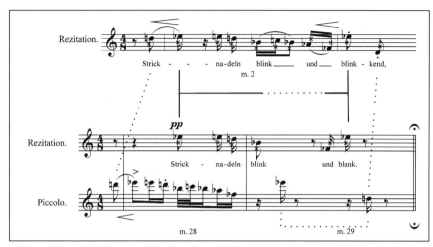

Example 7-11. **"Parodie," Sprechstimme, mm. 1–2; Sprechstimme and piccolo, mm. 27–28.**

beats. Through a judicious insertion of rests in the piccolo part, Schoenberg interlocks the piccolo's descending ninth with the Sprechstimme's ascending seventh. As a result, the final leap from F-flat$_4$ to E-flat$_5$ in the Sprechstimme is immediately followed by a D-natural$_6$ in the piccolo: the actual notes of the descending leap are inverted in this last musical parallel on the reversal of *blank* and *blinkend*.

NO. 18 DER MONDFLECK (THE MOON SPOT)

Einen weissen Fleck des hellen
  Mondes
Auf dem Rücken seines schwarzen
  Rockes,
So spaziert Pierrot im lauen
  Abend,
Aufzusuchen Glück und
  Abenteuer.

Plötzlich stört ihn was an
  seinem Anzug,
Er beschaut sich rings und findet
  richtig—

One white spot of the bright
  moon
On the back of his coat,

As Pierrot strolled in the temperate
  evening,
Searching for good fortune and
  adventure.

Suddenly disturbed by what is on
  his suit,
He inspects himself and finds
  immediately—

| Einen weissen Fleck des hellen Mondes | One white spot of the bright moon |
| Auf dem Rücken seines schwarzen Rockes. | On the back of his coat. |

Warte! Denkt er: das ist so ein Gipsfleck!	Wait! He thinks: it is only a plaster smudge!
Wischt und wischt, doch—bringt ihn nicht herunter!	Wipes and wipes, however—he cannot brush off!
Und so geht er, giftgeschwollen, weiter,	And so he goes further, filled with venom
Reibt und reibt bis an den frühen Morgen—	Rubbing and rubbing until the early morning—
Einen weissen Fleck des hellen Mondes.	One white spot of the bright moon.

The Text

"Der Mondfleck" is the thirty-eighth poem in Giraud's collection. In the third verse, Giraud calls Pierrot *Pierrot-Willette*, a reference to Adophe Willette (1857–1926), the Parisian caricaturist who undoubtedly influenced Giraud.[10] Hartleben omits this reference. Hartleben's translation is dedicated to Ferdinand Pohl (1862–1949), composer and music critic for the *Leipziger Tageblatt*.

Composition

"Der Mondfleck" was the twentieth melodrama composed, completed in its entirety on 28 May.

Musical Materials

"Der Mondfleck" is a marvel of contrapuntal invention, consisting of two fugues and a canon running simultaneously and grouped in score order by instrumental family (winds, strings, and piano). The first fugue is a two-voice fugue between the clarinet and piccolo. The second fugue is a three-voice fugue in the piano. The canon is a canon at the octave between the violin as leader and cello as follower. The two highest layers, the clarinet/piccolo fugue and the violin/viola canon, are palindromic. At the end of the sixth verse, where Hartleben has placed a hyphen before the second text refrain, Pierrot finds a white spot on the back of his coat. At that moment, in the middle of m. 10, both the wind fugue and string canon present all the material up to that point in retrograde. The fugue in the piano and the Sprech-stimme continue.

Schoenberg's use of fugue in "Der Mondfleck" is curious but inspired. Already by the end of the eighteenth century, conspicuous counterpoint sug-gested formality and learning as the fugue became increasingly isolated from its tradition and frozen in a set of procedures. Through the end of the nineteenth century, the fugue remained a compositional choice for traditional compos-ers such as Schumann and Brahms, but some progressive composers used the fugue to invoke the unpleasant connotations of academic music. Berlioz used a fugue to mock German contrapuntal sensibilities in *La damnation de Faust*. Wagner used fugato textures in *Die Meistersinger von Nürnberg* to character-ize the pedantic Beckmesser—a character that represents nineteenth-century music critics. Richard Strauss used a meandering fugue to represent science in *Also sprach Zarathustra*.

Unlike Wagner and Strauss, Schoenberg embraced the fugue both as a pedagogical tool and as an early precedent of the highly contrapuntal textures he cultivated in his own music. As a young man, Schoenberg would have read the article on the fugue in *Meyers Konversationslexicon*, which concluded:

> The fugue is essentially the meeting place [*Tummelplatz*] of all the contra-puntal arts, such that the simultaneous continuation of the subject and its counterpoint depends on the application of double counterpoint at the octave or twelfth and is amenable to canonic developments of all kinds up to the crab canon.[11]

The German word *Tummelplatz* refers to a meeting place for radicals and anarchists. Thus, this definition of fugue, which includes the potential for for-ward-thinking possibilities, is more suited to Schoenberg. "Der Mondfleck" embraces the potential of the fugue to integrate multiple contrapuntal proce-dures, as suggested by the *Meyers* definition, and puts these procedures in the service of dramatizing the poem.

The fugues in "Der Mondfleck" consist of expositions followed by epi-sodes and middle entries. As ex. 7-12 shows, the fugue between piccolo and clarinet begins with a subject that lasts for five beats. The subject consists of a head and a long tail with a defining rhythm that stands apart from the rhythms in the Sprechstimme and canon in the strings. The subject is presented in a stretto exposition, in which the answer (here in the piccolo) begins before the subject (in the clarinet) is complete.[12] Stretto expositions are unusual—the most famous example is probably the chorus *Gratias agimus tibi* from the *Gloria* in Bach's B Minor Mass—but a stretto exposition is precisely the sort of com-bination of fugue and canonic development that is suggested in the Meyers definition.

The overlapping answer in the piccolo is a fifth higher. The fifth is an important transposition relationship in tonal music, but has no particular importance in post-tonal music. Schoenberg answers the subject at the fifth in accordance with the traditional procedure. However, the answer at the fifth reveals a harmonic relationship between the head of the subject and answer. The head pairs two tritones with a final leap of a major seventh. Interestingly, the head contains four notes of the C-natural transposition of the whole-tone scale and one note from the C-sharp transposition of the whole-tone scale. The answer, a fifth higher, inverts this disposition (four notes from the C-sharp transposition; one note from the C-natural transposition). A comparison of the head for the subject and answer reveals that in each case, the note that is not part of the whole-tone scale is contained in the paired statement. This relationship is even clearer in the piano fugue, discussed below.

A series of short episodes and stretto middle entries follow the exposition. The middle entry in mm. 4–5 reverses the clarinet and piccolo and thus presents the subject and answer together as invertible counterpoint. The inverted pairing of subject and answer is a typical occurrence in the first middle entry of a fugue by Bach. The m. 4 reprise of the subject and answer is so literal and so early that one may call it a counterexposition, another eighteenth-century fugal device.

Example 7-12. "Der Mondfleck," mm. 1–3.

The middle entries shorten the temporal interval between the voices in the stretto, as shown in ex. 7-13.[13] In the exposition, there are two beats between the subject and answer. In m. 8, the entrances are separated only by one beat. In m. 9, incomplete entries—yet another fugue procedure—are separated by a mere eighth note. Shortening the distance between entries is a common device to intensify a fugue at the climax.

The three-voice fugue in the piano uses the same subject in 2:1 augmentation, with one exception: the sixteenth-note triplet in the head is transformed to sixteenth notes with the addition of a sixteenth rest. This small change makes the rhythms in the piano fugue more homogeneous than the

Example 7-13. "Der Mondfleck," detail, mm. 8–12.

rhythms in the clarinet/piccolo fugue. The lines in the piano fugue are frequently thickened with chords. In the exposition, the head is presented with parallel augmented triads. The augmented triads make the relationship between the whole-tone collections clear in that the last augmented triad of the head is the first augmented triad of the answer (inverted).

The fugue in the piano is less sectional and more developmental than the fugue in the winds. The entrance of the third voice, m. 3, alters the subject and leaves it incomplete. Some of the middle entries are almost exact, such as the middle-voice entry that begins in m. 8, but many of the middle entries are incomplete entries consisting of the parts of the head in stretto, as in mm. 9–11. The close stretto entries in mm. 9–11 mirror the close stretto entries in the clarinet/piccolo fugue at the same spot—approaching and leaving the axis of retrograde in the middle of m. 10.

The relationship of the piano fugue to the piccolo/clarinet fugue also reflects the generally accepted techniques catalogued in textbooks. For example, the fugues in "Der Mondfleck" combine like a double fugue in which one subject is in longer rhythmic durations than the other, a technique found, for example, in several of the *Contrapuncti* of Bach's *The Art of the Fugue*. Finally, the fact that the first fugue is reversed after m. 10 while the second fugue continues is loosely related to the *cancrizans* or crab canons from the *Musical Offering*. Schoenberg is clearly combining technical elements from a literature he knows well.

Unlike "Parodie," in which the Sprechstimme participates in the contrapuntal design, the Sprechstimme in "Der Mondfleck" is a contrapuntally independent element. As such, it presents a challenge for the reciter who must struggle to be heard in a comparatively low register in a consistently busy texture. However, the Sprechstimme begins a motive for *Einen weißen Fleck* that is based on the head of the subject and immediately varied for *des hellen Mondes*. This motive, like the head of the subject, is anticipated by the transition music at the end of "Parodie," mm. 31–32. The Sprechstimme then continues as free variation in short bursts of small durations.

The Sprechstimme also clarifies the role of the palindrome. In most of the poems, the first two stanzas form a sustained idea while the third stanza provides further commentary or a new direction. In "Der Mondfleck," the contrasting section—the retrograde of the first section—actually begins at the end of the second stanza when Pierrot realizes that he has the spot of moonlight on his coat; the reprise of the opening verses elides the textual cadence and begins the new idea. It is precisely at this moment, the reprise of the text in m. 10, that the canon and fugue in the winds suddenly reverse direction. Thus, just as the poem creates a new context for the same words, the contrapuntal devices create a new context for the same notes and rhythms.

NO. 19 SERENADE

Mit groteskem Riesenbogen	With a grotesque giant bow
Kratzt Pierrot auf seiner Bratsche,	Scrapes Pierrot on his viola,
Wie der Storch auf einem Beine,	Like a stork on one leg,
Knipst er trüb ein Pizzicato.	He snaps forlornly a pizzicato.
Plötzlich naht Cassander—wütend	Suddenly comes Cassander—furious
Ob des nächtigen Virtuosen—	About the nighttime virtuoso—
Mit groteskem Riesenbogen	With a grotesque giant bow
Kratzt Pierrot auf seiner Bratsche.	Scrapes Pierrot on his viola.
Von sich wirft er jetzt die Bratsche:	Hence he tosses presently the viola:
Mit der delikaten Linken	With a delicate left hand
Fasst er den Kahlkopf am Kragen—	He seizes the baldy by the collar—
Träumend spielt er auf der Glatze	Dreamily he plays on the shiny dome
Mit groteskem Riesenbogen.	With a grotesque giant bow.

The Text

"Serenade" is the sixth poem in Giraud's collection. Hartleben's translation, which is dedicated to the painter Paul Höniger (1865–1924),[14] makes a number of changes to the imagery. Giraud describes Pierrot as a *heron* and *acrobat*. Hartleben changes the imagery to *stork* and *virtuoso*. In a more dramatic change, Giraud describes Pierrot bowing Cassander's head as "putting zebra stripes on his head" (*Zèbra le bedon du gênant*). Hartleben discards this image entirely.

Like "Valse de Chopin," "Serenade" makes reference to musical imagery. However, whereas "Valse" uses the instrument that is implied, the piano, "Serenade" does not use viola but rather the cello. Visually, the cello bears a certain resemblance to a stork on one leg, since it rests on a pin. However, Allen Shawn has suggested that the use of a cello for a viola may have occurred to Schoenberg because when he was learning to play cello, he couldn't afford a decent instrument and fitted a viola with zither strings to serve as a cello.[15]

Composition

The eighth in order of composition, "Serenade" was composed on 25 April. The transition was added later. In "Serenade" Schoenberg used all five players for only the second time. He first used all five players for "Rote Messe," composed three days earlier but used the players with the substitute instruments (piccolo, bass clarinet, and viola). In "Serenade," he used all five standard instruments for the first time.

Musical Materials

"Serenade" is essentially a *concertante* work for cello with piano and Sprechstimme. The flute, clarinet, and violin enter only for a coda after the Sprechstimme ends. It begins with the longest introduction to any melodrama, including the most measures of instrumental music (although the instrumental reprise of "Der kranke Mond" after "Enthauptung" has a longer performance time). The sense of a slow Viennese waltz is communicated by observing the metrical accents. In the introduction, mm. 1–15, there is an attack on every quarter note, with the exception of m. 13, where the attack on the third beat is on the second eighth note. Moreover, the first beat in each measure is accented by traditional meter-affirming gestures, such as beginning with a low note (as in mm. 2, 4, 8, 10, 12, and 16); having a first beat anticipated by shorter durations at the end of the previous measure (as in mm. 3, 7, 8, and 12); or by use of an accented note that "resolves" down like an appoggiatura (as in the cello in m. 5 and in the piano, mm. 6, 8–9, and 14–15; see ex. 7-17, below). Naturally, the players must observe the sense of the meter, but a score note indicates that players should have a free presentation. A discrete use of rubato, especially in places marked with hairpins, would be appropriate both to the score direction and the Viennese waltz character.

The dreamy quality of the introduction and the melodrama that follows owes much to the use of whole-tone collections and the way those collections are framed by more chromatic collections or by a balance of both transpositions of the whole-tone scale. For example, the cello, mm. 1–3, presents the principal motive of the introduction. Four notes (B-flat, D, E, and G-sharp) from the whole-tone scale that begins on C-natural enclose three notes (A, E-flat, and G) from the whole-tone collection that begins on C-sharp. The symmetrical nature of these sets is such that any three notes from the group of four can be shown to be a transposition and/or an inversion of the group of three. As ex. 7-14 shows, the piano also balances the two transpositions of the whole-tone scale, both in the initial arpeggio and in the short lyrical figure in mm. 2–3, the upper notes of which are the same pitches as the three-note excluded subset in the cello, while the lower notes are members of the C-natural whole-tone scale, like the other notes of the cello.

The metrically accented first and last notes of the first phrase in the cello, B-flat to G-sharp in mm. 1–3, form a descending (enharmonic) second. The use of a second as an appoggiatura-like cadential gesture preceded by a turn is featured prominently in the introduction. After the appoggiatura gesture is

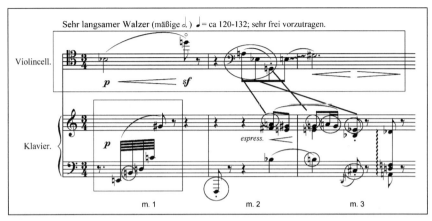

Example 7-14. **"Serenade," mm. 1–3.**

modeled in mm. 4–5, it is imitated and sequenced. Taken together, these references to Baroque ornamentation suggest an exaggerated playing style, as if Pierrot thinks quite highly of his playing.

With the entrance of the Sprechstimme, the form proper begins. (The entrance of the Sprechstimme is shown in chapter 3, ex. 3-1.) "Serenade" is presented in three sections that follow the stanzas with one exception: the third section actually begins with the second verse of the third stanza. As is typical, the sections of this song form are threaded by continuous variation, especially in the cello.

The motive forms found in the Sprechstimme emerge from the material first presented by the cello in the introduction. The initial entrance in mm. 16–18 is composed largely of the whole-tone scale on C. Against the Sprechstimme, the cello continues with the highly ornamented music from the introduction, ultimately culminating in the cadenza passage in m. 25.

The second section begins suddenly in m. 26. While marked *a tempo*, the aggressive presentation of the seven-note Pierrot figure in the cello, marked *brilliant*, tends to make the tempo brighter. Moreover, the cello and the piano superimpose two-four meter over the written three-four, which adds to the sense of an increased pace. The second section rises dramatically to the plateau maintained in mm. 30–34. There, for the text refrain, Schoenberg returns to elements from the introduction. The arpeggio in the piano recalls the introductory gesture in the piano to some degree, especially against the held note in the cello, but more striking is the arrangement of pitch elements on the downbeat of m. 30, shown in ex. 7-15, which resembles the symmetrical arrangement of whole-tone collections from m. 1. The Sprechstimme contributes to this pattern, in that each accented syllable is anticipated by notes from the same whole-tone scale. The Sprechstimme also presents a slight variant of the melody given for the same text in m. 16.

The final section begins with a false repeat, shown in ex. 7-16. In m. 35, the cello launches into a slight variant of the Pierrot figure with the same bracing presentation used to begin the second section. However, after only a measure, it suddenly pauses on a low trill. This false repeat is a Haydnesque joke, but it is also programmatic. The rushing notes of the cello happen as the Sprechstimme narrates Pierrot throwing his viola, and the fermata over the low trilling D creates a comic moment of deliberation while we contemplate what Pierrot will do next. Finally, this short passage serves to reprise and draw together many elements of the structure. The trill recalls the florid ornamentation of the introduction, which returns in the cello part for the third section. Moreover, the glissando into m. 37 recalls the glissando in m. 1; both use D as a boundary of a large range and both arrive with a "strangled" timbral effect—the harmonic in m. 1 and the G-sharp over an octave and a fifth above the open C string in m. 37. Finally, by delaying the true start of the section until the second verse of text, Schoenberg commences the third section with *Mit der delikaten Linken*, which begins like and has the same number of syllables as the text refrain, *Mit groteskem Riesenbogen*. Schoenberg capitalizes on the similarity by beginning the Sprechstimme with the same descent from G-sharp found in the text refrain.

The final section reprises and develops many elements from the first section, including the arpeggiation figures in the piano and the appoggiatura figures in the cello. The final text refrain begins, as shown in ex. 7-17, with

Example 7-15. "Serenade," mm. 30–31.

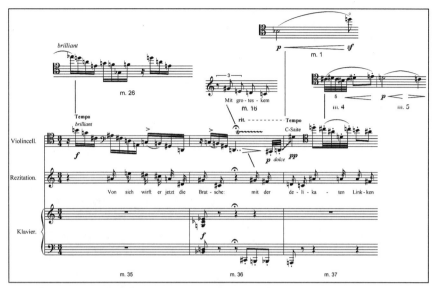

Example 7-16. "Serenade," mm. 1, 4–5, 16, 26, and 35–37.

a descent from G-sharp. However, the triplet rhythms have been augmented 3:1 to fit the entire measure; the quarter note and eighth note of the triplets found in mm. 30–31 (ultimately derived from the eighth-note triplets in m. 16) are expanded to a half note and a quarter note. With this augmentation and the repeat of the note F-sharp, the final text refrain recalls the appoggiatura rhythms in the cello from the introduction, which are offset by the similar accompaniment in the piano, now metrically askew.

In the short codetta beginning m. 46, the entering winds and violin add primarily chromatic elements. However, the last gestures of the piano and cello return to the counterpoised whole-tone sets at the beginning. As ex. 7-18 shows, each of these gestures has a small subset of adjacent notes that belong to the other transposition of the whole-tone scale. Note that the excluded subset in the piano, A, G, and E-flat in mm. 47–48, is also the excluded subset in the cello in m. 2 (ex. 7-14, above).

"Serenade" resembles "Gemeinheit" in many respects: both Part III melodramas make reference to traditional forms and genres, both feature the cello, and both poems speak of a clowning Pierrot having fun at the expense of Cassander. But the humorous aspects of "Serenade" are offset by lyrical passages. "Serenade" doesn't leave the same overall impression as "Gemeinheit" or "Raub." Rather, Schoenberg's setting suggests a more melancholy humor. In the larger context of Part III, "Serenade" also advances the characterization of Pierrot as homesick and prepares the way for his eventual return.

Example 7-17. **"Serenade," mm. 43–45.**

NO. 20 HEIMFAHRT (THE JOURNEY HOME)

Der Mondstrahl ist das Ruder,
Seerose dient als Boot,
Drauf fährt Pierrot gen Süden
Mit gutem Reisewind.

Der Strom summt tiefe Skalen
Und wiegt den leichten Kahn.
Der Mondstrahl ist das Ruder,
Seerose dient als Boot.

The moonbeam is the rudder,
Water-lily serves as boat,
Which carries Pierrot to the South
With good sailing wind.

The stream hums low scales
And rocks the light skiff.
The moonbeam is the rudder,
Water-lily serves as boat.

Nach Bergamo, zur Heimat,	Towards Bergamo, back home,
Kehrt nun Pierrot zurück,	Returns now Pierrot hence,
Schwach dämmert schon im Osten	Faintly dawns, already in the East
Der grüne Horizont.	The green horizon.
—Der Mondstrahl ist das Ruder.	—The moonbeam is the rudder.

The Text

"Heimfahrt" is the thirty-sixth poem in Giraud's collection. Hartleben simpli-fies Giraud's imagery, particularly in the third stanza. Giraud gives us a fanciful description of Pierrot as a "snowy king of mime" who "proudly combs his hair" (*Le neigeux roi du mimodrame* / *Redresse fièrement sa houppe*). While Hartle-ben retains the image of the green horizon, he omits Giraud's comparison to "flaming punch in a bowl" (*Comme du punch dans une coupe,* / *Le vague horizon vert s'enflamme*).

The imagery in "Heimfahrt," as presented in the German translation, strongly recalls the imagery in the first section of *Pierrot*. "Mondestrunken" presents the power of the moon as fluid and overflowing a still horizon. "Eine blasse Wäscherin" also has the moon as flowing and—not unlike an oar—lightly stirring a stream (*Leis bewegen sie den Strom*). Furthermore, "Der Dandy" presents Pierrot wielding the moonbeam, not as a rudder but as a make-up brush. "Der Dandy" also contains the only other references to Bergamo and the *green* of the East (or Orient), as found in "Heimfahrt." Thus, considering Schoenberg's origi-nal plan for twenty melodramas, "Heimfahrt" would have made a fine conclu-

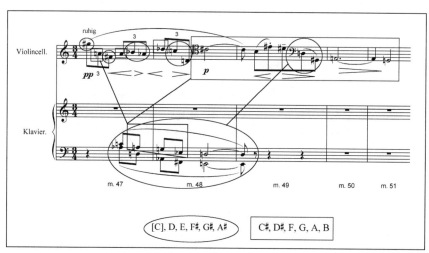

Example 7-18. "Serenade," mm. 47–51.

sion. As it stands, the summarizing and conclusive nature of "Heimfahrt" creates the impression that "O alter Duft" is an epilogue, even though "O alter Duft" immediately precedes "Heimfahrt" in Giraud's original ordering.

Hartleben dedicated his translation of this poem to Paul Scheerbart. Scheerbart was a poet and the cofounder of Verlag deutscher Phantasten, the small press that published the first edition of Hartleben's translation.

Composition

"Heimfahrt" was composed on 9 May, along with "Nacht," "Madonna," and "Raub."

Musical Materials

"Heimfahrt" is a barcarolle, meant to suggest the songs of Venetian *gondolieri*. Typically, barcarolles are in six-eight time and feature a texture that suggests the lapping of the waves. Here, the waves are suggested by the arpeggiation that begins in the pizzicato strings. The barcarole figuration makes "Heimfahrt" strongly metrical. The occasional syncopated superimposition of three-four meter, for example in mm. 10, 25, and 29, does little to disturb the metrical groupings of six-eight.

The repetition of the barcarolle figuration is more than just a stylistic feature of "Heimfahrt": it generates all the principal motivic material. While it begins with an ostinato, not unlike "Mondestrunken" or "Rote Messe," the barcarole figuration in "Heimfahrt" is immediately varied by an additive process in the piano left hand that builds a faster version of the figuration, as shown in ex. 7-19. Once complete, the faster version, in thirty-second notes, is used more frequently and with more variation. The original sixteenth-note version returns for closure at the end of the second and third sections.

The maintenance and development of the barcarolle figuration and its variants is largely found in the strings and piano. Above the figuration, the first two sections of "Heimfahrt" proceed as a concertina for winds. The flute and the clarinet alternate passages marked with the *Hauptstimme* brackets, with occasional counterpoint in the strings. Grace notes and notated turns, like the clarinet's turn at the end of m. 5, adorn the flute and the clarinet parts and add a certain sense of elegance, appropriate to the eighteenth-century origins of the barcarolle. Moreover, the concertina presentation of the winds complements the extended solo of the cello in "Serenade," which is emphasized by the solo of the cello in m. 8.

The principal motive developed in the winds, and later in the Sprechstimme, is actually derived from the highest notes of the barcarolle figuration, as shown in ex. 7-19. The entrance of the clarinet in m. 3 presents the motive composed-out as a melody. A statement of the motive begins the melody and is nested among the sustained notes in retrograde inversion. Another inversion is found in the piano, nearly synchronized with the entrance of the clarinet.

The melodrama proceeds in three sections that align with the three stanzas. Text-painting is an important part of the presentation. For the first section, the first words, *Der Mondstrahl*, are met with the entrance of the flute representing the moon with a soloistic flourish. Before the conclusion of that flourish, the word *Ruder* is met with the accelerated barcarolle figuration, which suggests the water

Example 7-19. "Heimfahrt," mm. 3–7.

lapping against the rudder. The image of Pierrot riding a water-lily boat is declaimed over a return of the barcarolle figuration in the piano, mm. 8–9, and the cello in m. 11. Over the entire first section, passages marked *Hauptstimme* develop aspects of the introductory melody in the clarinet. The flute's flourish, mm. 6–7, also shown in ex. 7-19, is a reflection of the leaps in the clarinet, mm. 3–4. The repetition of the G-sharp in the clarinet, mm. 3–4, is also found in the internal repetition of the flute, m. 7, and the cello, m. 8. Finally, all the solo instruments conclude with a melodic cadence that resembles an appoggiatura. With the word *Boot*, the clarinet plays a much altered reprise of the music from m. 3 and then imitates the cello's music from m. 8, as shown in ex. 7-20. At the close of the first section, the Sprechstimme is rhythmically aligned with the cello and piano in m. 10. The combination of Sprechstimme and cello is especially effective here as both descend to text-paint the notion of traveling south. When the cello reaches its lowest note, it begins a variation of the barcarolle figuration, while the flutter-tongue of the flute is paired with high trills in the piano to suggest the *good sailing wind* at the end of the stanza, m. 11.

The second section begins with the imagery of the stream humming low scales. The faster barcarolle figuration, first heard in m. 7, returns with scalar motion that is appropriate for the text. Unlike the first section, the second section does not divide the ensemble into concertino instruments with accompaniment. Rather, the clarinet, violin, and cello are used for voice-crossing *Klangfarbenmelodie* passages, in mm. 14 and 16. Example 7-21 shows how in these passages the most salient notes noodle around the pitch A. In m. 16, the Sprechstimme also

Example 7-20. "Heimfahrt," mm. 8–11.

participates in the noodling. The motive returns in the piano right hand in m. 13 for the text refrain, and the barcarolle figuration returns in m. 16.

The third section continues the grouping of clarinet, violin, and cello but also adds flashes of the soloistic passages from the first section. In m. 18, shown in ex. 7-22, the violin leads a homorhythmic grouping with a pitch-specific diminution of the motive from m. 3. Between those gestures, small flourishes in the piano add to a consistent macrorhythm of sixteenth notes. In m. 19, the trio grouping returns to a *Klangfarbenmelodie* presentation, which is complemented by the return of the flute in a soloistic role. The flute and violin switch roles in m. 20; the repeated notes in the ensemble—the antithesis of cross-voice *Klangfarbenmelodie*—accompany short motivic utterances by the violin before the return of the barcarolle figuration in m. 21.

After the dramatic repeated notes of m. 20, m. 21 has such a sense of arrival that it essentially concludes the third section. The last text reprise is the start of the coda. The homorhythmic groupings in mm. 22–24 are not presented as cross-voice *Klangfarbenmelodie*, but are voiced in score order. This passage is an ensemble challenge in that the flute, which is marked *Haupstimme* but playing in a low register, must still be heard. The flute's arrival on the note C-natural three times in a row against the last text refrain, mm. 22–23, recalls some of the repeated final gestures in the melodramas of Part I, especially the end of "Eine blasse Wäscherin"—the first melodrama encountered in the final

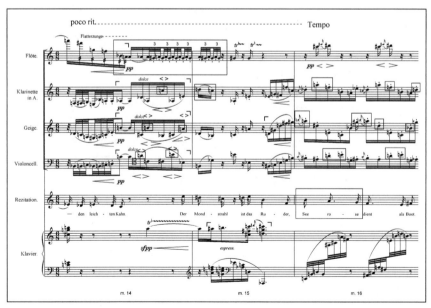

Example 7-21. "Heimfahrt," mm. 14–15; 16.

Example 7-22. "Heimfahrt," mm. 18–19.

order to use *Klangfarbenmelodie.* The coda continues with a brief repeat of the elements from the introduction—the barcarolle in the low strings, the motive in the clarinet, and the inversion in the piano. Finally, the last three measures of the coda form a link to "O alter Duft."

The last three melodramas are continuous, and the flute is the connecting instrument between each one, as shown in ex. 7-23. "Heimfahrt" is in the middle of this final group. It begins with the flute sustaining a C-sharp before giving way to a C-natural. Throughout "Heimfahrt" there are a number of C-sharps in the flute part that keeps the note active. "Heimfahrt" ends with the flute sustaining a C-sharp; the first note heard in the next melodrama is C-natural and C-sharp in the piano left hand, and the voice, doubled by piano, begins descending from B-natural. Finally, the first notes in the flute part in "O alter Duft" form a seven-note grouping with a chain of repeating C-sharps ornamented with an upper and lower neighbor before resolving to the quarter note—a C-sharp yet again.

NO. 21 O ALTER DUFT (OH ANCIENT FRAGRANCE)

O alter Duft[—]aus Märchenzeit,   Oh ancient fragrance[—]of a
                                      fairytale age,

Berauschest wieder meine Sinne!
Ein närrisch Heer von Schelmerein
Durchschwirrt die leichte Luft.

Intoxicate again my senses!
A knavish multitude of bedevilment
Swirls through the tranquil air.

Ein glückhaft Wünschen macht
    mich froh
Nach Freuden, die ich lang verachtet.
O alter Duft[—]aus Märchenzeit,

A favorable longing takes me
    cheerfully
To joys, which I long disdained.
Oh ancient fragrance[—]of a
    fairytale age,

Berauschest wieder mich!

Intoxicate me again!

All meinen Unmut gab ich preis;
Aus meinem sonnumrahmten Fenster
Beschau ich frei die liebe Welt
Und träum hinaus in selge
    Weiten . . .
O alter Duft—aus Märchenzeit!

All my frustrations I have eulogized;
From my sun-framed window
I marvel over the dear world
And dream further to glorious
    reaches . . .
Oh ancient fragrance—of a
    fairytale age!

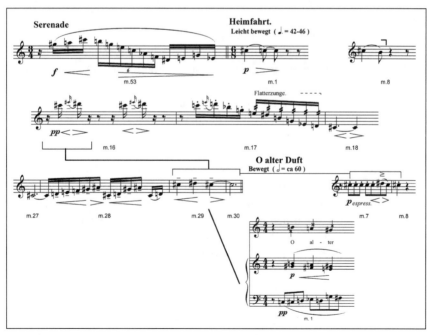

Example 7-23. The C-sharp connection of "Serenade," "Heimfahrt," and "O alter Duft."

The Text

"O alter Duft" is the thirty-fifth poem in Giraud's collection. Hartleben made a number of significant changes. The original poem was titled *Parfums de Bergame*. The imagery of a fairy-tale age does not appear in the French, which conjures a ghostly perfume (*O vieux parfum vaporize*). Hartleben shortened the eighth verse and completely reworked the last stanza. Giraud's last stanza conjures blue Elysian fields where the painter Jean-Antoine Watteau lives on forever (*Je revois les bleus Elysées / Où Watteai s'est éternisé*).[16] Hartleben's last stanza is more general and ultimately better suited for Schoenberg's purpose. Hartleben's translation is dedicated to Theodore Fontane (1819–1898), novelist and editor of the *Vossische Zeitung*.

There is a typographical error in most editions of the score: in m. 20, *geb* should read *gab*. The correct word is found in the text at the beginning of the score as well as Schoenberg's copy of the text and working draft (Sources Ab and B). Similarly, there is some confusion about the placement of hyphens. In adding the imagery of a fairy-tale age, Hartleben added the hyphens to the text refrain between *O alter Duft* and *aus Märchenzeit*; they do not appear in the original French poem. In the original edition of Hartleben's translation, the hyphens appear in each text refrain—the first, seventh, and thirteenth verses.[17] Schoenberg's copy of the poems was copied with the correct placement of the hyphen. However, in the 1911 edition of Hartleben's translation, the hyphen appears in only the last verse.[18] There are no hyphens in the poem as copied in the program distributed at the premiere.[19] Finally, in the first edition of the score, the hyphen is found only in the last verse of the poem. This small detail makes a difference; Schoenberg's reading of the poem without the hyphen affected his text setting, since his setting only reflects the hyphen in the last verse—the final measures of *Pierrot lunaire*.

"O alter Duft" is the only first-person poem in Part III, and the only first-person narration that follows "Gebet an Pierrot." "Gebet" is in the voice of a different character and addressed to Pierrot. Prior to "O alter Duft," the last poem with the presumed narrative voice of Pierrot is "Der kranke Mond," which is the conclusion of Part I. Moreover, the music of "Der kranke Mond" is reprised before the conclusion of Part II.

Composition

"O alter Duft," dated 30 May, was the last melodrama composed, although some melodramas had yet to be completed. Schoenberg's copy of the text contains a sketch of the principal motive and the piano in mm. 28–29.

Musical Materials

"O alter Duft" resembles a lied.[20] The voice serves as the *Hauptstimme* throughout and is accompanied by the piano. The other instruments play a subordinate role. The phrasing is regular, even periodic, which is more typical of homophonic music than the generally polyphonic texture of most of the melodramas.

The melodrama also resembles a lied in its succinct presentation of materials. Of the few melodramas that have Sprechstimme in every measure, including "Galgenlied" and the two contrapuntal melodramas "Parodie" and "Der Mondfleck," only "Gebet an Pierrot" is marked in as slow a tempo as "O alter Duft"—a curious connection between the first and last composed melodramas. However, "O alter Duft" is ultimately slower because it lacks the frenetic pace and sixteenth notes found in "Gebet." The repetition of the main motive gives the impression of a slower pace of compositional rhetoric and plays a determinate role in the form.

"O alter Duft" is in two broad sections with a codetta. The second section begins with an altered reprise of the first three measures. The form resembles a modified strophic lied form. However, because there are three stanzas, there is a superimposition of a three-section form. The starts of the second and third stanzas have similar music, which returns again for the coda.

Example 7-24.   A line graph of "O alter Duft."

As ex. 7-24 shows, the first section is presented in four phrases. The phrases end with either noticeably longer notes in the piano, as in mm. 3 and 6, or with a *ritardando*, as in mm. 9–10 or m. 13. In the first measure, two basic motive forms are presented—the descending quasi-diatonic thirds in the piano right hand and Sprechstimme, and the chromatic ascending line in the piano left hand, shown in ex. 7-25. In the second measure, two further details are added—the internal repetition of the right-hand line and the increasing leaps in the left-hand line. These two motive types dominate the materials both in their literal repetition and in their slight development.

"O alter Duft" contains a number of harmonic features that superficially resemble tonal structures. In addition to the parallel thirds of the main motive, a sense of tonality is engendered by the triads in mm. 3 and 6. The triad in m. 3, an E major triad in second inversion, belongs to the same key as the descending thirds in m. 1. Moreover, the Sprechstimme and piano right hand form other passing triads: the G major triad on beats one and three of m. 2 and the A major triad in mm. 4–5. Finally, the selective doubling of the piano and Sprechstimme in mm. 1–6 and again in mm. 8–9 anchors the pitches in the Sprechstimme and contributes to a sense of pitch centricity. Speaking to these tonal implications, Schoenberg's biographer, H. H. Stuckenschmidt, stated that "O alter Duft" was in E major with few qualifications. Alluding to a parallel between Pierrot's yearning for joys "once disdained" and Schoenberg's departure from tonality, Stuckenschmidt asks, "Perhaps tonality, a triad, consonances belonged to these despised joys at that time, at a critical stage in Schoenberg's development?"[21]

Stuckenschmidt's assertion is extreme, and an attempt at a tonal analysis would be increasingly frustrated after m. 6.[22] In m. 7 especially, where the text speaks of mischievousness, the sense of tonality disperses, and the Sprechstimme, while still essentially moving in rhythm with the piano, seems delib-

Example 7-25. "O alter Duft," mm. 1–3 (detail)

erately set against the piano in dissonant intervals. Except for the return of the original motive forms in mm. 14–16 and 26–27, "O alter Duft" cultivates post-tonal pitch collections that are not significantly different from the previous melodramas.

The second section begins in m. 14. This section is notable for using all the auxiliary instruments; the clarinet, flute, and violin are replaced with bass clarinet, piccolo, and viola. The music originally presented in mm. 1–10 is greatly condensed to six measures, mm. 14–19. The diminution is caused by the structure of the poem. The first ten measures contain four verses of the poem, whereas the reprise contains only two. Measure 19, where the third stanza begins, is parallel to mm. 9–10, the start of the second section.

The music for the third stanza, mm. 20–25, is more developmental than the music in the first section. The last reprise of the music for the text reprise, mm. 26–27, is varied by separating the descending thirds from the ascending chromatic counterpoint. In mm. 26, the descending thirds from the beginning are heard in the viola and cello. The cello may play the higher note of the thirds because of its affinity with the human voice: it takes the place of the Sprechstimme. The immediate repeat of the descending thirds—the fourth and fifth notes of the cello and viola—are presented in increasing durations, giving the impression of *ritardando*. A version of the chromatic bass line that usually appears with the descending thirds may be found two bars earlier in m. 24 in the piccolo, beginning over an E major triad in second inversion with a C in the bass. Thus, elements from m. 1 precede the incomplete reprise by two measures.

The last five measures of "O alter Duft"—the last five measures of *Pierrot lunaire*—are particularly rich in associations. As noted above, they are the first measures sketched by Schoenberg on his copy of the text. The descending thirds recur in the strings. As noted in chapter 4, David Lewin has demonstrated a relationship between the descending thirds in "O alter Duft" and the first notes of the Sprechstimme in "Mondestrunken." The chords in the piano are triadic and hint at a tonal context; the augmented chord at the end of m. 28 sounds like an enharmonic dominant of E major, which resolves to an E.[23] However, the resolution is complicated by notes in the Sprechstimme that do not share this tonal context.

Another association in the last measure is the role of C-sharp. As noted above, C-sharp is used in connecting the final three melodramas. The C-sharp in m. 27, in conjunction with the descending thirds in the strings, specifically resembles the transition between "Heimfahrt" and "O alter Duft." In the transition, a C-sharp was repeated after a neighboring D-sharp. That neighboring figure is recalled immediately by the clarinet in m. 3, the flute in m. 7, and the cello in m. 16. The neighbor figure is also reflected in the ascending line in the piano, m. 1 (shown in ex. 7-25). In that varied form, it can be seen further developed not only in the repetition of the ascending piano line, but also in the flute, mm. 14–16 (ex. 7-24), which is immediately imitated by the viola, mm. 17–18. That ascending line, beginning on C-sharp, is the motive that begins the second and third stanzas in the Sprechstimme as well as the coda. It completes a process of expanding the range of that motive from the initial chromatic segment in m. 10 to a leaping figure that spans an octave in mm. 27–28 as seen by comparing ex. 7-24 and ex. 7-26.

Finally, the leaps in the last measure resemble the quiet leaps found in the middle and end of "Der kranke Mond." The internal repetition of C-sharp, separated by higher notes that leap a minor third and a tritone, and the final F-natural strengthen the connection between the final measures, as shown in ex. 7-26. Alluding to "Der kranke Mond" at the end of "O alter Duft" completes

Example 7-26.   Connections in mm. 27–30 of "O alter Duft."

a pattern of weaving "Der kranke Mond" into the conclusion of each section. Moreover, the style and affect of "Der kranke Mond" are revisited and recontextualized at the end of the work. In this last melodrama, in which the moon is not even mentioned, Pierrot is finally free from the unrest first signaled in "Der kranke Mond."

The two solitary F-naturals in the Sprechstimme that end *Pierrot lunaire* represent the only instance of a melodrama ending with the Sprechstimme alone. The F in m. 30 is the sole instance of a measure in *Pierrot* that contains only the Sprechstimme. In a work of such timbral ingenuity and busy instrumental textures—a work that Igor Stravinsky famously remarked should be recorded without the Sprechstimme[24]—Schoenberg ends with the sound of the unaccompanied voice.

NOTES

1. Source Ab, 723. In the draft, there are two dramatic differences: the motive in the right hand is expressed as a dotted figure, which more closely resembles the violin's statement of the motive, and the B-natural, in the piano right-hand chord of fourths and in the violin's statement of the motive, is a B-flat. The violin provides the version of the motive with the B-flat in m. 3, and overlapping statements in the clarinet conform more to this version of the motive.

2. The written F-natural in the clarinet on the second beat of m. 18 is curious. Schoenberg uses F-sharp, the sounding D-sharp, that correctly completes the piano chord in m. 2, on the fourth beat of m. 17 and the fourth beat of m. 18 (which can be seen in ex. 7-3). The F-natural may be a slight variation or, in light of the prominent D-sharp simultaneously in the piano, it may be an effort to avoid octaves in the outer voices.

3. The harmonic in the left hand, found in every score prior to the *Gesamtausgaben* edition of 1996, is an engraving mistake.

4. "Menuet," *Meyers Konversationslexikon*, 4th edition.

5. Arnold Schoenberg, *Fundamentals of Musical Composition*, pb eds. Gerald Strang and Leonard Stein (London: Faber and Faber Limited, 1970), 141.

6. Schoenberg gives this schematic with repeat dots in *Fundamentals* (Schoenberg 1970, 141).

7. Dunsby 1992, 65.

8. Stephan Weytjens and Mark Dalaere, "Analytical Approaches to 'Pierrot lunaire,'" in *Arnold Schönberg in Berlin: Bericht zum Symposium, 28–30 September 2000*, ed. Christian Meyer (Vienna: Arnold Schönberg Center Privatstiftung, 2001), 123.

9. Dunsby 1992, 64.

10. See Youens, 101 &f.

11. "*Fuge*," *Meyers Konversationslexikon*, 4th edition.

12. Because it is a stretto exposition, it has been frequently described as a canon. Schoenberg himself briefly made this mistake. In the margin notes in his copy of Egon

Wellesz's *Arnold Schoenberg* (Leipzig: E. P.Tal & Co, 1921), Schoenberg noted that "there is even a double canon between piccolo and clarinet on one hand, violin and cello on the other." Later, he crossed out his first emendation to note that it was a fugue between piccolo and clarinet. See Brinkmann 1995, 299.

13. In the cello part, m. 12, the notes beamed below the staff reflect an error in the 1914 score; the notes beamed above the staff reflect Schoenberg's correction in his second copy of the score, Source D2, 63. The error can be seen by comparing the cello part on the first beat of m. 12 with the fourth beat of m. 8 in ex. 7-12.

14. Coincidentally, Höniger's most-known painting, *Im Cafe Josty*, depicts a café near the Berlin Choralion-Saal where *Pierrot luniare* premiered.

15. Shawn, 3–4.

16. Jean-Antoine Watteau (1684–1721) is perhaps best known for his painting *Pierrot* (alternately called *Gilles*). See Susan Youens, "Excavating an Allegory: The Texts of *Pierrot lunaire*," *Journal of the Arnold Schoenberg Institute* 8/2 (1984): 94–115.

17. Otto Erich Hartleben, *Pierrot lunaire* (Berlin: Verlag Deutscher Phantasten, 1893), 35.

18. Otto Erich Hartleben, Albert Giraud, and Otto Vrieslander. *Albert Giraud, Pierrot lunaire* (München: G. Müller, 1911), 35.

19. Arnold Schoenberg, *Pierrot lunaire,* Choralion-Saal, Berlin, Germany, 16 October 1912; Program at the Library of Congress, ML54.6.S36P4 1912 Case; "O alter Duft" is printed on page 12.

20. After the New York premiere, the British critic and early Wagner scholar Ernest Newman dismissed "O alter Duft" as little more than "a platitudinous German Lied wrenched a little out of shape." Quoted in David Metzer, "The New York Reception of 'Pierrot lunaire': The 1923 Premiere and Its Aftermath," *Musical Quarterly* 78/4 (1994): 678.

21. Stuckenschmidt 1978, 201.

22. Jim Samson has grouped "O alter Duft" with a number of post-tonal works with "suppressed tonal structures" in "Schoenberg's 'Atonal' Music," *Tempo* 109 (1974): 18. He later grouped "O alter Duft" with works that "'explain' their atonal music by presenting it in traditional guise, with a conventional phrase and rhythmic structure and quasi-tonal part-movement," in *Music in Transition: A Study of Tonal Expansion and Atonality, 1900–1927* (Oxford: Oxford University Press, 1977; reprint 2002), 221. Allen Forte summarily dismissed the role of tonality in the first bars of "O alter Duft" by noting, "[T]he entire opening, with its surface 'simplicity' may have been intended to dupe some unsuspecting critic," in "Sets and Non-Sets in Schoenberg's Atonal Music," *Perspectives of New Music* 11/1 (1972): 54.

23. Both Stuckenschmidt (1978, 201) and Brinkmann (1997, 142) analyze the last three events in the piano part as an (presumably imperfect) authentic cadence.

24. Robert Craft, *Memories and Commentaires* (London: Faber and Faber Limited, 2002), 224.

Afterword

$\mathcal{I}$n the summer of 1900, Alma Schindler, then twenty-one years old, was studying composition and composing lieder. She had not yet met her future husband, Gustav Mahler, and while she had met Arnold Schoenberg and had begun flirting with Alexander Zemlinsky, she had not yet begun studying with Zemlinsky. One Saturday, 16 June, she made the following annotation in her diary: "Composed quite a lot. Two songs. Texts by Richard Dehmel and Rainer Maria Rilke. Half song, half recitation, half chorale—I seem to have come up with an entirely unique art-form."[1]

Alma Mahler would never reach her full potential as a composer, but as a composition student, her experience was not unlike the experiences of more illustrious composers. Like them, she read contemporary poetry and felt it deeply. Indeed, it is remarkable that she set poems by many of the same poets that Zemlinsky and Schoenberg chose—poets generally overlooked by Hugo Wolf and Gustav Mahler. And like so many composers of her era, she idolized Wagner and looked to his prosody—his Sprechgesang—for inspiration. Perhaps this passing whim, hastily jotted in her diary, indicates that she was groping for the same ineffable sound that had vexed Humperdinck and would vex Schoenberg—a joining of speaking and singing that transcended Wagner's Sprechgesang.

If so, the ineffable sound was probably as welcome as a ghost—and just as hard to document. Alma didn't try to notate the sound; her song was published in traditional notation. Humperdinck and Schoenberg tried to notate this sound—tried to eff the ineffable—and a century later, we still try to recreate this imagined sound.

Information theorists have an idiomatic definition of *noise*: in any transmission of information, noise is unintended content that disrupts the message. The word *noise* has so often been associated with *Pierrot* that we hesitate to invoke it here. Nevertheless, music notation is a message; it is a set of instructions to create a desired sound. Many musicians believe that the instructions for Sprechstimme cannot be followed. Perhaps the message is incomplete or flawed. Perhaps we cannot understand the message. Or perhaps there is noise in the message.

When Schoenberg wrote "Gebet an Pierrot" he had a sound in mind. That new sound was conceptually related to the sound he had first imagined for *Gurrelieder*, but it had changed over time. His musical language had changed. His aesthetics had changed and were changing back. He had new ideas about timbre. And perhaps most significantly, his imagination was excited by the ideas of Albertine Zehme, who had independently conceived a similar idea. It was not a breathtakingly original idea, but Zehme had thought it through in language that was remarkably similar to Schoenberg's writings. And she had acted on her idea.

While we can never know what Schoenberg heard in his head on 12 March 1912, it seems likely he did not hear it at the October premiere. He heard noise. Not the noise that tender-eared critics would describe, but rather the difference between what he imagined and what Zehme achieved. Every statement made after the fall of 1912—his letters to Berg, his twice-drafted preface for the score, his later writings and statements, and even his own recording—have added more noise. These fragmentary bits of information have not clarified, but have rather obfuscated what seems clear from the notation: the Sprechmelodie in *Pierrot lunaire* is pitched speech.

These "one times seven" chapters will hardly be the last words on the subject. Sprechstimme, like *Klangfarbenmelodie* and *Grundgestalt*, is a concept that exists at the boundaries of language. Both Zehme and Schoenberg, in independent writings, observed that words had become more important than sounds. Zehme wanted to restore sound to its former position of prominence. Schoenberg took to task no less a mind than that of Arthur Schopenhauer for trying to translate the language of music into the abstraction of words. The message of music notation is beyond language; language is noise. And yet words are all we have.

NOTE

1. Mahler-Werfel, 294. According to Antony Beaumont, the Dehmel setting was probably "Wie das Meer ist die Libe," published in 1924 by Josef Weinberger as "Lobegesang," the fourth of Alma's *Fünf Gesang*. Note also that Alma made this reference before hearing Thuille's *Lobetanz* or owning the score, as briefly mentioned in chapter 1.

Bibliography

Arnold Schönberg. Munich: R. Piper & Co., 1912. Translated by Barbara Z. Schoenberg. In *Schoenberg and His World*, edited by Walter Frisch, 195–261. Princeton: Princeton University Press, 1999.

Auner, Joseph. "'Heart and Brain in Music': The Genesis of Schoenberg's *Die glückliche Hand.*" In *Constructive Dissonance: Arnold Schoenberg and the Transformations of Twentieth-Century Culture,* edited by Juliane Brand and Christopher Hailey. Berkeley: University of California Press, 1997.

Auner, Joseph H. "In Schoenberg's Workshop: Aggregates and Referential Collections in *Die glückliche Hand.*" *Music Theory Spectrum* 18/1 (1996): 77–105.

———. "Schoenberg's Compositional and Aesthetic Transformations, 1910–1913: The Genesis of *Die glückliche Hand.*" PhD diss., University of Chicago, 1991.

———, ed. *A Schoenberg Reader: Documents of a Life.* New Haven: Yale University Press, 2003.

Bailey, Kathryn. "Formal Organization and Structural Imagery in Schoenberg's *Pierrot lunaire.*" *Studies in Music from the University of Western Ontario* 2 (1977): 93–107.

Berg, Alban. *Arnold Schönberg. Gurrelieder Führer.* Leipzig and Vienna: Universal Edition, 1913.

Berg, Alban, and Arnold Schoenberg. *The Berg-Schoenberg Correspondence: Selected Letters.* Edited by Juliane Brand, Christopher Hailey, and Donald Harris. New York: W. W. Norton & Company, 1987.

Besch, O[tto]. *Englebert Humperdinck.* Lepizig: Breitkopf & Härtel, 1914.

Bierbaum, Otto Julius, ed. *Deutsche Chansons (Brettl-lieder) von Bierbaum, Dehmel, Falke, Finckh, Heymel, Holz, Liliencron, Schröder, Wedekind, Wolzogen.* Berlin und Leipzig: Schuster & Loeffler, 1900.

Boss, Jack. "Schoenberg's op. 22 Radio Talk and Developing Variation in Atonal Music." *Music Theory Spectrum* 14/2 (1992): 125–49.

Boulez, Pierre. *Notes of an Apprenticeship.* Edited by Paule Thévenin. Translated by Herbert Weinstock. New York: A. A. Knopf, 1968.

————. *Orientations: The Collected Writings by Pierre Boulez*. Edited by Jean-Jacques Nattiez. Translated by Martin Cooper. Cambridge: Harvard University Press, 1986.

————. "*Pierrot lunaire* and *Le marteau sans maître*," translated by Martin Cooper. In *From Pierrot to Marteau*, edited by Leonard Stein. Los Angeles: Arnold Schoenberg Institute, 1988.

————. "Timbre and Composition—Timbre and Language." Translated by R. Robertson. *Contemporary Music Review* 2 (1987): 161–71.

Brand, Juliane, and Christopher Hailey, eds. *Constructive Dissonance: Arnold Schoenberg and the Transformations of Twentieth-Century Culture*. Berkeley: University of California Press, 1997.

Brinkmann, Reinhold. *Arnold Schönberg. Pierrot lunaire, op. 21: Kritischer Bericht, Studien zur Genesis, Skizzen, Dokumente*, Reihe B Band 24, *Arnold Schönberg Sämtliche Werke*. Edited by Rudolph Stephan. Mainz: B. Schott's Söhne, 1995.

————. "The Fool as Paradigm: Schönberg's *Pierrot lunaire* and the Modern Artist." In *Schönberg and Kandinsky: An Historic Encounter*, edited by Konrad Boehmer, 139–67. Vol. 14, *Contemporary Music Studies*, edited by Peter Nelson and Nigel Osborne. Amsterdam: Harwood Academic Publishers, 1997.

————. "On Pierrot's Trail." Translated by Paul A. Pisk. *Journal of the Arnold Schoenberg Institute* 2/1 (1977): 42–48.

————. "What the Sources Tell Us . . . A Chapter of *Pierrot* Philology." *Journal of the Arnold Schoenberg Institute* 10/1 (1987): 11–27.

Busoni, Ferrucio. *Ferrucio Busoni: Selected Letters*. Edited and translated by Antony Beaumont. New York: Columbia University Press, 1987.

Byron, Avior. "Demystifying Schoenberg's Conducting." *Min-Ad: Israel Studies in Musicology Online* 2 (2006) at http://www.biu.ac.il/HU/mu/min-ad/06/Byron_Schoenberg.pdf (accessed September 2, 2007).

————. "*Pierrot lunaire* in Studio and in Broadcast: Sprechstimme, Tempo and Character." *Journal of the Society for Musicology in Ireland* 2 (2006–7): 69–91.

————. "The Test Pressings of Schoenberg Conducting *Pierrot lunaire*: Sprechstimme Reconsidered." *Music Theory Online* 12/1 (2006) at http://mto.societymusictheory.org/issues/mto.06.12.1/mto.06.12.1.byron.html (accessed March 4, 2006).

Byron, Avior, and Matthias Pasdzierny. "Sprechstimme Reconsidered Once Again: '. . . though Mrs. Stiedry is never in pitch.'" *Music Theory Online* 13/2 (2007) at http://mto.societymusictheory.org/issues/mto.07.13.2/mto.07.13.2.byron_pasdzierny.html (accessed September 1, 2007).

Cerha, Friedrich. "Zur Interpretation der Sprechstimme in Schönberg's *Pierrot lunaire*." In *Bericht über den 1. Kongress der Internationalen Schönberg-Gesellschaft, Wien: 4–9 Juni, 1974*, edited by Rudolph Stephan, 25–33. Vienna: Verlag Elisabeth Lafite, 1978.

Cherlin, Michael. "Dialectical Opposition in Schoenberg's Music and Thought." *Music Theory Spectrum* 22/2 (2000): 157–76.

Craft, Robert. *Memories and Commentaires*. London: Faber and Faber Limited, 2002.

Cramer, Alfred William. "Music for the Future: Sounds of Early-Twentieth-Century Psychology and Language in Works of Schoenberg, Webern, and Berg, 1908 to the First World War." PhD diss., University of Pennsylvania, 1997.

————. "Schoenberg's 'Klangfarbenmelodie': A Harmonic Principle of Early Atonality." *Music Theory Spectrum* 24/1 (2002): 1–34.

Dahlhaus, Carl. *Schoenberg and the New Music: Essays.* Translated by Derrick Puffett and Alfred Clayton. Cambridge: Cambridge University Press, 1987.

Delaere, Mark, and Jan Herman, eds. *Pierrot lunaire: Une collection d'études musico-littéraires.* Louvain: Éditions Peeters, 2004.

Dunsby, Jonathan. *Pierrot lunaire.* New York: Cambridge University Press, 1992.

————. "*Pierrot lunaire* and the Resistance to Theory." *Musical Times* 130/1762 (1989): 732–36.

————. "Schoenberg's Pierrot keeping his *Kopfmotiv.*" In *Pierrot lunaire: A Collection of Musicological and Literary Studies,* edited by Mark Delaere and Jan Herman. Louvain: Éditions Peeters, 2004.

Forte, Allen. "Sets and Non-Sets in Schoenberg's Atonal Music." *Perspectives of New Music* 11/1 (1972): 43.

Frisch, Walter. "Brahms, Developing Variation, and the Schoenberg Critical Tradition." *19th-Century Music* 5/3 (1982): 215–32.

————. *The Early Works of Arnold Schoenberg, 1903–1908.* Berkeley: University of California Press, 1993.

————. ed. *Schoenberg and His World.* Princeton: Princeton University Press, 1999.

Fürlus, Eckhard. "Nachwort." *Pierrot lunaire.* Albert Giraud. Translated [into German] by Otto Erich Hartleben. Edited by Eckhard Fürlus. Bielefeld: Aistesis Verlag, 2005.

Giraud, Albert. *Pierrot lunaire: Rondels bergamasques.* Paris: A. Lemerre, 1884.

————. *Pierrot lunaire.* Translated by Otto Erich Hartleben. Berlin: Verlag Deutscher Phantasten, 1893.

Goltz, Jennifer E. "The Roots of *Pierrot lunaire* in Cabaret." PhD diss., University of Michigan, 2005.

Gorrell, Lorraine. "Performing the Sprechstimme in Arnold Schoenberg's *Pierrot lunaire,* op. 21." *Journal of Singing* 55/2 (1998): 5–15.

Green, Martin, and John Swan. *The Triumph of Pierrot: The Commedia Dell'arte and the Modern Imagination.* University Park: Pennsylvania State University Press, 1993.

Guilbert, Yvette. *How to Sing a Song: The Art of Dramatic and Lyric Interpretation.* New York: Macmillan, 1919.

Haimo, Ethan. "Atonality, Analysis, and the Intentional Fallacy." *Music Theory Spectrum* 18/2 (1996): 167–99.

————. "Schoenberg's *Pierrot lunaire:* A Cycle?" In *Pierrot lunaire: A Collection of Musicological and Literary Studies,* edited by Mark Delaere and Jan Herman. Louvain: Éditions Peeters, 2004.

————. *Schoenberg's Transformation of Musical Language.* Cambridge: Cambridge University Press, 2006.

Hartleben, Otto Erich, Albert Giraud, and Otto Vrieslander. *Albert Giraud, Pierrot lunaire.* München: G. Müller, 1911.

Höhn, Andreas. "Im Dienst der Krone und der Kunst: Albertine und Felix Zehme." *Leipziger Blätter* 39 (2001): 39.

Horwitz, Karl. "[The Teacher]," translated by Barbara Z. Schoenberg. In *Schoenberg and His World*, edited by Walter Frisch. Princeton: Princeton University Press, 1999. Originally published in *Arnold Schönberg*. Munich: R. Piper & Co., 1912.

Humperdink, Englebert. *Die Köningskinder: Klavierauszug*. Leipzig: Max Brockhaus, n.d. [1897].

Humperdinck, Wolfram. *Englebert Humperdinck: Das Leben meines Vaters*. Franfurt Am Main: Verlag Waldemar Kramer, 1965.

Jelavich, Peter. *Berlin Cabaret*. Studies in Cultural History. Cambridge: Harvard University Press, 1993.

Klement, Alfred von. *Die Bücher von Otto Erich Hartleben: eine Bibliographie, mit der bisher unveröffentlichten Fassung der Selbstbiographie des Dichters*. Salò: Halkyonische Akademie für unangewandte Wissenschaften, 1951.

Korte-Böger, Andrea, ed. *Engelbert Humperdinck zum 70. Todestag (Veroffentlichung des Geschichts- und Altertumsvereins fur Siegburg und den Rhein-Sieg-Kreis e.V)*. Siegburg: Franz Schmitt, 1992.

Krämer, Ulrich. "Zur Notation der Sprechstimme bei Schönberg." In *Schoenberg in der Sprechgesang*, edited by Heinz-Klaus Metzger and Rainer Riehn. Musik-Konzepte 112/113. Munich: Edition Text u. Kritik, 2001.

Kravitt, Edward F. "The Joining of Words and Music in Late Romantic Melodrama." *Musical Quarterly* 62/4 (1976): 571–90.

Kurth, Richard. "Pierrot's Cave: Representation, Reverberation, Radiance." In *Schoenberg and Words: The Modernist Years*. Vol. 11, *Garland Reference Library of the Humanities*, edited by Charlotte Marie Cross and Russell A. Berman. New York: Garland Publications, 2000.

Lessem, Alan. "Text and Music in Schoenberg's *Pierrot lunaire*." *Current Musicology* 19 (1975): 103–12.

Lesure, François, Emily Good, Gertraut Haberkamp, Malcolm Turner, and Emilia Zanetti, eds. *Dossier de presse de 'Pierrot lunaire' d'Arnold Schönberg*. Geneva: Minkoff, 1985.

Lewin, David. "Some Notes on *Pierrot lunaire*." In *Music Theory in Concept and Practice*, edited by James M. Baker, David Beach, and Jonathan W. Bernard, 433–57. Eastman Studies in Music. Rochester, NY: University of Rochester Press, 1997.

Luisa of Tuscany [Louise Antoinette Marie]. *My Own Story*. New York: G.P. Putnam's sons, 1911.

Mahler-Werfel, Alma. *Alma Mahler Diaries, 1898–1902*. Edited and translated by Antony Beaumont. Ithaca, NY: Cornell University Press, 1999.

———. *Gustav Mahler: Memories and Letters*, 3rd ed. further enlarged. Edited by Donald Mitchell. Translated by Basil Creighton. Seattle: University of Washington Press, 1975.

Mäkelä, Tomi. *Klang und Linie von Pierrot lunaire zu Ionisation: Studien zur funktionalen Wechselwirkung von Spezialensemble, Formfindung und Klangfarbenpolyphonie*. Interdisziplinäre Studien zur Musik, Vol. 3. Frankfurt am Main: Lang, 2004.

McColl, Sandra. *Music Criticism in Vienna, 1896–1897: Critically Moving Forms*. Oxford Monographs on Music. Oxford: Clarendon Press, 1996.

McDonald, Malcolm. *Schoenberg*. London: J.M. Dent, 1976.

Metzer, David. "The New York Reception of 'Pierrot lunaire': The 1923 Premiere and

Its Aftermath." *Musical Quarterly* 78/4 (1994): 669–99.

Metzger, Heinz-Klaus, and Rainer Riehn, eds. *Schoenberg und der Sprechgesang*. Musik-Konzepte 112/113. Munich: Edition Text u. Kritik, 2001.

Morier, Henri. *Dictionnaire de poétique et rhétorique*. Paris: Presses Universitaires de France, 1975.

Mothes, Rudolf. "Lebenserinnerungen," n.d. Archiv der Stadt Leipzig, Leipzig, at http://www.quelle optimal.de/mothes.html (accessed July 23, 2007)

Newlin, Dika. "Arnold Schoenberg's Debt to Mahler." *Chord and Discord* 2/5 (1948): 21–26.

———. *Bruckner, Mahler, Schoenberg*. New York: W. W. Norton, 1947; Revised Edition. New York: W. W. Norton, 1978.

Nono-Schoenberg, Nuria, ed. *Arnold Schönberg 1874–1951: Lebensgeschichte in Begegnungen*. Klagenfurt: Ritter, 1992.

Nordau, Max. *Degeneration*. 2nd ed. New York: D. Appleton and Company, 1895.

Novalis. *Sämmtliche Werke*. Vol. 3. Edited by Carl Meissner. Florence und Leipzig: Eug. Diederichs, 1898.

Porter, Andrew. "Munching a Beanstalk." In *From Pierrot to Marteau*, edited by Leonard Stein. Los Angeles: Arnold Schoenberg Institute, 1988.

Ramazzotti, Marinella. "Klangfarbenverschmelzung von Stimme und Instrumenten in *Pierrot lunaire*." *Report of the Symposium: Arnold Schönberg in Berlin, 28.–30. September 2000, Journal of the Arnold Schönberg Center* (March 2001): 145–59.

Rapoport, Eliezer. "On the Origins of Schoenberg's Sprechgesang in *Pierrot Lunaire*." *Min-Ad: Israel Studies in Musicology Online* 2 (2006) at http://www.biu.ac.il/HU/mu/min-ad/06/Sprchgsng.pdf (accessed September 2, 2007).

Reich, Willi. *Schoenberg: A Critical Biography*. Translated by Leo Black. New York: Praeger, 1971.

———, ed. *Arnold Schoenberg: Schöpferische Konfessionen*. Zürich: Verl. Die Arche, 1964.

Richter, Gregory, trans and ed. *Albert Giraud's Pierrot lunaire*. Kirksville, MO: Truman State University Press, 2001.

Rosen, Charles. *Arnold Schoenberg*. New York: Viking Press, 1975.

Rosewall, Michael. "Schoenberg's Enigma: The Performance of Sprechstimme." *Journal of Singing* 59/1 (2002): 31–38.

Samson, Jim. "Schoenberg's 'Atonal' Music." *Tempo* 109 (1974): 18.

———. *Music in Transition: A Study of Tonal Expansion and Atonality, 1900–1927*. Oxford: Oxford University Press, 1977.

Schmidt, Christian Martin. "Analytical Remarks on Schoenberg's *Pierrot lunaire*." In *From Pierrot to Marteau: An International Conference and Concert Celebrating the Tenth Anniversary of the Arnold Schoenberg Institute*, University of Southern California School of Music, March 14–16, 1987. Edited by Leonard Stein. Los Angeles: Arnold Schoenberg Institute, 1987.

Schoenberg, Arnold. "Analysis of the Four Orchestral Songs Opus 22." Translated by Claudio Spies. *Perspectives of New Music* 3/2 (1965): 1–21.

———. "Art and the Moving Pictures." *California Arts and Architecture* (April 1940): 12, 38, 40.

————. "Attempt at a Diary." Translated by Anita Luginbühl. *Journal of the Arnold Schoenberg Institute* IX/1 (1986): 7–52.

————. *Berliner Tagebuch.* Edited by Joseph Rufer. Frankfurt, Berlin, and Vienna: Propyläen-Verlag, 1974.

————. *Fundamentals of Musical Composition.* Edited by Gerald Strang and Leonard Stein. London: Faber and Faber Limited, 1970.

————. *Harmonielehre.* Translated as *Theory of Harmony* by Roy C. Carter. Berkeley: University of California Press, 1978.

————. *Letters.* Selected and edited by Erwin Stein. Translated by Eithne Wilkins and Ernst Kaiser. London: Faber and Faber Limited, 1964.

————. "Preface." In *Die vereinfachte Studier- und Dirigier-Partitur* [of Vier Lieder für Gesang und Orchester op. 22]. Vienna: Universal Edition, 1919.

————. *Sämtliche Werke.* Mainz: B. Schott's Söhne; Vienna: Universal Edition, 1966.

————. "Self Analysis." Appendix 1 in *Schoenberg: A Critical Biography.* New York: Da Capo Press, 1981.

————. *Style and Idea: Selected Writings of Arnold Schoenberg.* Edited by Leonard Stein. New York: St. Martin's Press, 1975; Paperback reprint, Berkley: University of California Press, 1984.

Schuller, Gunther, and Eduard Steuermann. "A Conversation with Steuermann." *Perspectives of New Music* 3/1 (1964): 22–35.

Simms, Bryan R. *The Atonal Music of Arnold Schoenberg, 1908–1923.* New York: Oxford University Press, 2000.

Smith, Joan Allen. "Schoenberg's Way." *Perspectives of New Music* 18/1–2 (1979): 258–85.

Stadlen, Peter. "Schoenberg's Speech-Song." *Music and Letters* 62/1 (1981): 1–11.

————. "Schönberg und der Sprechgesang." In *Bericht über den 1. Kongress der Internationalen Schönberg-Gesellschaft: Wien, 4–9 Juni, 1974,* edited by Rudolph Stephan, 202–12. Vienna: Verlag Elizabeth Lafite, 1978.

————. "Die von Schönberg intendierte Ausführungsart der Sprechstimme im 'Pierrot lunaire'." In *Stimme und Wort in der Musik des 20. Jahrhunderts,* edited by Hartmut Krones, 109–26. Wien: Boehlau, 2001.

Steegmuller, Francis, ed. "*Your Isadora*": *The Love Story of Isadora Duncan & Gordon Craig.* New York: Random House, 1974.

Stein, Erwin. "Die Behandlung der Sprechstimme in *Pierrot lunaire*." *Pult und Taktstock* 4 (1927): 45–49. Reprinted in Stein, Erwin. *Orpheus in New Guises.* London: Rockliff, 1953.

————. *Orpheus in New Guises.* Westport, CT: Hyperion Press, 1979.

————. "Vom Melodram." *Musikblätter des Anbruch* 10 (1928): 370–72.

Stein, Leonard, ed. *From Pierrot to Marteau: An International Conference and Concert Celebrating the Tenth Anniversary of the Arnold Schoenberg Institute,* University of Southern California School of Music, March 14–16, 1987. Los Angeles: Arnold Schoenberg Institute, 1987.

Stephan, Rudolph. "Zur jungsten Geschichte des Melodrams." *Archiv für Musikwissenschaft* 17 (1960): 183–92.

Sterne, Colin C. *Arnold Schoenberg: The Composer as Numerologist.* Lewiston, NY: E. Mellen Press, 1993.

Steuermann, Edward. *The Not Quite Innocent Bystander: Writings of Edward Steuermann.* Edited by Clara Steuermann, David Porter, and Gunther Schuller; Translations by Richard Cantwell and Charles Messner. Lincoln: University of Nebraska Press, 1989.

———. *"Pierrot lunaire* in Retrospect." *Juilliard News Bulletin* 1 (Feb. 1963): 6–8.

Stravinsky, Igor, and Robert Craft. *Dialogues and a Diary.* London: Faber, 1968.

Stuckenschmidt, Hans Heinz. *Arnold Schoenberg.* Translated by Edith Temple Roberts and Humphrey Searle. New York: Grove Press, 1960.

———, ed. *Ferruccio Busoni: Entwurf einer neuen Ästhetik der Tonkunst. Faksimile einer Ausgabe von 1916 mit den handschriftlichen Anmerkungen von Arnold Schönberg. Im Anhang Transkription der Anmerkungen und Nachwort von H. H. Stuckenschmidt.* [Frankfurt am Main]: Insel Verlag, 1974.

———. *Schoenberg: His Life, World and Work.* Translated by Humphrey Searle. New York: Schirmer, 1978.

Thompson, Oscar, and Nicolas Slonimsky, eds. *The International Cyclopedia of Music and Musicians.* 5th ed. New York: Dodd, Mead, 1949.

Thuille, Ludwig, Otto Julius Bierbaum, and Herm Bischoff. *Lobetanz: ein Bühnenspiel in 3 Aufzügen.* Berlin: A. Denekey Musikverlag, 1897.

Viertel, Salka. *The Kindness of Strangers.* New York: Holt, Rinehart, and Winston, 1969.

Vilain, Robert. *"Pierrot lunaire:* Cyclic Coherence in Giraud and Schoenberg." In *Pierrot lunaire: Une collection d'études musico-littéraires.* Edited by Mark Delaere and Jan Herman. Louvain: Éditions Peeters, 2004.

Vrieslander, Otto. *Pierrot lunaire: 46 Dichtungen nach Albert Giraud.* Munich: Henrich Levy, 1904.

Wagner, Erika. "Treffen mit Schönberg anläßlich der Aufführung des *Pierrot lunaire."* *Pult und Taktstock* 7–8 (1924): 284–85.

Wagner, Richard. "The Destiny of Opera." In *Richard Wagner's Prose Works.* Vol. 5, *Actors and Singers.* Translated by William Ashton Ellis. London: Kegan Paul, Trench, Trüber & Co., 1896.

Webern, Anton. "Schoenberg's Music," translated by Barbara Z. Schoenberg. In *Schoenberg and His World,* edited by Walter Frisch. Princeton: Princeton University Press, 1999. Originally published in Webern, Anton. *Arnold Schönberg.* Munich: R. Piper & Co., 1912.

Weytjens, Stephan. "Text as a Crutch in Schoenberg's *Pierrot lunaire?"* In *Pierrot lunaire: Une collection d'études musico-littéraires,* edited by Mark Delaere and Jan Herman. Louvain: Éditions Peeters, 2004.

Weytjens, Stephan, and Mark Dalaere. "Analytical Approaches to '*Pierrot lunaire.*'" In *Arnold Schönberg in Berlin: Bericht zum Symposium, 28–30 September 2000,* edited by Christian Meyer. Vienna: Arnold Schönberg Center Privatstiftung, 2001.

Williams, Elizabeth Otis. *Sojourning, Shopping & Studying in Paris; A Handbook Particularly for Women.* Chicago: A.C. McClurg & Co., 1907.

Wolf, Hugo. Wolf Hugo to Melanie Köchert, 19 July 1891. In *Letters to Melanie Köchert,* ed. Franz Grasberger, English ed. and trans. Louise McClelland Urban. New York: Schirmer, 1991.

Wolzogen, Ernst von. *Ansichten und Aussichten, ein Erntebuch; Gesammelte Studien über Musik, Literatur und Theater.* Berlin: F. Fontane & Co, 1908.

————. *Wie ich mich ums Leben brachte. Erinnerungen und Erfahrungen.* Braunschweig: Georg Westermann, 1923.

Wood, Ralph W. "Concerning 'Sprechgesang.'" *Tempo* 2 (1946): 3–6.

Wörner, Karl H. "Arnold Schoenberg and the Theater." Translated by Willis Wager. *Musical Quarterly* 48/4 (1962): 444–60.

Youens, Susan. "Excavating an Allegory: The Texts of *Pierrot lunaire.*" *Journal of the Arnold Schoenberg Institute* 8/2 (1984): 94–115.

————. "The Texts of *Pierrot lunaire*, Op. 21." *Journal of the Arnold Schoenberg Institute* 8/2 (1984): 94–115.

Zehme, Albertine. *Die Grundlagen des künstlerischen Sprechens und Singens.* Leipzig: Verlag Carl Merseburger, 1920.

Index

About the Authors

*R*ecognized as one of the most authoritative interpreters of vocal music of the twentieth century, Phyllis Bryn-Julson commands a remarkable repertoire of literature spanning several centuries. Ms. Bryn-Julson has appeared with every major European and North American symphony orchestra under many of the leading conductors, including Esa-Pekka Salonen, Simon Rattle, Pierre Boulez, Leonard Slatkin, Leonard Bernstein, Claudio Abbado, Seiji Ozawa, Zubin Mehta, Gunther Schuller, and Erich Leinsdorf. She has collaborated with Pierre Boulez and the Ensemble Intercontemporain for much of her career. Ms. Bryn-Julson has made over one hundred recordings, including two well-received recordings of *Pierrot lunaire*. Her recording of Schoenberg's *Erwartung* with Simon Rattle won the 1995 best opera Grammaphone Award. Her recording of the opera *Il Prigioniero* by Dallapiccola won *the Prix du Monde*. She has been twice nominated for Grammy awards for best opera recording (*Erwartung*) and best vocalist (Ligeti, *Vocal Works*). Ms. Bryn-Julson has taught at the Peabody Institute of the Johns Hopkins University for twenty-five years.

Paul Mathews teaches at the Peabody Institute of the Johns Hopkins University, where he currently serves as the associate dean of academic affairs. A composer of chamber music and chamber opera who has been recognized by ASCAP and Meet the Composer, his recent scholarship investigates the dialectic of French and German orchestration in the late nineteenth century, and he is the author/editor of *Orchestration: An Anthology of Writings*.